The Greatest Escape

The Greatest Escape

Adventures in the History of Solitude

David Balcom

iUniverse, Inc.
New York Lincoln Shanghai

The Greatest Escape
Adventures in the History of Solitude

iUniverse, Inc.

For information address:
iUniverse, Inc.
2021 Pine Lake Road, Suite 100
Lincoln, NE 68512
www.iuniverse.com

Cover art: Thomas Cole; *The Fountain of Vaucluse*, 1841; oil on canvas, 69 x 49 1/8 in. (175.3 x 124.8 cm); Dallas Museum of Art, gift of J.E.R. Chilton.

ISBN: 0-595-30990-9 (Pbk)
ISBN: 0-595-66233-1 (Cloth)

Printed in the United States of America

To my wife, Natalia,
who graces our solitude
with love and music

Take an ax to the prison wall.
Escape.
Walk out like someone suddenly born into color.
Do it now.

—Jalaluddin Rumi, Eleventh Century

There is another Loneliness
That many die without—

—Emily Dickinson, 1868

CONTENTS

PROLOGUE—Eastside Hermit to the Reader xv

OVERTURE 1

- Nietzsche's Call 3
- Petrarch's Life of Solitude 10

A BRIEF HISTORY 31

- Prehistoric Solitude 34
- Hermits of India 48
- Greece and Rome 65
- Ancient China 83
- The Desert Fathers 95
- Sufi Soloists 104
- Medieval Europe 116
- Scholars and Ch'an Masters 132
- Modern Recluses 144

ON CLOISTERPHOBIA 155

- The Hermit Bashers 157
- Reply to Cloisterphobes 172
- Extreme Solitude 189

PSYCHOLOGY 199

- Parade of Hermits 201
- Creativity 209
- Joy 227
- Enlightenment 242

SOLITUDE IN SOCIETY 269
- Alienation 271
- Inner Solitude 283

Sources, Further Reading 293
- Primitives 293
- India 294
- Greece, Rome 296
- China, Japan 298
- Christians 299
- Sufis 301
- Modern Europeans 302
- Modern Americans 304
- Historians, Philosophers, Psychologists 305

Notes 307

ACKNOWLEDGEMENTS

I completed the research for this book over the course of more than two decades, drawing mainly on the resources of the New York Public Library; bookstores in Manhattan too numerous to mention, many of which are now out of business; and, over the last few years, books purchased through the Internet, mainly at the Website of Barnes & Noble. I owe special thanks to my wife, Natalia Nikova, and my editor, Bruce Macomber, for their honest commentary, encouragement, and help in translating my wayward thoughts in solitude into relatively well organized prose. Thanks in particular to Bruce, as well as my friend Edward Doherty, for their meticulous editing assistance. I was greatly aided in translations from Italian by Agnese Barolo and in those from Spanish by Misha Lepetic. I acknowledge with gratitude the following reprint permissions for poetry quotations: Penguin Books for *Songs of the South*, Coleman Barks for his translations of Rumi in *The Essential Rumi*, Copper Canyon Press for *The Collected Songs of Cold Mountain*, Tuttle Publishing for *Zen Art for Meditation*, and Shambala Publications for *The Heart of Awareness.* I also thank the Dallas Museum of Art for permission to reproduce Thomas Cole's *The Fountain of Vaucluse* on the cover.

Prologue

Eastside Hermit to the Reader

Some junctures in life turn out to be propitious crossroads that prompt one to think more deeply than usual and, often, to act in ways that may at first seem strange or out of line. Mine came in the summer of 1979, when I made my fourth journey of relocation between Asia and America, moving from Kuala Lumpur, Malaysia, to New York, amid the psychic turbulence of a shaky marriage and questions about my employment in public relations. My firm kindly paid up-front money to help me find a place to live, which turned out to be a small garden apartment on the Upper East Side of Manhattan, where I have resided ever since.

As I sat in my garden that summer, I realized how lonely I was. Like Dante, at the midpoint of his life as expressed in the *Divine Comedy*, I "awoke to find myself alone in a dark wood." At age thirty-four, I had lost my way.

Most of all, I felt alien. I knew that migration between societies inevitably has that effect, as one loses touch with friends and associates, and all the news, references, values, and assumptions that make up life in one location are suddenly replaced by different people and all the trappings of a different day-to-day society. But this time, the effect was particularly strong. Perhaps it stemmed from my sudden realization that although I still had my youthful energy and more than half of my life lay ahead, its trajectory now seemed downward, as the prospect of aging, sickness, and death sat down beside me, prompting a mood that was at once reflective and fearful.

Nevertheless, I continued to work in public relations and over the years developed a relatively successful career, mainly on Wall Street. I remarried, found new jobs, new friends, and replanted myself in American culture.

At the same time, to address my continuing sense of loneliness, I pursued a more "spiritual," more personal avocation. I was, and am still, skeptical of modern self-help literature that bids us to fight loneliness by finding ways to be more active in society, to join clubs and support groups, or to find a mate. That, I thought, would only be an attempt to fight fire with fire and a part of me was already active in society. I also had a hunch, which I believed worth examination, that an excessive need for social relations lies at the root of the problem. Self-help authors are fond of pointing out the difference between loneliness and solitude. Well, I thought, perhaps the latter state might be the best therapy for the former.

I had long been attracted to such masters of solitude as Henry David Thoreau, Marcel Proust, and the Chinese hermit-poet Han Shan, who took plunges into solitude and found good things there. So, being optimistic by nature, I began researching and, in a sense, making friends with more such figures throughout history. In the New York Public Library and in bookstores across Manhattan, I sought out hermits, solitaries, and literary recluses who had spent some time in solitude, had positive-minded experiences there, and who left records of those experiences either in their own writing or in the writings of others about them. I now call them Friends of Solitude.

Having collected the writings and researched the biographies of more than a hundred such Friends from several of the world's major civilizations—Indian, Chinese, Greco-Roman, Christian, Islamic, European, American—I have found what some might term an "embarrassment of riches." My find includes the thoughts, works, and spiritual adventures of premodern Friends from Yajnavalkya to the Buddha in India, Lao Tzu to Wang Wei in China, Pythagoras to Epicurus in Greece, Horace to Marcus Aurelius in Rome, and Saint Anthony to Meister Eckhart in the Christian West.

With the Renaissance and the rise of Protestantism, both Christian monasticism and eremitism faded away in Europe and the idea that solitude might hold any value whatever virtually disappeared. Nevertheless, though generally unrecognized, solitude played an important part in the lives of many of the greatest Western philosophers and poets over the last half millennium. Montaigne, Rousseau, Kierkegaard, Nietzsche, Emerson,

Wordsworth, Valéry, Rilke, Dickinson, Jeffers, and many others were secular Friends and their work in solitude has enriched Western culture and literature inestimably.

This volume is a summation of what I found.

In different ways, each of the soloists I have studied unearthed rich treasure troves in solitude—astonishing powers and prophecies, important discoveries, world-piercing revelations on which the great religions are built, profound aesthetic perceptions, abiding joy, intense fulfillment, moral perspective, and other gains at once so far-reaching and so subtle as to be as difficult to explain as life or death.

These Friends of Solitude comprise a vast range of religious-minded figures, along with secular-minded philosophers and poets. They tended to have conflicting viewpoints on life. They lived in times and cultures that were poles apart and had different beliefs and objectives. In each specific case, they had somewhat different experiences in their aloneness. Yet beneath the chatter of cultural influence and historical circumstance lies, I believe, a common thread that being alone, whether religious or secular in orientation, can provide fertile ground for creative inspiration, therapeutic tranquillity, equanimity, and, perhaps, enlightenment. That commonality springs from human givens—the astonishing fact of existence, death's inevitability, the singleness of consciousness in the plurality of society, and the subtle workings of the senses and the mind, which may require a quiet mood to function in top form.

As you might expect, there are many who strongly oppose the idea that solitude holds any value whatever. In fact, these "hermit bashers" argue passionately that solitude is irresponsible, conducive to madness, and a destructive force against society. I encourage them to have their say, then take time to examine and rebut their objections. I suggest the outlines for a psychology of positive-minded solitude that attempts to provide good, commonsense reasons why the "fruits of solitude" are real and not always the product of fantasy, as some modern psychologists contend. And I propose that the life of solitude—either through periodic retreats or continuing inner solitude in society—may be the best answer to cries that modern world is inevitably a "lonely crowd." Such a life is certainly not irresponsible and there is no good reason whatever that Friends of Solitude should feel guilty for "rejecting" society. It is often they—perhaps we—who provide the greatest creative energy, spiritual uplift, and nourishing literature and philosophy. I will argue that we who may enjoy an occasional detachment from society to think and sort things out rarely detract, but often add, to the social good.

Accordingly, I invite you to join our hypothetical society: The Friends of Solitude, a loosely configured "group" in which, paradoxically, most of its members are not aware of their associates.

As a resident of Earth in the twenty-first century, you may be too skeptical or shy to accept such an unusual offer. I acknowledge that, depending on one's mental constitution and sensibility, intentionally choosing to be alone for some time may not be for everyone. And be forewarned that, like Saint Anthony in the deserts of Egypt or Petrarch at the Fountain of Vaucluse, your lonely quietude may be bothered by demons of lust, vainglory, or melancholy. Your fears and vanities will follow you into solitude. And time alone may kindle unwelcome eloquence in that part of your soul that heretofore held only a gnawing feeling that you are wasting your life. But I encourage you to have an open mind on the subject. There are ways around these difficulties, and many facets to the experience of time alone.

Generally speaking, the accommodations make little difference. Many hermits, particularly those with religious zeal, preferred to live intensely ascetic lives in solitude. Other recluses chose more comfortable retirement, often accompanied by family or a few close friends, but they enjoyed the fruits of solitude nonetheless. Some Friends lived in utter solitude for years at a time; others chose periodic retreats; still others found an inner detachment that coexisted with social life. The essential thing is to be apart from society for some time, physically, mentally, or spiritually.

Nor is the character and content of solitary experience the main point. There are thoughtful working solitudes and "thoughtless" ones that aim at the profundity of "no-mind." There are philosophical or aesthetic meditations and spiritual contemplations aimed at achieving enlightenment or receiving God's grace. There are contrite solitudes that seek to repent of human sins and heretical solitudes that stand on their own two feet. There are psychic journeys intended to produce altered states of consciousness.

There is the simple joy of doing nothing, appreciating life away from the crowd. I will argue for diversity and balance.

But how is it, I have often been asked, that a PR man has taken such an interest in time alone as to parade himself as a champion of solitude, that most private of anti-relations? My answer is that I believe there is nothing to prevent the marriage of the contemplative with the active life. Each can be an important counterpoint to the other.

I take my cue from the apparent contradictions in the lives of two enigmatic Yankees: the composer Charles Ives, and the poet Wallace Stevens. Ives produced brilliant, iconoclastic symphonies in his creative time alone, but his musical career had all the while to share time in the head of a Hartford, Connecticut, insurance executive. Stevens, who termed himself "the poet striding among the cigar stores," was also an insurance executive in Hartford. Like Ives, his antipathies were integral—an everyday business world, which he cultivated by choice, found its opposite in an abstract sphere of words. The tangible everyday life in him was refracted in twinkling unashamed constructions of the "unreal." "I taste at the root of the tongue the unreal of what is real," he wrote. In my way, I try to do the same.

Today, as I sit in my garden, retired, in a sense, writing and alternately doing nothing, I can say that my explorations in the history of solitude have been beneficial to me. I know that being alone has been and will ever be a wellspring of human creativity and that it will be therapeutic, not for the sake of happiness alone, but for a kind of quickened awareness, which is larger than sadness and deeper than cheerfulness.

That has not so much cured my sense of loneliness as it has shown me that it is a mirage. At the dawn of the twenty-first century, the most common response to loneliness is to stand and fight. We strive in every way to fill the dreaded "emptiness" of our lives with an exciting bustle of activities and entertainment. We spend most, if not all, of our time in a frenetic atmosphere, which tantalizes an animal thirst for life but rarely affords time for a deep, cool drink. Too often, we are like those parched travelers who attempt to dive into a lake they think they see in the desert, only to find themselves head deep in sand.

My belief now, more than ever, is that there should be no cause of alarm once the mirage is recognized. If one is careful not to be mystified by the rising heat waves, one can walk stridently, even pleasantly, onward, as the true contour of the land unveils itself before you get there. And if you are alert and patient, you are likely to find your thirst-quenching spring. The profoundest slight-of-mind is to transform loneliness into solitude. That is what Emily Dickinson, quoted in the epigraph to this book, calls "Loneliness," with a capital "L," a state, she says, that "Is richer than could be revealed/By mortal numeral."

Perhaps this detached posture of thought, empty and energetic at the same time, could, if widely taken up, bear a larger fruit in this America of ours by fostering a thoughtful synthesis between solitude and society. But my praise of solitude is not intended to change society. Rather it is a personal offering. Here is an apology for and guide to the greatest of all escapes…solitude.

OVERTURE

Oh, if there were someone to tell us the history of that subtle feeling called solitude.

—Friedrich Nietzsche, *Daybreak*, 1881

Nietzsche's Call

I was surprised to stumble some years ago upon Friedrich Nietzsche's call for a history of solitude. It came from Nietzsche, of all people, that hard-minded, existential philosopher of the Will to Power; not the kind of person, I thought, who would want anything to do with a subject that suggests asceticism and withdrawal from the world. But there it was. That sentence still has an enchanting ring.

Nietzsche himself, I soon discovered, might have been the best of all possible someones to fulfill his call. "But I need solitude," he wrote, "which is to say, recovery, return to myself, the breath of a free, light, playful air."[1] Indeed, like Heraclitus in the Temple of Artemis, the Buddha under his Bodhi Tree, or Thoreau at Walden Pond, Nietzsche felt and thought best and most deeply when alone. Like many another Friend of Solitude, his attraction to aloneness began early in life. At age fourteen, a friend wrote that the future philosopher's "fundamental character trait was a certain melancholy, which was apparent in his whole being." From earliest childhood onward, the friend continued, young Friedrich "liked solitude and used it to give himself up to his own thoughts."[2]

That attraction was also fueled by circumstance: Nietzsche suffered throughout his life from severe headaches, which sometimes took him to the point of blindness and obliged him to stay at home in his room. The illness was so irksome that after only a few years as a professor of philology at Basel University, he retired at age thirty-five to a decade of lonely, intense, and highly productive philosophizing. He lived on his professorial pension and stayed mainly in single-room boardinghouses in Switzerland during the summer and along the Italian and French coasts of the Mediterranean during the winter. Nietzsche's description of his philosopher-saint Zarathustra may, I think, be applied just as well to his life during that period: "He enjoyed and quaffed his solitude."[3] In fact, in his characteristically self-proud and aggressively grandiloquent manner, Nietzsche later proclaimed: "I am solitude become man."[4]

It is not surprising, therefore, that he begins his call with an exclamatory "Oh"—which implies that there was something great at work in his lonely meditations, and by extension a similar potential in all being alone. If only someone could reveal its workings; if only someone could break the story on solitude—that would be a prize indeed! As Nietzsche wrote elsewhere, we might be able to "live peacefully and cheerfully, even amidst the turmoil." For the best thing in life, he said, quoting Goethe, is "the deep quiet in which I live and grow against the world, and harvest what they cannot take from me by fire or sword."[5] He also stressed that loneliness may have creative value: "O you poor devils in the great cities of world politics, you gifted young men tormented by ambition…however much you desire to do great work, the profound speechlessness of pregnancy never comes to you! The event of the day drives you before it like chaff." [6]

To be genuinely productive, according to Nietzsche, many forces need to come together in the thinker: imagination, self-uplifting, abstraction, the critical faculty, contemplativeness, comprehensiveness, and even "love for all that exists"—so many inward qualities that they are not likely to achieve their mysterious confluence without the forging time of extended solitude. That is why every philosopher, says Nietzsche, is a hermit.

But the wording of his call also contains a cautionary note. The subjunctive "if there were" implies that the telling of a history of solitude may be impossible. That suggestion is developed in this passage from his book *Beyond Good and Evil*:

> One always hears in the writings of a hermit something of the echo of the desert, something of the whisper and shy vigilance of solitude; in his strongest words, even in his cry, there still resounds a new and more dangerous kind of silence and concealment. He who has sat alone with his soul day and night, year in year out, in confidential discord and discourse, and in his cave—it might be a labyrinth, but it may be a gold mine—become a cave-bear or treasure-hunter or a treasure-guardian and dragon, finds that his concepts themselves at last acquire a characteristic too light color, a smell of the depths and of must,

> something incommunicable and reluctant which blows cold on every passerby.[7]

Such a hermit may sense that his hearers would be unable to grasp the beauty and delicate integrity of his meditations. He may perceive that his thoughts are dangerous, that his listeners may threaten him if they do not like what they hear. The hermit may also sense that he does not fully understand his thoughts. In the tricky depths of his cave, he will always be attracted to yet another, deeper grotto.

At the same time, it is obvious that Nietzsche aims to pique our interest. For the hope remains that if we listen carefully, we may hear the faint echoes from the hermit's cavern. We may learn to go spelunking in our own depths. That is why we would need a history of solitude—to provide, as it were, a treasure map to the rich mysteries of solitary musing in the past. With such a map, we might join the ranks of what Nietzsche calls the "born, sworn, jealous friends of solitude."[8]

It is clear that the friends Nietzsche has in mind would be philosophers. The history of solitude would be an account of those twinkling moments in which spiritual sportings are conceived in the ardent meditations of tough-minded philosopher-hermits such as him. To my mind, however, the brotherhood and sisterhood of the Friends of Solitude should not be so limited. The writings of hosts of less heroic soloists throughout the long history of solitude are also worthy of our attention. They may enter the recesses of time alone with reverence and humility, with a sense of aesthetic wonder, or with a sense of humor. Accordingly, I researched many less curmudgeonly philosopher-soloists and treated them as Friends: Epicurus, Montaigne, and Kierkegaard in the West, for instance, along with relatively good-natured Eastern thinker-hermits, such as the Chinese Taoist Chuang Tzu and the Indian philosopher of the *Upanishads*, Yajnavalkya.

Although most solitary poets are not the kind of "cruel investigators" that Nietzsche tends to prefer, their works contain some of the most penetrating and inspiring philosophies of solitude in all the eremitic literature. I included them in my research, too, with the hope that this broader look into the history of solitude might help to prepare us for reading between the lines of great poets, from Horace to Rumi, whose work was nourished in solitude and is best heard from that perspective.

It is also clear that any comprehensive history of solitude must make room for religious hermits, including yogis, gymnosophists, and world-renouncing *sadhus* in the panoply of the Hindu religion who must have numbered several millions at least over the past three or four millennia. A complete history should make room for Christian hermits, which probably adds another million or so if one were to count all those who were "called to solitude" during the first millennium and a half after Christ. For the same reason, I included clever Sufi soloists such as Rabi'a and al-Ghazali, along with the uncountable numbers of primitive shamans who, I will venture to say, have employed solitude as a technique in their still unbroken chain of ecstatic spiritual methodology going back thirty-five millennia at least.

Nietzsche, for one, hated religious hermits, whom he called "drunkards of god." He noted that their ascetic self-deprivation may be courageous, but he thought it misguided. He didn't like their orthodoxy. I say, nevertheless, that the religious hermit's rigorous experience in solitude may have much to tell us about the subtleties and dangers there, and, indeed, about the soaring spiritual flights of mystic inspiration that even Nietzsche experienced, albeit with a sense of skepticism and embarrassment. Moreover, many religious hermits—the Buddha, for instance—were free-thinking heretics in their day.

By the same token, should not an artist or scientist working alone in his or her study be included among the Friends? Shouldn't all writers be included, along with painters and hunters in the forest or, for that matter, anyone walking alone in the mountains—or anywhere? Of course. I have a feeling (which has kept me going for these many years) that if we heard the full history of these and other Friends of Solitude, we might gain the ability to penetrate hidden depths behind any communication of a thoughtful, reclusive artist, scientist, philosopher, or poet. And what is most important, I believe such a history might help us to turn the trick of cocking our own souls to the subtle or maybe not so subtle murmurs and songs, the grunts and groans, of our own consciousness. Nevertheless, I have only included those Friends or associates of solitude who left a record of their experiences, or otherwise helped us to better understand the phenomenological history of solitude itself.

It is not surprising that most everyone who has considered these matters at all deeply has recognized that solitude is a slippery concept. At one extreme, it is reasonable to say that everyone is a hermit. As individual self-conscious organisms, we are born, we live, we die essentially alone. No one can fully know another—solitude is congenital. Yet, in a different sense, no one can be completely solitary. No man, says John Donne, is an island set wholly apart from the mainland of human existence. Neither gestation nor birth can occur in a total isolation. A mother must be present. From that point on, an infant human requires nurturing. Without other humans to talk with, language cannot be learned, and thinking itself would be severely curtailed if not impossible.

We humans, therefore, live in two worlds. Our relationship with others is a conundrum: we are necessarily social and essentially alone. Being a Friend must be a relative detachment somewhere between these two poles, with the emphasis, in a positive way, on the alone side.

Accordingly, we will allow the possibility—explicitly advocated by many Friends of Solitude from Kierkegaard to Robinson Crusoe to the god Krishna of the Bhagavadgita—that, by being mentally and spiritually detached, one may be a hermit while still remaining very active in the world. Through a clever mental gymnastic, one can rechannel society's noise and distraction out of consciousness—to become "solitary amid the crowd." Even in that case, the Friend will probably find some time to be away from society, physically. But how much time is enough? My answer is simple: It doesn't matter.

The most infinitesimal solitude you can imagine may be sufficient. In "The Oversoul," Emerson writes:

> The spirit sports with time,—
>
> > Can crowd eternity into an hour,
> > Or stretch an hour into eternity.

"The soul," he adds, "knows only the soul; the web of events is the flowing robe in which she is clothed."[9]

It is said, further, that Mohammed's audiences with Allah were each quicker than the time it takes for the water in an overturned glass to fall to the table. The Messenger typically received these divine communications while meditating in a desert cave or in his house wrapped up in a blanket, but he could have been anywhere.

If duration is not key, motivation is. You're not really a Friend unless you've either chosen isolation or, if it were thrust upon you, you came to appreciate its therapeutic, creative powers. For instance, the mobster John Gotti lived for more than a decade in solitary confinement in a maximum-security prison in Colorado; but I doubt that he suddenly fell in love with his aloneness or that he would not rather have been a free man in Brooklyn. On the other hand, witness the literary and philosophical output of such men as Machiavelli or Solzhenitsyn. Exiled or imprisoned for political reasons, they used their time alone to compose books that changed the course of the societies from which they were divorced.

For others, an unexpected solitude can deliver a shock that forces a salutary contemplation on the nature of life and things. Among my favorite examples is that of Admiral Richard E. Byrd. In 1934, on a scientific expedition to Antarctica that went awry, he was forced to spend four months alone in a small hut near the South Pole in temperatures around 85 degrees below zero, with no hope of rescue. Amid the extreme trials of that misadventure, as recounted in his book *Alone*, Byrd had many transformative "peak experiences" akin to the enlightenment reported by shamans and religious hermits. One night, for instance, while listening to Beethoven's fifth symphony on his gramophone and contemplating the starry night, Byrd recalled:

> As the notes swelled, the dull aurora on the horizon pulsed and quickened and draped itself into arches and fanning beams which reached across the sky until at my zenith the display attained its crescendo. The music and the night became one; and I told myself that all beauty was akin and sprang from the same substance.[10]

A full history of solitude would no doubt include an examination of all the high points and low points in what Byrd terms the "laboratory of solitude." But to limit the scope of this project amid the overwhelming flood of eremitic literature in human record I decided to focus mainly upon those who have chosen solitude, left a record of their experience, and have something useful or inspirational to tell us about time spent alone.

I have also steered clear of monastic solitudes as they have appeared most notably over the last two millennia in Buddhism and Christianity. Tellingly, the word "monk" derives from the Greek *monachos*, one who lives alone. No doubt, life in a monastery is a form of solitude, corporate aloneness with others; yet it is a different type and quite another world. The supportive discipline of monastic life helps monks and nuns to sit still amid the chaos of their own minds. It also provides a vehicle for passing on spiritual methodology and concepts between teacher and disciple. But a monk is not a hermit.

If Nietzsche himself planned to write such a history of solitude, however delineated, he never got around to it. Alas, from syphilis, an overdose of his special version of ecstatic philosophy, or some other yet undiagnosed cause, he collapsed into madness in 1889, at the age of forty-five, never to philosophize cogently again.

What Nietzsche didn't know was that the first history of solitude—*De Vita Solitaria* (*The Life of Solitude*)—had already been written five centuries earlier by Francesco Petrarcha.

Petrarch's Life of Solitude

In 1337, at the age of thirty-three, Francesco Petrarcha (Petrarch)—admirer of Dante and acquaintance of Boccaccio; poet, philosopher, humanist, and Friend of Solitude—acquired a small piece of land and a modest house at The Fountain of Vaucluse, in modern-day Provence. Except for a few outward excursions, notably to Rome where he was crowned poet laureate, Petrarch resided in "retirement" there until 1341, then from 1345 to 1347, and again in the early 1350s.

His life at Vaucluse was far from retirement in the modern sense. Petrarch said that he wrote or began in earnest all of his major work at Vaucluse, where the quiet life gave him time to "finish certain works which were half done or merely projected."[11] It was there that he wrote his famous love poems to Laura (collected as the *Canzoniere*); numerous biographies of illustrious men, notably Roman generals and statesmen; his *Triumphs,* on love, chastity, and death; voluminous letters entreating friends to share his retreat; a dialogue with Saint Augustine, *Secretum* (*The Secret*); and *The Life of Solitude.*

Located some twenty miles east of Avignon, Vaucluse is a fine and majestic spot for a quirky, aesthetic-minded, reclusive genius. As the name implies (the Romans called it *Vallis Calusa*, meaning "valley enclosed"), the place is a U-shaped canyon with steep limestone cliffs on three sides enclosing a valley carved out over time by the action of the river Sorgue. The river begins at the fountain, a large and still-not-fully-explored underground spring that collects in sinkholes in the dry land to the north, then erupts suddenly from a cave-like gorge at the upper end of the valley.

This peaceful abode has long "inspired awe and amazement in strangers," the poet wrote in a letter of invitation to his friend Philippe de Cabassoles, who was then bishop of the nearby town of Cavaillon. Quoting Seneca, Petrarch explained that the fountain, "a place not built with hands but hollowed out into spaciousness by natural causes, will deeply move the soul by a certain intimation of the existence of God." "If that is true, he added, "where, I ask, is there a cave more suited to inspiring religious awe?" "Here you may enjoy in a rare union the privileges of being free and a lord, a dignitary in solitude."[12]

From the fountain, the Sorgue flows on, a haunting, crystalline emerald green (colored by the water parsnip), today, past a paper mill, erected in the eighteenth century, and riverside cafés where fleshy tourists, clad in halters, shorts, and sunglasses, sip Pernod and Coca-Cola, then past a modern reconstruction of Petrarch's cottage (now a museum) and further on to the village, Fontaine de Vaucluse.

High on a cliff overlooking the valley is the remains of a castle, where some say Petrarch lived. Most historians agree, however, that the poet resided in a more modest accommodation, a house just below the castle along the left bank of the river (as illustrated in the painting on the cover of this book, "The Fountain of Vaucluse," by the nineteenth-century Hudson Valley painter Thomas Cole). It is approachable on foot only through a tunnel, the remains of a Roman aqueduct that opens onto a grassy area bounded on one side by the rocky cliffs and the other by the Sorgue.

Petrarch confessed the he loved the place—so much so that he said he had never been happy anywhere else. In his voluminous letters, it often sounds as though Vaucluse—not Laura—was the true love of his life. "You will see me content from morn to eve," he wrote to his Roman friend Giovanni Colonna, "wandering among the meadows, hills, springs, and woods."

> I flee men's traces, follow the birds, love the shadows, enjoy the mossy caves and the greening fields, curse the cares of the Curia, avoid the city's tumult, refuse to cross the thresholds of the mighty, mock the concerns of the mob. I am equidistant from joy and sadness, at peace by day and night. I glory in the Muse's company, in bird-song and the murmur of the water nymphs.[13]

Petrarch was certainly attracted to seclusion. But like most Friends, he was both pulled and pushed into solitude. He came to Vaucluse from Avignon, where he had been jilted in love and fastidiously ignored over the course of a decade by Laura. But there were many other influences on his particular desire for a secular retirement that had been totally forgotten in Western civilization since the fall of the Roman Empire.

In Avignon, he wrote a few poems and studied the classics. He may have worked in some way as a lawyer or court secretary; but with a sophisticated classical education, good looks, and a knack for charming conversation, he was more likely what is known in Provençal as a *gai sabor*, a gay-blade who slipped, as one historian puts it, into a life of "elegant dissipation."[14]

In 1333, he toured Europe, discovering in Liege two lost speeches of Cicero. One of them, "Pro Archia," contains the following passage on the value of literature and gentlemanly leisure:

> These studies sharpen youth and delight old age; they enhance prosperity and provide a refuge and relief in adversity; they enrich private life and do not interfere with public life; they are our companions at night, on journeys, and in our country retreats.[15]

The work must have reminded Petrarch of the writings on the value of solitude that he came across in his readings of classical authors. Despite his humanistic leanings, though, Petrarch was a devout late-medieval Christian. In fact, he was a cleric. So, although he does not mention it, he probably did not miss the fact that the hills and abundant limestone caves along the Lebrun Valley had been home to Christian hermits since at least the ninth century and probably much earlier. By Petrarch's day, monasteries and associated churches had been built adjacent to many of the hermitages, as can be seen today at the nearby monastery of Saint Hilaire.

Petrarch also neglects to mention another local influence that may have spurred his independent-minded views on solitude, as well as his worldly love. In his student days, he spent a summer in the Pyrenees Mountains of Languedoc, then a last vestige of the Provençal-speaking Albegensians. Most of their ancestors, once spread throughout Provence, had been massacred during the local Crusades two centuries earlier, ostensibly for their heretical belief that right-thinking and right-feeling men and women could rise on their own powers to spiritual heights of enlightenment, and because of their suspicious emphasis on the virtues of human in addition to divine love. In Languedoc, or certainly in Avignon, the poet would have heard the Provençal love songs of troubadour poets, such as Arnaut Daniel.

It is known that Petrarch read the poets of the region, because a work in the Vatican containing poems and biographies of these "Masters of the Gai Saber" is full of marginalia in Petrarch's hand. One is tempted to think, therefore, that he would have heard this audacious statement by Daniel:

> I am Arnaut, who loves the wind,
> And chases the hare with the ox,
> And swims against the torrent.[16]

And he probably knew this religiously incorrect line by the twelfth-century troubadour Pierre Vidal:

> Good Lady, I think I see God when I gaze on your delicate body.[17]

Petrarch's "good lady," of course, was Laura de Sade. If she lived at all and was not, as some maintain, merely a platonic ideal concocted to fill a poetic need, Laura was probably married when he met her in 1327 and until her death by plague in 1348. Petrarch, however, never married. He had taken a formal vow of chastity when ordained a member of the clergy three years after he met Laura. The fact that his illegitimate son had just been born could have had something to do with his first retirement to Vaucluse. The poet insisted, however, that it was Laura, "the glorious woman in my life," who caused him to seek refuge in a woody retreat:

> Still she stands before my eyes, terrifying me, assailing me, nor does she show any sign of leaving me in peace. She had captured me by no feminine guile, but by her simple ways and by her rare beauty. I bore her yoke for ten years, though scorning myself for my subjection. I was wasted by my disease, the fever-glow had penetrated to my very marrow. I hoped to die; and then longing for liberty invaded my afflicted breast and planted there the courage to rebel.[18]

In such a pass, continues the poet, "my only hope lay in flight":

> As the benighted steersman fears the lurking reefs I recoil in terror from her face, from her words that fire the mind, from her gold-clouded head, from her necklaced throat, her quivering shoulders, her eyes delighting in my death.
>
> In this desperate pass I perceived a rock upon a secret shore, a refuge against disaster. And now, hidden among the hills, I weep my past life.[19]

Petrarch was also fleeing, more in disgust than terror, from the place where Laura resided. "I came here eagerly," he wrote from Vaucluse, "partly because my ears were battered and my mind afflicted by the city's tumult." The city is Avignon, one of the most important in Europe during the fourteenth century, when a second papacy resided there. Petrarch was born in Florence and associated Italy with the glory of the Roman Empire, so the papal schism was to him another vulgar sign of the depths to which European civilization had sunk. Avignon was dirty and noisy, filled with luxuries and vain distractions. It was also home to some early friends who, he said, "had driven me to the brink of perdition." He critiqued the city for the soul-sickness it induced in its nervous inhabitants, and he harbored a vehement repugnance for city life:

> Everywhere in the squares of cities crowds of fools may be encountered in whose mouths no words occur more often than the familiar ones of the grammarian's formula, *piget, tædet, pœnitet* [I am troubled, I am weary, I am sorry], or the phrase from Terrence, "I do not know what to do."[20]

It may also have been significant that the year before his first retreat to Vaucluse, Petrarch received an unexpected lesson from Saint Augustine. He and his brother Gherardo made a day trip hiking to the top of nearby Mount Vaucluse (2,000 meters above sea level). For some reason, Francesco had brought along a copy of the saint's *Confessions*, and when he reached the top he opened the book at random to a passage in the tenth book that reads: "And men go about admiring the high mountains...but they themselves they abandon."[21]

As with many another recluse before Petrarch's time, age could also have had something to do with it. He was thirty-three when he first went to Vaucluse, just about the traditional "midpoint" of life (set by Aristotle, Dante, and Jung at thirty-five), when a newly middle-aged man may have a tendency to believe that time has pushed him into a "darkening wood." That predicament naturally prompts reflection on the swift passage of time and an urge to get serious about how he will spend his remaining days.

THE APOLOGIA

During his first stay at Vaucluse, Petrarch focused on writing his more ponderous Latin oeuvre, his letters to friends, and poems on his love for Laura. The idea of writing on the virtues and pleasures of solitude came during his second stay, partly the result of long discussions on the subject with Philippe de Cabassoles. The idea coincided with Petrarch's growing interest in the Bible and the literature of the church fathers (including the Christian hermits of Egypt). It also coincided and with his visit to the Carthusian monastery of Monterieux, where Gherardo then lived as a monk.

The result of that visit was a short work praising religious solitude: *De Otio Religioso* (*On Monastic Tranquillity*), which is essentially a sermon on a passage in the forty-sixth Psalm: "be still and see that I am God."[22] Petrarch was inspired by the high-minded spiritual silence of the monastery and by the finality of the monks' liberation from worldly affairs. But that did not dissuade him from his attraction to the literary retirement of which he had grown so fond. "I want a solitude not utter," he said, "a leisure not inert and useless, but a retreat which may be profitable to many."[23]

The Life of Solitude is Petrarch's apologia for that sort of secular retreat. He terms the book a "celebration of a life of solitude and leisure," a little mirror in which "you shall behold the entire disposition of my soul, the full countenance of a serene and tranquil mind."[24] Written as an exceptionally long letter to Philippe, it begins with this inclusive manifesto that cleverly applauds both religious and secular seclusion:

> I believe that a noble spirit will never find repose save in God, in whom is our end, or in himself and his private thoughts, or in

> some intellect united by a close sympathy with his own. For though the pleasures of society be covered with the most entangling lime and full of sweet and alluring baits, yet they lack the force to detain powerful wings upon the ground.[25]

For many Christians of Petrarch's time, and even today, it would be patently heretical to think that anyone, no matter how noble, would have the option of finding repose "in himself." But Petrarch is persistent. He continues his demonstration of the "blessedness of solitude" with an extended antithesis that recalls the long-standing medieval debate between the active and the contemplative life, wherein the latter always comes out on top. But instead of contrasting worldly life with that of religious contemplation, which was the norm, he slyly pits the tranquil, contemplative, moral life of the retired man (himself) with a day in the life of the busy man amid the noisy, sinful, active life in the city (his earlier self in Avignon).[26]

The busy man in this tale "awakes in the middle of the night, his sleep interrupted by his light and by terror of nightly visions. No sooner is he up than he settles his body to the miserable bench and applies his mind to falsehood." Meanwhile, "the retired man—a man of leisure—awakes in a happy mood, refreshed by a moderate rest and a short sleep, unbroken unless when he is aroused at intervals by the songs of the night-haunting Philomel [the nightingale]."

When daylight comes, the busy man is beset by enemies and friends; he is greeted, solicited, pulled and jostled, assailed with arguments, and rent asunder. But "the retired man, with a store of leisure and of calm, goes blithely into a nearby wood and enters joyfully upon the propitious threshold of a serene day."

As lunchtime comes, the busy man "composes himself amid his piles of cushions in a huge hall over which ruin impends; he sits with countenance overcast, eyes dull, forehead clouded, nose wrinkled, and cheeks pale, parting his sticky lips with difficulty, scarce lifting his head." The retired man, by contrast, is "quick-witted and alert because of the previous day's fast…In place of tumult he has peace, silence instead of clamor, himself alone instead of a crowd. He is his own companion, his own storyteller, his own table guest." And so it goes for them, "as the hours fly and the day slips past."

Having established the retired man's moral superiority with humorous clarity, Petrarch sneaks in a new element: worldly pleasure. He concedes that such retired men live outside the religious regimen of the cloister, but he maintains nonetheless that they can be "friends of God" and may begin, in this life, to feel the delights of the life eternal. It is not impossible, Petrarch writes, always directing his appeal to Philippe, that

> any one of their number, to whom there clings no trace of the dust of this world, should be raised up with the assistance of the divine mercy to such height that, though still confined to earth, he may hear the chorus of angels singing harmoniously in heaven and behold in an ecstasy of mind what he is unable to express when he comes back to himself.[27]

Aside from an occasional mystic transport, the retired man will have many other commendable delights to chose from as he stands on the high tower of solitude watching the troubled actions of men beneath his feet:

> To travel back in memory and to range in imagination through all ages and all lands; to move about at will and converse with all the glorious men of the past and so to lose consciousness of those who work all evils in the present; sometimes to rise, with thoughts that are lifted above yourself, to the ethereal region, to meditate on what goes on there and by meditation to enflame your desire, and in turn to encourage and admonish yourself with a fervent spirit as though with the power of burning words—these are not the least important fruits of the solitary life, though those who are without experience do not appreciate it.[28]

The retired man may also take delight in sharing his retreat with a like-minded friend. "Not the smallest part of my pleasure," he told his friend Giovanni, "is that I rarely see a human creature."[29]

Rhetoric aside, Petrarch never lived completely alone at Vaucluse. His invitations to friends were often accepted and he reveled in the companionship, provided it was an occasion for serious talk on lofty matters, such as the Greek and Roman classics, poetry, Christian morality, the Crusades, or the beauty of the surrounding countryside. I know of no other passage from the Petrarchan invitations to solitude than this one that better illustrates his deep need for such friendship. To my mind, it should be regarded as one of the all-time great epigrams of eremitic literature:

> Not only will you, Philippe, be the support of my quiet, you, only you, will be my quiet, not only the comfort of my solitude, but my solitude: and I will seem to be truly alone when I am with you.[30]

Others shared Petrarch's retreat, too. During his first stay at Vaucluse, he brought along his brother, who was also grieving over lost love and had not yet taken orders as a monk. He hired a local man to manage his affairs, and the man's wife served as cook. In choosing them, he may have thought to make sure that the surroundings would not kindle his sensitive tastes for feminine beauty. The woman had a bright soul, he wrote to another friend, but added that "if you could see that face, so dry and sunburned, so lacking in vital juices, you would think you were looking at the Libyan or Ethiopian desert. If Helen had such a face, Troy would still be standing."[31]

He had a canine friend at Vaucluse, a royal wolfhound given to him by Cardinal Colonna, who in turn had received the dog as a gift from the king of Portugal. The dog stood guard over his house, occasionally caught a duck or snagged a fish out of the river for dinner, and accompanied Petrarch on his daily walks, once removing the sword from the hand of an attacker.

Petrarch's cottage also contained friends, of a sort, in one of the finest personal libraries of classical literature in Europe. Among the great benefits of books, says Petrarch, is that they do not ask for food or drink and are content with a narrow portion of one's house, yet they provide inestimable treasures of mind. In their authors, one has unfailing companions

> always prepared to be silent or to speak, to stay at home or to accompany him in the woods, to travel, to remain in the country, to converse, to amuse, to cheer, to comfort, to advise, to dispute, to consult, to teach the secrets of nature, the memorable deeds of history, the rule of life and the contempt of death, moderation in prosperity, fortitude in adversity, equanimity and steadfastness in all our actions.[32]

Indeed, says Petrarch, "isolation without literature is exile, prison, and torture; but supply literature, and it becomes your country, freedom, and delight."[33]

Petrarch stresses, however, that his closest friend in solitude was his own reflective mind: "In my solitude, I not only entertain but take pains to summon noble thoughts, than which no companionship can be imagined more agreeable and charming, and without which life is miserable whether in cities or in the woods."[34] But beyond such appeals to personal welfare, he suggests that solitude can supply what he calls a "divine fertility of intellect"[35] that is conducive to creative work, specifically for philosophical thought and literary composition. Who doubts, he asks, that these pursuits can be carried on anywhere more successfully than in solitude? There at least, he says,

> I can speak from experience, for I know what spurs it supplies to the mind, what wings for the spirit, what leisure time for work—things which I know not where to seek save in solitude.[36]

In fact, Petrarch argues that "leisure or freedom, call it what you will, is the source of literature and the arts." He cites Aristotle's contention that the mathematical arts were highly developed in Egypt because of the life of leisure granted to ancient Egyptian priests. He adds that according to "one of our own priests," Cheremon the Stoic, some high-minded Egyptians were allowed to "put aside all business and thoughts of the world and lived always in the temple, studying nature and its causes and making computations of the stars."[37]

Remarkably, Petrarch's next step is to push the envelope even further by arguing gingerly but effectively for something virtually unheard of at the time: individual freedom of thought. Again and again in *The Life* he takes pains to warn Philippe that solitude may not be for everyone and that he himself is not absolutely sure he is on the right track. "I only appear as a painstaking inquirer," he writes. Although he believes he has always sought the truth, he admits that "the recesses in which it is hidden, or my own preoccupations or a certain dullness of mind may have sometimes stood in my way, so that often in my search for the thing I have been bewildered by false lights." He recommends solitude, therefore, not in the spirit of one who lays down the law but as a student and investigator. For to define is the province of a wise man, and he is neither wise nor neighbor to the wise, but, again in Cicero's words, "a man fertile in conjectures."[38]

> I am not so much proposing a rule for others as exposing the principles of my own mind. If it commends itself to anyone, let him follow its suggestion. Whoever does not like it is free to reject it and, leaving us to our solitude, to embrace his own anxious cares and live to his own satisfaction in scorn of our rural retreat.[39]

If that is the way these busy men want to live, they are welcome to it, says Petrarch. His entreaties are directed to the likes of Philippe de Cabassoles:

> I shall be glad to persuade the few. It is indeed not reasonable to induce all men to lead one kind of life, particularly the life of solitude, and so I do not speak for everybody, but for you and myself, and for those few with whose dispositions these unusual habits agree. For us, surely, if we follow not the foolish opinion of the crowd but our own nature, nothing is more appropriate.[40]

LAURA AND A WRITING CURE

In *The Life,* Petrarch presents us with an elegant and heartfelt plea for what may best be seen as his official view of solitude. But it is essentially an idealized, promotional work with more than a bit of self-justification thrown in. Neither there nor, for the most part, in his shorter letters do we hear the full story of Petrarch's life at Vaucluse.

He left no account, for example, of how he financed his retirement. Most likely, the house was purchased or rented for him by Cardinal Colonna, who may also have supplied an ongoing grant-in-aid to cover Petrarch's relatively modest daily expenses. As a cleric he earned a perpetual stipend, which may have helped him to continue his avocation of book collecting. But the position was virtually a sinecure and, appropriately, Petrarch never heard confession. He refused to be named bishop, or to take any benefice that involved the cure of souls: "I have enough to do," he said, "looking after my own."[41]

Indeed, caring for his hypersensitive worldly heart was among Petrarch's chief occupations at Vaucluse. To get a feel for that aspect of his retirement, we must turn particularly to his personal reflections in the *Canzoniere.*

If Petrarch fled Avignon to get away from Laura, he was in for a surprise. The demons of worldly life followed him into his retreat; and their soul-pounding clamor was all the more magnified in solitude, as he tells us in poem 35, probably written shortly after he arrived at Vaucluse for the first time:

> Alone and lost in thought I pace
> deserted fields with slow somber steps,
> my eyes alert so I can flee whatever trace
> of human footprint marks the sand.
>
> I find no other way to shield my pain
> from the prying glances of mankind,
> for in my face where joy is drained
> they will discern what burns inside.[42]

Petrarch the poet keeps on hunting for the perfectly lonely spot that Love and his thoughts of Laura dare not enter. Of course, he knows he will fail. But his work on the *Canzoniere* provides a different solace, one probably borrowed from the poets of the gai sabor. In the solitudes of Vaucluse, he is like an injured animal that has gone off to lick its wounds. Like a modern psychotherapist who seeks a "talking cure," Petrarch's sophisticated laments are a personal writing cure. And like a highly sophisticated version of the country-western troubadours of today, he seems to have hoped that by expressing every aspect of his most painful feelings, they might be extracted from his aching heart.

"From thought to thought, mountain to mountain, Love leads me on," he writes in poem 129. He concedes that every path he trods runs counter to a tranquil life, but he finds some relief in solitude. For

> if there is on some solitary slope a river
> or a spring between two crags in a shady vale,

my frightened soul finds comfort there;
    and at Love's invitation
it laughs, weeps, fears, or feels assured[43]

In his love-agony, he is also moved to bring the power of fantasy to his aid. The force of his half-delirious imagination was capable, he said, of causing Laura to materialize before his eyes. His poetry turned inward then to produce the psychic compensation of all aesthetes: beauty for its own sake, albeit, in this case, by means of a sylvan hallucination.

"In the shade of a tall pine or a hillside," he writes, also in poem 129, "there I sometimes stop, and in the first stone I see I portray her lovely face with my mind." When he comes back to himself, he finds his breast wet with tears. Nevertheless, says Petrarch,

    …as long as I
hold my disordered mind to the first thought
and look at her, forgetting myself,
Love seems so close by
that my soul is happy with the deception;
In so many beautiful places do I see her,
that should the image last, I would ask for no more.[44]

Over the years, the agony and the lamentation continue; and Petrarch takes the trouble to make a faithful record in verse of every nuance of his mourning. But he tells us in poem 270 that Laura's death in 1348 changed things:

    Death released me, Love, from all your laws;
she who was my lady has flown to Heaven,
leaving my life sad and free.[45]

Assuming a philosophical frame of mind, Petrarch considers that his suffering for Laura may have taught him an important lesson on life's fine, if transient, pleasures. In poem 290 he finds this optimism in a meditation on death:

So it goes! Now I'm delighted and pleased
by what once distressed me; I who clearly see

that to find salvation I had torment,
and waged a war for my eternal rest...

But blinding Love and my deaf mind
led me so far astray by their powers
that I had to go where Death is.
Blessed be she who steered my desires
toward a better shore and reined in
my passions so that I might live![46]

Through the memory of her untimely death, Laura begs him from heaven "to scorn the world and its sweet hooks." But Petrarch tells us elsewhere that his change of heart came earlier. In his "Letter to Posterity," he writes that around the age of forty "I renounced abruptly not only those bad habits, but even the very recollection of them—as if I had never looked at a woman. This I consider to be among my greatest blessings, and I thank God, who freed me while I was still sound and vigorous from that vile slavery which I always found hateful."[47]

Notably, this purported renunciation occurred just around the time his second illegitimate child was born, probably at Vaucluse to an unnamed mistress. So that event is more likely to explain the abruptness of his resolution. Also, while Petrarch says that his passions were still strong, one can wonder whether the natural effects of age on sexual biology might not have had something to do with it. All of those things must have made it easier for him to fulfill his desire to repent worldliness and to embrace God, as Saint Augustine does in his *Confessions*. That hope, as he wrote to his friend and professor of theology Dionisio da Borgo San Sepolcro, first occurred to him on his ascent of Mount Ventoux, just before he came to Vaucluse:

> The time, perhaps, will come when I can review all the experiences of the past in their order saying with the words of your St. Augustine: "I wish to recall my foul past and the carnal corruption of my soul, not that I love them, but that I may the more love you, O my God.[48]

The *Canzoniere* can thus be read as Petrarch's confessions. The poet, no doubt, always makes it less clear than does the saint as to whether he is reviewing his past with repugnance or wistful pleasure. In the last poem of the series, though, he continues to say that his love for Laura was all part his spiritual education. At first, she had been his exquisite worldly torment; then a guiding light from heaven; finally, his salvation. In poem 366, he closes the *Canzoniere* with a prayer to a higher lady who has finally replaced Laura in his desires:

> Bright Virgin, stable through eternity,
> star above our tempestuous sea,
> guide to every faithful helmsman:
> see what fearful storm I face,
> alone, without a tiller,
> close to my last screams.
> Still my wayward soul relies on you,
> sinful as it is, I cannot deny,
> yet able to pray, O Mary,
> that your enemy will not scorn me.
> Remember that our sins made God,
> to save our souls,
> take on human flesh
>   in your virginal cloister.[49]

Always a rather idiosyncratic recluse, Petrarch relished the fame his writings gave him across Europe; but it was his serious Latin verse that brought him glory. His poems about Love and Laura were not widely known and probably remained unpublished until late in his life. Yet to his great credit he seems to have gone on recording this very human side of his character, not worrying over much about the worldly contradictions of a cleric in love. The important thing, he seems to have believed, is a minute self-searching examination of all the vicissitudes of the individual life in the flesh, a life made potentially holy, after all, by the mysterious fact that God, too, once lived in an earthly body.

AUGUSTINUS

As time went on, Petrarch's grander literary schemes took second place to more personal, less schematic writings. In one mood, he continued to write his formal Latin poetry and essay-like letters. In another, he seems sincerely to have despaired of communicating with his contemporaries at all: "I talk much, I write much, but less to benefit these desperate, wretched times than to relieve and unburden my own mind."[50]

Petrarch's *The Secret* is a product of this later period; and, like the poems to Laura, it was not originally written for publication. Its subsequent influence on European thought and letters was nothing compared with that of the *Canzoniere*, but its value to us in elucidating Petrarch's inner conflicts and experiences is equally great. In the love-lyrics, he questions and apparently ends up denouncing worldly love. In *The Secret*, he even questions his views on solitude.

Like the comparison between the busy man and the retired man in *The Life*, the work embodies a contrast of two characters. In this case, we hear a direct dialogue between Petrarch's worldly self (Franciscus) and Saint Augustine (Augustinus), who represents the poet's unrealized ideal of himself: a true man of the Church, understanding the unfixable ways of the world, and living in controlled detachment by the grace of God.

Franciscus admits a love of the world and an inability to will otherwise. Despite all his talk of the nobility of solitude, his simple lifestyle, and his stoic recognition that wealth cannot be a source of happiness, he admits that he is still tied to the miseries of the world by two "fetters of gold." One is his love of Laura; the other is his desire for fame, as symbolized by the laurel wreath with which he was crowned poet laureate.

Even in the midst of his supposedly delightful solitude, says Franciscus, he is beset by melancholy. In modern terms, he has a case of ennui, the same psychic ailment identified as *acedia* by the Christian hermits of the Egyptian deserts and experienced in related forms by solitaires of every age. Ironically, it is a malady hardly different from that assigned in *The Life* to the busy man of the city. Franciscus describes it as

> that inward discord of which we have said so much, and that worrying torment of a mind angry with itself; when it loathes its

> own defilements, yet cleanses them not away; sees the crooked paths, yet does not forsake them; dreads the impending danger, yet stirs not a step to avoid it.[51]

In such times, he says,

> I take not pleasure in the light of day, I see nothing, I am as one plunged in the darkness of Hell itself, and seem to endure death in its most cruel form...I so feed upon my tears and sufferings with a morbid attraction that I can only be rescued from it by main force and in spite of myself.[52]

Analyzing his interlocutor's ailment, Augustinus concludes that he places too much emphasis on the false and fleeting sweetness of worldly pleasures. His life is not his own but is mired in the need to please others. He is distracted from higher thoughts by his desire for fame. One remedy offered by Augustinus also parallels that of *The Life*:

> If the tumult of your own mind within should once learn to calm itself down, believe me this din and bustle around you, though it will strike upon your senses, will not touch your soul.[53]

Offering another stoic-minded consolation, he bids Franciscus to remember that the dread of evils yet to come and all the terror of his heaped up calamities are indeed normal misfortunes within the world. It is his interpretation of them that reflects an over-vivid imagination and self-involvement. Franciscus should, after all, look on the bright side.

"Assuredly," says Augustinus, "if you look carefully at the lives of others as well as your own, and reflect that there is hardly a man without many causes of grief in this life, and if you except that one just and salutary ground, the recollection of your own sins—always supposing it is not suffered to drive you to despair—then you will come to acknowledge that Heaven has assigned to you many gifts that are for you a ground of consolation and joy, side by side with that multitude of things of which you murmur and complain."[54]

As for the complaint that Franciscus is pulled by fate in every direction and cannot call his life his own, Augustinus prescribes that "[you] will find no small consolation in reflecting that the same complaint has been made by men greater than yourself, and that if you have of your own free will fallen into this labyrinth, so you can of your own free will make your escape."

But as Petrarch knew only too well, one's will is a matter of human passion as much as reason—and the worldly will is not so easily bent to Heaven. Precisely, says Augustinus. With shrewd metaphysical exactitude, he reasons that ultimately all the innumerable shapes and images of things—thus the whole of earthly fate—enter through the senses and are pressed together into what he labels the "penetralia of the soul." The soul, he says, is "neither born for this nor capable of so many deformed things." It is weighed down and confused by the clamor of the senses:

> Hence, this epidemic of phantasms, dispersing and shattering your thoughts with an array of deadly concerns, blocks the road to the clarifying meditations by which the soul ascends to the one, only and supreme light.[55]

How can the blockage be removed? Petrarch's secret confessions in the *Canzoniere* were intended to help clarify things by unburdening his lovelorn heart. In *The Life*, he seems to have hoped that the hidden recesses of solitude could stimulate clarification if he could only control his thoughts: "The mind must be left aside. The mind, I say, must be left at home, and I must humbly pray God to create in me a clean heart and renew a right spirit within me. Then at last I shall have penetrated the secrets of the solitary life."[56]

In the *Secretum*, Petrarch offers a more specific method for controlling tempestuous thoughts. The objective, says Augustinus, is "to descend sufficiently deeply" into the soul so as truly to see beyond the residue of everyday affairs that has built up there, thus to get down to the reality of existence:

> We must picture to ourselves the effect of death on each several part of our body frame, the cold extremities, the breast in the sweat of fever, the side throbbing with pain, the vital spirits running slower and slower as death draws near, the eyes sunken and

> weeping, every look filled with tears, the forehead pale and drawn, the cheeks hanging and hollow, the teeth staring and discolored, the nostrils shrunk and sharpened, the lips foaming, the tongue foul and motionless, the palate parched and dry, the languid head and panting breast, the hoarse murmur and sorrowful sigh, the evil smell of the whole body, the horror of seeing the face utterly unlike itself—all these things will come to mind and, so to speak, be ready to one's hand, if one recalls what one has seen in any close observation of some deathbed where it has fallen to our lot to attend. For things seen cling closer to our memory than things heard.[57]

To be sure that technique achieves its purgative effect upon the soul, Augustinus offers the following test:

> Every time you meditate on death without the least sign of movement, know that you have meditated in vain, as about any ordinary topic. But if in the act of meditation you find yourself suddenly grow stiff; if you tremble, turn pale, and feel as if you have already endured its pain…then you may be assured that you have not meditated in vain.[58]

But while the saintly side of Petrarch can wrap himself in such high-minded considerations, Franciscus—the mainly honest, living man—must not truly have been equal to the medicine. For on the subject of giving up worldly fame (his chief desire—thus, all the literature Francesco left us), he waffles:

> My principle, concerning the glory we may hope for here below, is that it is right for us to seek while we are here below. One may expect to enjoy that other more radiant glory in heaven when we shall have arrived there, and when one will have no more care or wish for the glory of earth.[59]

Augustinus argues that earthly success may run counter to his heavenly goals, that he should put virtue before glory. But Franciscus, coming to the end of the dialogue, appears to grow impatient. "I will attend to myself as much as I can and gather up the scattered fragments of my soul," he says;

but then he remembers that "even as we speak a crowd of important affairs, admittedly mortal, awaits my attention." And so the poet-philosopher leaves the matter—unresolved.

LADY SOLITUDE

Here, then, in a secluded transalpine hermitage of late medieval Provence two cracks appear that will eventually fell the fortress of the church and medieval European morality. One is a worldly compromise with otherworldly religion; the other, an almost Protestant insistence on personal experience. Both presage the Renaissance in Europe, if they do not mark its birth in the solitudes of Vaucluse.

Overall, the record of Petrarch's life of solitude introduces us to the range of values, themes, and variations of the solitary life—the pitfalls, the psychological games, the exalted freedom that makes the soul more content with simple existence and with nature, the time to work and think, the "divine fertility of intellect," the thoughts of life and death, and the search for a remedy or a higher form of life.

Petrarch is of interest because he encompasses so many of the possibilities of solitude. To him it is a great blank page. In *The Life* he even anthropomorphizes time alone as a fertile goddess:

> Solitude is indeed something holy, innocent, incorruptible, and the purest of human possessions. To whom does she reveal herself amid forests, for whom does she display her charms and thorns?...With whom, finally, does she ingratiate herself, who does she seek to please, except the person who has penetrated the inmost recesses of solitude and for whom therefore there is no solitude?

Lady Solitude, continues Petrarch,

> aims to deceive no one; she neither simulates nor dissimulates; she adorns nothing, she glosses nothing, she pretends nothing. She is utterly naked and unadorned.[60]

The Lady, then, is essentially an open, ancient, empty, pregnant state of mind with multitudinous values and possible experiences and forms—depending on the individual. Not everyone has the appropriate temperament, but Petrarch holds on to the belief that there is a chosen few—"in all respects but numbers superior and triumphant over the rest"—who will feel the Lady's attraction. And so he concludes his apology with the following appeal to Philippe:

> Let the others be constantly in a state of restlessness and agitation, let us establish ourselves with feet firmly planted on the rock; let them be always motionless, let us make some progress; let them in their perplexity be always seeking counsel, let us at length carry wholesome counsel into practice…
>
> You can, indeed you can, if you prefer, cut all the knots at one stroke instead of untying them one by one. We are engaged with a hydra; there will be no end unless we cut off its ever-sprouting heads in the style of Heracles![61]

A BRIEF HISTORY

But what vistas of mystical sensation, what luminous mental landscapes, what avenues of planetary reverie are opened up when one follows these voyagers through the void!

—John Cowper Powys,
A Philosophy of Solitude, 1933

PETRARCH'S *THE LIFE OF SOLITUDE* was the world's first apologia for time alone; it was also the first work to answer Nietzsche's later call for a history of solitude. Petrarch bills his chronicle as "a compact enumeration over the most holy and famous men who by their presence have given distinction to solitude." Among several dozen such soloists, he discusses the ancient Hyperboreans of the Far North, Druids of Gaul, and the gymnosophists of India, along with Greek philosophers such as Democritus and Heraclitus; Romans such as the poet Horace, the philosopher-playwright-statesman Seneca, and Caesar Augustus; as well as the early Christian hermits of Egypt and even the Savior himself. Understandably, though, he lacked sufficient information—and, in some cases, the inclination—to cover all the Friends of Solitude whose biographies and writings are available today, thanks to modern advances in literary and cultural research. The following short history is intended to fill that gap, taking Petrarch's work as a starting point and, in some cases, correcting his account.

Prehistoric Solitude

There is much controversy in the literature of solitude on the question of who, exactly, was the first hermit, recluse, or solitary.

Petrarch naturally begins with Adam, "that general parent of the human race, than whom, as long as he was alone, no man was happier, but as soon as he received a companion, none more wretched." Adam was probably not as happy as Petrarch assumes, for according to The Book of Genesis, God said that it was not good for him to be alone and created Eve to "soothe his loneliness." His troubles were soon compounded when Eve bid him partake of apples from the Tree of the Knowledge. As a result, "the eyes of them both were opened" and they became "as gods knowing good and evil." In other words, they gained human consciousness. But we might more rightly term Adam the first alienated man rather than the first positive-minded Friend of Solitude. After eating the apples, God "put enmity" between him, Eve, and all other creatures, whereby Adam was as sorely anguished in that solitary state and as alienated from God—and other men—as any modern existentialist.

Long before Petrarch, Saint Jerome insisted that the Egyptian solitary Paul was the first hermit, having fled to a desert at the age of fifteen to escape persecution against Christians during the reigns of the Roman emperors Decius and Valerian in the third century. Known subsequently as Saint Paul the First Hermit, Jerome says that he beat the much more famous hermit Saint Anthony to a Christian retreat by more than two decades. But Jerome was writing for a specifically Christian audience. It was obviously not in his interest to bring up any earlier figure—the philosopher Pythagoras, for instance, or Democritus, both of whom chose to live alone for a time and profited by the experience. For Jerome, since they did not know Christ, they could not be true hermits.

More recently, Jean-Jacques Rousseau speculated in *The Social Contract* that solitude was "the first state of humankind." Contented in their freedom from society, he reasoned that the first conscious humans would only have come together for procreation or other activities of benefit to a community of individuals. When they did so, it was by an implicit contract which could be nullified if the terms of the agreement were not fulfilled. Rousseau's aim, of course, was to establish the right of individuals to overturn the will of a corrupt or unrepresentative government; but his position does not square with more modern and eminently reasonable theories that would have humans emerging millions of years ago from a simian heritage that was plainly communal from the outset, certainly without a social contract, explicit or implicit.

Any conjecture as to the state of human affairs in prehistoric times, let alone speculation as to the degree of solitude, is tricky business. But I would argue that compared with the three ideas above, there is much more evidence for a theory that tens of thousands of years ago at least a few human beings would have spent some productive and even joyful time alone, as do shamans of primitive cultures today.

Modern anthropologists and archaeologists tell us that cavemen well before the Paleolithic period had brains that were about the size of ours and physically little different. Given the artifacts they left behind, it is not unreasonable to believe that they also possessed consciousness, much as we do. As such, they would have been aware of the prospect of death, disease, and starvation; they would have been disturbed by the enmity and violence between men and frightened of the world to which they were born without explicit guidelines on how to live. In such a state, it is not difficult to imagine further that one courageous soul would have been separated from his community and, if not terrified to death, would have been amazed at the expanse of nature. At the same time, he may have had an inkling that he might somehow communicate with the force behind the world before him and thereby find answers, or at least explanations, for the fix in which he found himself. That man or woman would have been the first Friend of Solitude.

There is evidence for that scenario in the "paintings" recently discovered in two hundred or so caves in Northern Spain and Southern France dating back to the Middle Paleolithic period, 10,000 to 40,000 years ago. Some have presumed that this cave art was the work of primitive artists who chose for some reason to ply their craft secretly, deep inside the earth, perhaps for their own aesthetic enjoyment. But many others reason that the artifacts on the cave walls were the work of shamans who were aiming to get through to the other, controlling world of spirits.

The caves are treacherous and dark and many of the chambers where the paintings are found can be reached only by crawling on hands and knees through very narrow passageways. Moreover, the paintings could only have been created or observed by the light of flickering torches. So, first off, it is clear that the experience must have been both scary and essentially solitary, even if more than one person were present. Secondly, there is much evidence from anthropological reports of shamanism among contemporary primitive groups and from ancient history that solitary descents into the earth are employed to facilitate consciousness-altering spiritual journeys. These are used for the initiation of youth into the culture of the tribe, for the initiation of neophyte wizards into the mysteries of shamanism, and by shamans themselves as part of their spiritual work of healing and magic.

Among the most apposite examples of the latter is the Iglulik Eskimo story of the discovery of shamanism, as recorded in Greenland in the 1920s by the Danish explorer Knud Rasmussen. It was during a period of extreme hardship and starvation, according to Rasmussen's Iglulik informant, the shaman Aua, that one man took it upon himself to find a solution. "He demanded," said Aua, "to be allowed to go behind the skin hangings at the back of the sleeping place," saying that he was going to travel down to the "Mother of the Sea Beasts." Aua explains:

> No one in the house understood him, and no one believed in him. Nevertheless, he had his way, and passed in behind the hangings. Here he declared that he would exercise an art which afterwards would prove to be of great value to mankind; but no one must look at him. It was not long, however, before the unbelieving and inquisitive drew aside the hangings, and to

> their astonishment perceived that he was down into the earth. He had already gone so far down that only the soles of his feet could be seen.

How the man ever hit on this idea no one knows, adds Aua. But the shaman himself said that he was helped by spirits he had entered into contact with out in "the great solitude."[1]

Rasmussen further records that shamans among the Eskimos of Hudson's Bay routinely employ a similar tactic by sending their psychic selves downward to a mystically charged lower-world. There they are able to connect with "helping spirits" who provide them with magical powers. For the greatest shamans, according to another of Rasmussen's informants, "a way opens right from the house in which they evoke their helping spirits; a road down through the earth, if they are in a tent on shore, or down through the sea, if it is in a snow hut on the sea side, and by their route the shaman is led down without encountering any obstacle."[2]

On the other side of the planet, shamans among aboriginal peoples of Australia are often initiated into shamanhood via a similar descent into the earth. For the Arunta tribes, according to a nineteenth-century report by Bishop Spencer and F.J. Gilllen, one of the most potent initiation procedures includes becoming a temporary hermit in a cave in the Australian outback. The neophyte doctor spends a night at the mouth of the sacred cave. Amid considerable trepidation he finally falls asleep toward daybreak when spirits known as *Iruntarinia* (ancestral reincarnations) pierce him several times with spears and take the novice deep into the cave, where they provide him with a completely new set of intestines. Once the neophyte returns to his senses from "a bout of insanity," he becomes a shaman. The most powerful of such medicine men can suck evil magic out of his fellows, thus curing them of disease. But many also have the power of "climbing at nighttime by means of a rope, invisible to ordinary mortals, into the sky, where he can converse with the star people."[3]

A contemporary observer, Michael Harner, who purports to be a shaman himself, maintains that descent to the underworld via caves, hollow tree stumps, animal holes, or cavities made especially for the purpose are common to shamanic practice throughout the world.[4] He refers to

Eskimo examples, along with those of a Tavgi Samoyed shaman of Siberia, who said that on his first experience in a quasi-trance state typical of shamanic journeys (what Harner calls the SSC, shamanic state of consciousness) he visualized a hole in the earth that entered into an underground stream on which he flowed to a "sunny" underworld. In his books and classes on shamanism, Harner teaches his students how—lying face up on the ground amid repetitive sounds of drumming provided by an accomplice or a CD player—to put themselves into the SSC and find their way in spirit down to the lower world through whatever entrance happens to come to their minds.

Along the same lines, the ancient Anasazi Indians of the American Southwest built underground chambers for ceremonial purposes. Most such compartments, called *kivas,* have holes in their floors known as *sipapu,* which lead down into the underworld. Many American Indians, such as the Hopi of Arizona, still hold various rites in the kivas. Only initiated members of the tribe or neophytes undergoing initiation are allowed to witness; but it is known that the proceedings involve elaborate, inventive, colorful costumes representing figures in the spirit world, along with the enactment of symbolic events, all of which would seem analogous to the paintings in the caves of Southern France. Harner believes that the rites are often accompanied by descent into the underworld via the sipapu.

I am by no means the only one to make this connection between prehistoric cave art and the spirit flights of shamans. Among the first was Horst Kirschner, who proposed in a 1952 paper, "An Archaeological Contribution to the Early History of Shamanism," that there were distinct shamanic elements in the religions of Paleolithic hunters. He referred particularly to the representation in the cave at Lascaux of a shamanic trance and to mysterious objects found there which appear to be sticks for drumming in shamanic ceremonies.

More recently, Jean Clottes and David Lewis-Williams propose in their 1998 book *The Shamans of Prehistory: Trance and Magic in the Painted Caves* that the paintings in the Paleolithic caves have a psychedelic quality, which they interpret as depicting altered states of consciousness and mystical excursions. They note that the vast cave complexes include large areas where prehistoric shamans may well have demonstrated their spiritual discoveries to members of their group, including youthful initiates, the outline of whose small hands appear painted on the cave walls. The authors also propose that crannies in far reaches of the caves were employed for shamanism. These small, dark nooks, which would fit only one person at a time, have scratchings on their ceilings that appear to be the residue of solo spirit journeys intended to get through the rock to a deeper reality on the other side.

THE POWER IN CAVES

There is further evidence, particularly from ancient Greek literature, that caves were put to similar use in more recent but still very ancient times. Petrarch suggests that the Druids of Gaul were "accustomed in caves and ravines to instruct the noblest men of the nation in wisdom and eloquence and natural science and the motions of the stars and the mysteries of the gods and the immortality of the soul and the state of future life."[5] Petrarch did not name his sources, but they came no doubt from his reading in classical literature. A closer look at multitude of sources now available reveals many similar accounts, but with greater detail, of sages and poets who may in some way have been continuing a very archaic tradition of spiritual spelunking in Europe.

For example, we know that the cave of Ida on Crete was a particularly popular spot for fostering divine connections. Zeus is said, in one tradition, to have been "born" in the Idean cave, and excavations have shown that it was a sacred place even before the arrival of the Greeks. Later, King Minos and his brother Rhadamanthus, both regarded as sons of Zeus and revered lawgivers, were said to have retreated to the same cave every nine years to renew their royal powers and lawmaking wisdom through direct contact with Zeus.

Much later, Epimenides (c. 600 B.C.), a semi-legendary prophet-philosopher, is reported by several ancient sources to have "slept" like an ancient Rip van Winkle for fifty-seven years there, wherein he cultivated remarkable powers as a purifier, lawmaker, and philosopher. During the forty-sixth Olympiad, according to Diogenes Laerteus, Athenians called

Epimenides to their city asking him to purify it of a pestilence, a feat he successfully performed by sacrificing sheep to local divinities. At the same time, Epimenides was a thinker (or, as Aristotle described him, a "theologian") to whom are attributed both poems and philosophical works—the latter including *On Minos and Rhadamanthus*. The implication is clear that Epimenides' powers of reasoning as well as his wonderworking (the two never obviously divided until later in the history of Greek thought) came as a direct result of his years in seclusion. "Some," says Diogenes, "are fond to maintain that he did not go to sleep but withdrew himself for a while."[6]

Several other philosophers in the shadowy world of Greek antiquity spent time in caves and appear to have profited thereby. Diogenes reports that Pythagoras went to the cave of Ida to study with Epimenides. Later, after his journeys to visit seats of wisdom from Babylon to Egypt, the philosopher settled on the island of Samos, where, according to the fourth-century Syrian philosopher Iamblichus, he "made a cave the private site of his own philosophical teaching, spending most of the night and day-time there and doing research into the uses of mathematics."[7]

Perhaps it was there that he discovered his theorem and other verities of geometry, numbers, music, and astronomy. Central to Pythagoras' philosophical method, as the Cambridge classicist W.K.C. Guthrie explains, was the belief that assimilation to the divine is attained through "active contemplation" involving an actual change in the philosopher's own nature.[8] Pythagoras would have had any number of precedents from which he may have borrowed the idea that solitary time in caves could enhance contemplation. One of his teachers, Pherekydes, portrayed caves, or what he called hollows in the Chthoni (the "earth mother"), as receptacles of the divine hand of creation. According to the later Greek philosopher Porphyry, Pherekydes regarded such caverns as focal points for cosmic energies and the reception of souls leaving and returning to earth through metempsychosis.[9]

Similarly, the Greek sage Zalmoxis is reported to have built a secret underground chamber in his homeland of Thrace, where he lived for three years. He did this, according to Herodotus, to demonstrate that men are immortal and when we die we merely go temporarily to another place.

Thracians assumed that Zalmoxis had died; so when he emerged after four years, they were persuaded to believe his theory. Herodotus presents Zalmoxis' underground sojourn as a ruse, but one wonders why the sage would have spent so much time alone if he did not find some philosophical or magical benefit in solitude.

It was through a cave that the mythical poet and prophet Orpheus descended to the underworld to retrieve his lover Eurydice. And after the maenads of Dionysius beheaded Orpheus for attempting to introduce the religion of Apollo to Thrace, his head was "laid to rest" in the sacred cave of Antissa, where he is said to have "prophesied day and night." Likewise, most ancient Greek oracles resided in caves. Ancient Taoists typically lived in caves in the mountins of China, and many Christian hermits made their homes in caves out in the deserts of Egypt.

Clearly, there is something special, if not archetypal, about solitary experience in caves. Writing about Zalmoxis and Zeus' birth in the Idean cave, Mircea Eliade speculates that "the cave at the summit of the mountain signifies the most typical site of the divine epiphany, the place where, after a period of occultation, a redeeming god, a prophet, or a cosmocrator makes his appearance."[10] The cave, says Eliade, represents both the other world and the entire universe. Not only is it dark and subterranean, it is a place shut off from ordinary life, which makes it a "world-in-itself," an *imago mundi* "full of 'riches' and countless virtualities."[11]

ABOVE GROUND

Although dark caverns have long been powerful sites for evoking powers in solitude, there is no particular reason to believe that such powers may not be encouraged above ground. Clottes and Lewis-Williams cite many examples of hallucinogenic art from primitive peoples around the world akin to that found in Paleolithic caves. These tend to occur on rocky surfaces outside caves. Of course, Paleolithic shamans might well have produced similar public artifacts that would have been washed away by millennia of weathering.

In fact, spiritual descendents of the first shaman among the Igluliks say that they too found their powers out in the great solitude of the tundra, where the only caves are man-made igloos. And in many cases it was that experience alone which sufficed. Aua told Rasmussen that he tried to become a shaman with the help of teachers. He visited many famous shamans and gave them valuable gifts in hopes that they would train him in the ways of the shaman. But after these attempts failed, Aua said that he sought an untutored solitude, where, at first, he became very melancholy:

> I would sometimes fall to weeping, and feel unhappy without knowing why. Then, for no reason, all would suddenly be changed, and I felt a great, inexplicable joy, a joy so powerful that I could not restrain it, but had to break into song, a mighty song, with only room for the one word: joy, joy! And I had to use the full strength of my voice. And then in the midst of such a fit of mysterious and overwhelming delight I became a shaman. I could see and hear in a totally different way.[12]

Aua explained that he had attained what the Igluliks call *quamaneq*, the shaman-light of brain and body:

> It was not only I who could see through the darkness of life, but the same light also shone out from me, imperceptible to human beings, but visible to all the spirits of earth and sky and sea, and these now came to me and became my helping spirits.[13]

Aua added that a shaman cannot become truly powerful until he is capable of "seeing the body as a skeleton"—in other words, contemplating the reality of death, as he did in his melancholy sojourn on the tundra and as Augustinus advised Petrarch to do at Vaucluse. Without that capability, said Aua, the necessary helping spirits will never come to visit, and the shaman will be powerless.

Another of Rasmussen's informants, the Hudson's Bay Eskimo Igjugarjuk, likewise achieved his enlightenment in a soul-wrenching experience in the great solitude. He told the explorer that he spent a full month sitting in an igloo far out in the tundra wearing only light clothing and consuming only one drink of water the whole time. His body shriveled literally to a skeleton; and when his novitiate was finished his instructor had to carry him away on a sledge, because he could not walk.

Igjugarjuk complained that too many shamans attach weight to tricks designed to astonish the audience ("they jump about the floor and lisp all sorts of absurdities and lies in their so-called spirit language"). "For myself, I do not think I know much," he said, stressing that knowledge of things cannot be sought in such a superficial manner:

> True wisdom is only to be found far away from people, out in the great solitude, and it is not found in play but only through suffering. Solitude and suffering open the human mind, and therefore a shaman must seek his wisdom there.[14]

Igjugarjuk doesn't emphasize the joys of solitude. He seems to have been a bit more glum than Aua. But Aua stresses that not only was his first enlightenment a joyful experience, he found a similar sense of elation whenever he went into solitude to call forth his helping spirits. Each shaman has different helping spirits, suited, perhaps, to their personalities. Aua's support in time alone came from a shark and a female shore sprite called an *aua*. To summon them, he sang the following song:

> Joy, joy,
> Joy, joy!
> I see a little shore spirit,
> A little aua,
> I myself am also Aua,
> The shore spirit's namesake,
> Joy, joy!
>
> I would keep repeating these words until I burst into tears, overwhelmed by a great dread; then I would tremble all over, crying only: "Ah-a-a-a-a, joy, joy! Now I will go home, joy, joy!"[15]

When Aua lost a son, he stayed for a long time alone at the grave site far away from his village. Overcome with grief, he felt as though he could not leave the spot and that he would remain for the rest of his life "like a mountain spirit, afraid of humankind."[16] But one day, after his song of joy came to him, he returned to himself and again felt longing for his fellow man.

SOLITARY INITIATION

If shamans of the Paleolithic discovered the power of solitude, it would have been natural for them to employ that power, not only for their own purposes but also to initiate youth into adulthood and the mythic culture of the tribe.

That is what we find in modern anthropological reports of primitive initiation rites around the world. One of the most dramatic examples occurs among the Pangawe of Tanzania, where, four days before the rite begins, novices are marked with a "consecration of death." On the first day of the initiation, they must drink a nauseous potion; then when the novices vomit, they are chased through their village with cries of "you must die" and pushed into a house filled with ants' nests, where they are badly bitten. The novices are taken to individual cabins in the jungle where they remain completely naked and in absolute solitude for a month. They are then painted white and ushered back to the village to participate in dances—but must otherwise reside alone in their huts for three months.[17]

Another eloquent example occurs in New Guinea among the Nor-Papua, who build a special house for the circumcision of boys in the form of the Monster Barlun, complete with belly and tail. The boys are forced to remain in the house, where the monster is thought to swallow then disgorge them as reborn individuals. In some cases, the devouring monster-spirit has a flute-like voice—which is probably irrelevant to anything, except that I like this image of the spirit of solitude as a devouring, transforming chimera with a strange voice: the Monstrous Song of Solitude, you might say.[18]

On occasion, such initiation rites can be so powerful and self-transforming that they enable the novice to develop the creative and innovative powers of a shaman. Such was the case with one young brave in North America who, according to an Ojibwa Indian tale, undertook the *ke-ig-uish-im-o-win* rite of passage through fasting in solitude. During the first few days of the fast, the boy strolled in the forest collecting images for his nightly dreams. But on the third day the Spirit of Corn, dressed in yellow and green, appeared and bid the youth to wrestle, then to kill, and finally burry him. His fast over, the boy tended the grave until shoots of corn grew up that would feed his undernourished family and provide a new source of food for his tribe.[19]

Solitude must have been a very important, if risky, part of cultural life among the Ojibwas. For according to another tale, one initiate became so enamored of solitude out in the forest that he decided to leave his tribe altogether. On the ninth day of his lonely fast, the boy reported to his father that his dreams forbade evil and requested to be allowed to leave. But despite repeated pleas his father insisted he stay. When the rite was completed, the father came to collect his son, only to find that he had turned into a robin (with the power of speech). "Regret not the change you behold," said the boy. "I shall be happier in this state than I could have been as a man. I shall always be a friend of man and keep to their dwellings…I will cheer you by my songs and strive to inspire in others the joy and lithesomeness I feel as a bird."[20]

The Tibetan *chöd* rite offers still another useful example of initiation in solitude because it provides insight into what initiates are asked to visualize in their retreats. The chöd is a sort of mystery play for one in which the neophyte, or "actor," is directed first to find a "solitary, awe-inspiring place" free of the influences of genie, demons, and worldly ambitions. There he or she should use clarity of intellect to conjure the following mental picture:

> Then imagine this body, which is the result of your karmic past,
> To be a fat, luscious-looking corpse, big enough to embrace the universe.
> Then, Phat!—visualize the radiant intellect within you
> As being the Wrathful Goddess and as standing apart from your body,
> Having one face and two hands and holding a knife and a skull.
> Think that she severs your head from your body
> And sets your severed skull like an enormous caldron over three skulls placed like the legs of a great tripod embracing the Three Regions,

> And cuts your corpse into bits and flings them inside your skull as offerings to the deities.[21]

As the initiate implements this grizzly sacrifice, he is directed to evoke the mystic power of two mantras—*Aum-Ah-Hum* and *Ha-Ho-Hri*—whereby his body and intellect are "wholly transmuted into *amrita*, the nectar of the gods, sparkling and radiant." Having thereby freed himself of all vestiges of self, intellect, and other noisome worldly illusions, the neophyte should learn through psychodramatic experience that *samsara* (the material world of the senses) and *nirvana* (the transcendental world of spirit) are one. This realization delivers the neophyte to a state of enlightenment, because in the sacrifice he or she has simultaneously rejected and accepted both the material and the spiritual world in order to see them in an entirely new light.

The spiritual objective of the rite is expressed in Buddhist terms. Nevertheless, its rather violent modus operandi, along with the presence of demons and spiritual beings, clearly suggest that it is an adaptation of archaic ecstatic practices of Tibet's shamanic Bon religion. The ease with which Buddhist philosophy is overlaid on the rite's shamanic origins suggests that both are pointing to a similar, albeit ineffable, mystic experience in solitude. Some philosophers such as Henri Bergson have even speculated that all religion and its associated rituals are in essence reenactments of such primal mystic experiences. Religion, says Bergson in *The Two Sources of Morality and Religion*, is "the crystallization, brought about by a scientific cooling, of what mysticism had poured, while hot, into the soul of man."[22] In that light, the chöd script and solitary initiation practices may be seen as methods for evoking such mystic experience directly, while the other rites and spiritual practices of religion would be an attempt to evoke only a taste of those experiences.

In their interpretation of the markings on the walls of the Paleolithic caves, Clottes and Lewis-Williams suggest that a similar scenario may have been at work there. The far reaches of the caves, where copious markings also occur, were generally accessible by only one person at a time. But there are also many larger caverns in which several individuals could assemble to reenact experiences that more adventurours adepts would have conjured alone in the recesses of the cave systems.[23]

At the same time, we can presume that the need for primary mystical experiences persisted throughout the Paleolithic age and that later shamans would have sought solitude, to cultivate such experiences, either inside or outside the caves. It is impossible to know whether this actually occurred or what the circumstances of such prehistoric uses of solitude might have been, but considering that tens of thousands of years separated the Paleolithic age from that of the earliest known religion and philosophy, it is clear that much could have occurred. And given the persistent desire of conscious humans to understand and control the mysteries of death and existence, it is reasonable to speculate that the use of time alone for adventurous mystical purposes did occur.

In fact, in each of the major civilizations of India, China, and Greece, we find evidence of the origins of religion and philosophy in myths and legends of shaman-like individuals who are said to have lived in solitude apart from their societies. As we will see, these independent sages were engaged first and foremost in enhancing their own goodness and spiritual well being; but the value of their solitude was widely recognized by interested observers, especially by powerful kings and noblemen.

Hermits of India

THE FIRST HERMITS to make a strong appearance in the written history of solitude appear in India. They are the *munis*, or "silent sages," of the Hindu Vedas, who probably date back at least to the second millennium B.C. According to verse 136 of the tenth book of the Vedas, called the "Munisukta," a group known as *kesins,* or long-haired ascetics, were naked hermits who wore "dirty red rags." Like shamans, they were friends of "this god and that" and were capable of "revealing everything" and "declaring the light." They moved like heavenly nymphs or wild beasts. And when gods entered them they became "stallions of the wind" and "friends of hurricanes."[1]

The Vedas are not clear about whether the munis and kesins were different groups or whether they may have derived from the same ecstatic tradition. Nor are they entirely clear about what these ancient spiritual explorers were thinking or doing. But there are indications in the wording of many of the oldest Vedic hymns, where the seers are described as ascetics, and where *soma* and other hallucinogenic drugs are frequently mentioned. Solitude—including both withdrawal from society and inner quietude—seems also to have played an important role, since the kesins are described specifically as being "maddened with silence." In such a state, the kesins proclaimed, "We have mounted the wind! Our bodies are all you mortals can see!"[2]

There is also evidence that the seers' spirit flights were powered by some form of mystic wordplay. In his book *Poetry and Speculation of the Rg Veda*, Willard Johnson holds that the seers of the Vedas were "conscious enigmatizers." The enigmas they invented, known as *brahmans*, are like Zen koans designed to jolt the mind from common categories of thinking so as to "wander" and to evoke an understanding or vision of Brahman, the essential ground and power of the universe.

In several places in the *Vedas*, we hear of sacrificial symposia in which the seers gathered to compete at provoking "mental flashes" intended to "yield this highest power of understanding." In one such verse, which Johnson believes to be among the earliest recorded milestones in Indian mysticism, the contestant acknowledges that he does not fully understand the thread of the brahman nor how it is woven. So, he elicits the help of Agni Vaisvanara, god of the sun and light, who is also known as the original poet-seer:

> Only Agni truly understands the thread
> and how to weave; he should solve the brahmans
> which are to be explained according to reality
> as it is,
>
> He really sees the reality to which
> the enigma takes aim, he is the protector
> of the immortal, moving here below and
> above observing through another.[3]

Later, a similar spirit of mystic spontaneity is evident in the Forest Books of the Upanishads, which I would term the first great works of eremitic literature. The wisdom expressed therein is attributed to seers of Vedic times stretching back, significantly, to the god Brahma. The ancients passed their spiritual knowledge on through several dozens of generations to the most prominent figure of the Forest Books, the reclusive sage Yajnavalkya, who probably lived circa 700 B.C.

Yajnavalkya is known for leaving his wives and family to become a full-time mystic philosopher dedicated to finding the spiritual essence underpinning the sacrifices and rituals of the day. If he did not retreat permanently to the forest, he certainly retreated inwardly to search for the essence of his spiritual soul (*atman*), thus to achieve union with the infinite (*brahman*). This is expressed in his famous conclusion that atman *is* brahman—in other words, one's soul, properly understood, is identical with the spiritual essence of things and therefore constitutes a door that opens into the immortality, freedom, and peace of the all-powerful brahman.

Wherever he was located, it is clear that Yajnavalkya's retreat was punctuated with visits by followers who hoped to benefit from the fruits of his meditations. His interlocutors included curious women as well as men and nobles such as King Janaka, all of whom came to question his philosophy in hopes that they could follow his penetrating mystic logic to enlightenment. As he embarked on his philosophic retreat, it is recorded that Yajnavalkya granted his wife Maitreyi a boon, whereupon she asked him to explain the "secret of immortality." He answered:

> Lo, verily, not for love of a husband is the husband dear, but for the love of the Soul a husband is dear...The Soul is not this, it is not that. It is ungraspable, for it cannot be grasped. It is indestructible, for it cannot be destroyed. It is unattached, for it does not attach itself. It is unbound. It does not tremble. It is not injured.[4]

"After speaking thus," according to the *Brihadaranyaka Upanishad*, "Yajnavalkya departed." Thereafter, Yajnavalkya did not become an anti-worldly curmudgeon. For one thing, he had a philosophical sense of humor. When the female sage Gargi continues to pry with straightforward questions about the nature of the world, he warns her: "Gargi, do not question too much, lest your head fall off!"[5] Pressed by another interlocutor, Kahola, on the means to brahmanhood, he only replies cryptically: "By that means by which he does become such a one."[6]

Ancient accounts also suggest that Yajnavalkya lived in style. When, on several occasions, King Janaka awarded him "a thousand cows" for his insightful repartee, it is clear that he cheerfully accepted his winnings.

POWER HERMITS

Around the same time, according to the Hindu Mahabharata, other eremitic seers and transcendental athletes were following a somewhat different track. I call them power hermits because they sought solitude not only to plumb the nature of truth or human happiness but also to build up energy, both spiritual and physical.

Like the philosophy of the Upanishads, this avenue in solitude seems to have ancient roots, particularly in its application of an extreme form of asceticism known in Sanskrit as *tapas*. According to verse 190 in the tenth book of the Rig Veda, the whole world was created by the power of tapas. As the verse puts it, "Order and truth were born from heat as it blazed up. From that was born night; from that heat was born the billowy ocean."[7]

The word tapas also refers to the "heat" that a *tapasvin* can build up within himself, often with astonishing physical effects. Among the most sensational examples is the tapas of the warrior Arjuna. According to the Mahabharata, he journeyed up into the Himalayas, where he ate only fruit every fortnight, then subsisted on a dead leaf for a month, and finally on wind, when he spent a month meditating, while standing on the tips of his toes, arms raised without support. As a result, he was able to produce what must be the first weapon of mass destruction, known as the *Pasupata* or "Brahma's Head." The storytellers of the Mahabharata relate that it was "gruesome, of terrible power, which at the horrible end of the Eon will destroy the entire world...From its mouth, when properly spelt, issue forth thousands of tridents, awful-looking clubs, and missiles like venomous snakes."[8]

As often happens in Hindu mythology, nearby seers, who seem always to have been present in the mountains of India, became worried about what Arjuna might do with all his accumulated energy. So they went to the god Siva, lord of ascetics, to ask him to put a stop to Arjuna's tapas, whereupon Siva assumed the guise of a mountain hermit armed with a bow to test the hermit-warrior's intentions. Arjuna succeeded in assuring the god that he "did not desire heaven, nor sovereignty, nor long life," but merely worldly power. Siva then allowed him to retain the magic weapon, but issued a warning that further attests to its modern proportions:

> You must never let it loose at any man in wanton violence, for if it is a person of insufficient power, it might burn down the entire world. There is no one in all three worlds with their moving and standing creatures who is invulnerable to it, and it can be launched with a thought, a glance, or a bow.[9]

This psychic power, or at least the perception of it, was employed in ancient India not only for military might but also for statecraft. For according to Hindu legend, many Vedic priests not only supervised the sacrifices of their kingdoms, they also served as *purohita* (ministers of state) whose function it was to counsel and protect the king with magical powers. Among the most important, and most interesting, of these were the warring hermit-ministers Vasistha and Visvamitra. Like Romulus and Remus for Rome, they are recognized in Hindu mythology as playing an important role in the founding of Indian civilization—but in a very different way.

A key story in the Mahabharata centers on Visvamitra, a strong-willed member of the baronial *kshatria* caste of warriors and statesmen. One day while out hunting with his retinue in the forest he happened upon Vasistha, a brahmin who was residing in his hermitage with his magical cow Nandini. Visvamitra became so enamored with Nandini that he offered his entire kingdom in return for the cow. When Vasistha refused, Visvamitra directed his soldiers to take her by force, but on Vasistha's order, Nandini transformed herself into formidable armies, which surrounded the soldiers and drove them off. On seeing this great miracle that sprang from brahmanic power (that is, the power of tapas), Visvamitra became so discontented that he concluded the following:

> A curse on the power that is baronial power! Brahmanic power is *power*. On weighing weakness and strength, asceticism appears the superior power![10]

So Visvamitra relinquished his prosperous kingdom and went off into the forest, where he put all his worldly pleasures behind him and set his mind on asceticism and meditation. Eventually, he became so perfected by his austerities that "he burned all the worlds with his fiery might and attained to brahminhood."[11]

Of course, this tale of super-solitude does not stop there. The Hindu gods began to fear that Visvamitra was building up so much power that he too threatened the well-being of the universe. So the great god Indra elicited the help of Menaka, a callipygian girl "distinguished in the divine talents of Heavenly Nymphs." Listen, he told her,

> that great hermit Visvamitra, who possesses the splendor of the sun, has been performing awesome austerities that make my mind tremble...Lest he topple me from my throne, go and seduce him! Obstruct his tapas! Do me the ultimate favor! Seduce him with your beauty, youth, sweetness, fondling, smiles, and flatteries, my buxom girl, and turn him away from his austerities![12]

Menaka agreed, albeit reluctantly, given the seer's stupendous powers. But as always occurs in Hindu mythology, the eremitic seduction turned out to be successful. In fact, it resulted in 650 years of lovemaking and the conception of Sakuntala, who is recognized by many as the "mother of India." Visvamitra raised the girl and one day when Sakuntala had reached maturity, another noble, King Dushanta, happened to meet her while the hermit was away gathering fruits. One thing led to another and the result was the conception of Bharata, whose progeny are the subject of the Mahabharata, the great epic of Hindu civilization.

EREMITIC EPIDEMIC

These two benefits of solitude—powerful magic and enlightenment—were highly attractive to early Indian kings. By the middle of the first millennium B.C., they also attracted large numbers of thoughtful Indians with no pretensions at all to kingly status. The result was an epidemic of eremitism more extensive and experimental than the world had ever known, and possibly more lavish than the world will ever know. According to Buddhist sources, there were 4,900 types of hermits during this period:

> They went naked. They were of loose habits, performing their bodily functions and eating food in a standing posture, not crouching down or sitting down as decent people did. After taking meals they lick their hands instead of washing them. If asked to come nearer or wait a moment when they go round for alms, they would go away...These ascetics feed on potherbs, or wild rice, or *nivara* seeds or leather parings, or powder of rice husks; on rice-scum, on flour of oil seeds, on grass, cowdung, or fruits

> and roots. They wear coarse hempen cloth, coarse mixture cloth, discarded shrouds, discarded rags, bark cloth, antelope hide, *kusa* fiber, human hair blankets, horse-hair blankets or garments made of owl's feathers. They pluck their hair and beard, crouch on heels, are addicted to exerting themselves, lie on beds of iron spikes or thorns, use plank beds, sleep on the ground, or sleep on one side...[13]

This popular outbreak of asceticism was accompanied by a flowering of thought, including a continuation of the orthodox brahmanic philosophy of the Upanishads and philosophical explorations of a host of heterodox sects and stand-alone philosophers, all of whom were world-renouncing hermits.

The field of thinking was wide open. Some hermits, such as Makhali of the Cow Pen, argued against the laws of karma, maintaining that no actions of any kind have an effect on the random level of suffering to be endured in this life or the next. Men and women will find an end to pain only after eighty-four hundred-thousand eons, he said, when their existence finally unwinds like a ball of yarn and comes to an end. Agita the Hairshirt reasoned that individuals will not have to wait so long, since there is no next life at all. "Both the foolish and the wise," he argued, "on the dissolution of the body, are annihilated and destroyed, and nothing comes again into being."[14]

The origins of this eremitic nihilism remain obscure, but observers such as W.S. Urquhart, point out that there were pessimistic tendencies latent within Vedic thought itself, which gave rise to "a growing sense of helplessness of the individual and the poverty and wretchedness of his life in the presence of universal forces."[15] Joseph Campbell traces it to "a mood of world-and life-negation" that overcame the Indus Valley when the Vedic Aryan warrior folk invaded circa1500–1200 B.C. and some in the non-Aryan population were prompted to find a practical answer to the problem of escape from sorrow.[16] A.L. Basham finds what seems to me to be the most likely cause in the social, political, and economic upheaval of the opening centuries of the first millennium. "It was a time," he says in his book *The Wonder That Was India*, "of great social change, when old tribal units were breaking up. The feeling of group solidarity, which the tribe gave, was removed and men stood face to face with the world, with no refuge in their kinsmen. Chieftains were overthrown, their courts dispersed, their lands and tribesmen absorbed into greater kingdoms." Despite the great growth of material civilization at this time, Basham adds, "the hearts of many were failing them for fear of what should come to pass upon Earth."[17]

In a passage from the *Maitri Upanishad*, King Brihadratha sums up that sense of worldly despair:

> In this ill-smelling insubstantial body...which is afflicted with desire, anger, covetousness, delusion, fear, despondency, envy, separation from the desirable, union with the undesirable, sorrow, and the like, what is the good of enjoyment of desires?
>
> We see that this whole world is decaying, as are these gnats and mosquitoes, as are the trees that arise and perish...Among other things, even great oceans dry up, mountain peaks fall away, the pole star changes its position in the heavens, stars burn out, the earth is submerged, the celestials retreat from their station.
>
> In this cycle of existence what is the good of enjoyment of desires, when after a man has fed on them he returns here to earth?[18]

HETRODOX HERMITS

Amid this upheaval of asceticism and pessimism, two prominent figures arose who, so many believed and still believe, provided an optimistic solution. Each represented a culmination or synthesis of the religious and philosophical explorations during the early eremitic epidemic. In their solitary meditations and through their debates with fellow vagabonds, both concocted ingenious philosophies and methodologies for rising from the tribulations of worldly life to a state of blissful enlightenment—in one case, very much in the material world; in the other, beyond being altogether. One was Vardhamana (or Mahavira, "Great Hero"), purported founder of Jainism; the other was Shakyamuni, the muni of the Shakya clan, who became the Buddha.

Mahavira is known in Jainism as a *kaivalin* (isolated one) and the twenty-ninth and most recent *tirthankara* (teacher). He is the most forthrightly fanatical ascetic hermit that I can find in all the literature of eremitism. He went naked. He abstained from sex and ate little or nothing at all. He made every effort never to harm the least of creatures, leaving rules that many Jains follow to the present day—for instance, that one should not step in mud puddles for fear of harming anything that may be living there. Likewise, one should not raise one's arms abruptly for fear of scaring birds. If, riding in a boat, a fellow traveler gets angry and decides to throw one overboard, the proper follower of Mahavira should jump into the water before the upset traveler has a chance to push him in.

Mahavira's rules are no doubt difficult to follow and, to most of us, preposterous in their life-negating demands. But if one agrees with the premises, there is, after all, a powerful logic to the Jain system, which potentially anyone can follow (although it may take a hundred or more reincarnations). For if life is suffering and evil and if one's actions in the world build up through karmic causality, as the Jains and many other Indians believe, then the way to end suffering is to avoid evil entirely, thereby shifting the laws of karma into reverse. According to Jain theology, isolation serves to cut off the natural accumulation of bad karma, that metaphysical residue of one's foul deeds which, as punishment, leads to future suffering: to rebirth as a pariah, for example, or as one of those little creatures to be found in mud puddles. By avoiding this karmic buildup, so the theology goes, one can cleanse one's conscience in the present life and, more importantly, increase the chances of rebirth in successively more exalted spiritual lives to come.

The reward for such thoroughgoing asceticism is nothing short of miraculous. Mahavira "knew and saw all conditions of all living beings in the world, what they thought, spoke, or did at any moment."[19] Thus prepared, he died sometime in the early fifth century B.C., the result of ritual starvation, to become an enlightened monad at the tip of the universe, which in Jain theology is in the shape of a man. Presumably, he still resides there, aware of but unbothered by what we write here.

It was long thought by Westerners that Mahavira and the Buddha were the same person. Both were pampered princes in Northern Indian kingdoms circa the fifth century B.C. who renounced the rights to their thrones, cut off their hair, and took up the life of wandering mendicancy. Both spent a decade or so in diligent ascetic isolation and meditation before they achieved enlightenment. And both rejected the brahmanic atman-is-brahman philosophy, along with the concept of God altogether.

But what might be termed their anti-theology differed markedly. Buddha advocated Jain-like ascetic purity only as a starting point on which he built his philosophy of spiritual isolation. The aim, sitting in a "lonely spot" and thinking subtle, powerful thoughts, is not to rise to the heavenly tip of the universe or to become brahma by knowing the soul, as Yajnavalkya would have it. Rather, the aim, in so many words, is to reside in the "nothingness" of nirvana, the indefinable essence of things that is beyond understanding.

When Shakyamuni "crossed over to the other shore" of enlightenment it is said that the earth shook and the gods rejoiced. Thereafter, the Buddha spent years preaching his path to enlightenment to hosts of followers. The full scope of that teaching is, of course, too complex to elucidate in a few words, but one critical element along that path is particularly relevant here. It is the realization, as the Buddha explained again and again, that everything that is "effected and thought out"—that is, everything in the ordinary world of life—is impermanent, but that a kind of permanence can be obtained by living in what might be termed the "ultimate solitude."

Buddha explains how that may be done in a recorded dialogue with King Ajatasattu, known as "Fruits of the Life of a Recluse." One moonlit night, according to the Pali text, the king, accompanied by five hundred of his women on five hundred she-elephants, journeyed to the mango grove of Jivaka, the children's physician, where the Buddha was camped with 1,250 monks. The purpose of his visit was to ask the Buddha a single question: What is the advantage of living the life of a recluse? To make a very long answer short, he tells the king that the recluse may achieve "a state of joy and ease born of detachment" as a result of his ascetic discipline and world renunciation. At a still higher level of attainment, the recluse may "suppress all reasoning and investigation," then "hold aloof from joy," so as to enter a state of "attentive equanimity."

Finally, he may give up happiness and sadness completely to enter "a state of pure mindfulness and equanimity beyond both pain and pleasure." At that point, says the Buddha, as the recluse applies his mind to "insight knowledge," he is "tranquil, purified, cleansed, flawless, free from defilements, supple, ready to act, firm and imperturbable."[20]

In this way, the recluse can become an *arhat*, or "worthy one"—in which case, his mind is freed of sensuousness, external existence, and "delusive ignorance." Dwelling in serenity, he may bend his mind to such things as the ability to mentally reproduce his own body, to penetrate the minds of others, or to remember all his existences as well as those of others, past, present, and future. Then, at the very highest level, he may turn his attention to the "knowledge of the destruction of the Deadly Floods."

> In him, thus set free, there arises the knowledge of his emancipation, and he knows: "Rebirth has been destroyed. The higher life has been fulfilled. What had to be done has been accomplished. After this present life there will be no beyond!"[21]

Such, then, is the value of solitude, according to the Buddha. Apparently, the king got it, because the Buddha proclaimed that he would have achieved enlightenment then and there, were it not for his confession that he had murdered his father. Nothing is said about the five hundred women being an impediment in that regard; but, as we will see, worldly trappings are not necessarily barriers to enlightenment, provided one is able to maintain inner solitude and right-mindedness.

COMPROMISE, SOPHISTICATION

Petrarch knew something about the hermits of India through his reading in classical western literature, enough to include two chapters about them in *The Life of Solitude*. Hindu gymnosophists, he wrote, "are accustomed to philosophize while wandering about naked (which is precisely what their name denotes), through the remote, shady wildernesses of

India." Referring to a book that he says was signed by Saint Ambrose, Petrarch also mentions "a tribe of Brahmans…distinguished by continence and purity and by contempt of riches, and greatly to be respected for their severe silence."[22]

He did not condone the Hindus' nakedness and was careful to condemn what he took to be their widespread practice of suicide by self-immolation, something that Alexander is reputed to have witnessed with admiration during his campaigns in Persia and India.[23] "On the other hand," he writes, "I like their contempt of the world, which cannot be too great in a right-minded man; I like their solitude, I like their freedom, which no people enjoys to an equal degree; I like their silence, I like their leisure, I like their repose, I like their habit of fixed contemplation."[24]

Petrarch goes on to speculate that because there were numbers of such men in the past, "what prevents the existence of one today?" That conjecture was correct. Since Alexander's brief conquest, the Buddha's path to enlightenment had spawned a major religion; but by the fourteenth century, Buddhism had already disappeared in India, having been subsumed back into Hinduism. Meanwhile, the skepticism and spiritual exploration that fueled India's eremitic epidemic went on as before. And the history of solitude continued to develop and ripen along many lines simultaneously—including a reaction to the arrogant antiworldliness of the hermit, and a sense of humor.

Among the best examples of the latter direction is the curious tale of Cyavana, a seer who sat so long out in the forest in the *vira*, or heroic yoga posture, that an anthill formed around him. One day, according to the third book of the Mahabharata, King Saryati was walking in the same forest with his retinue of four thousand women, when his daughter Sukanya walked by the hermit, who "watched her in his solitude." Enamored, he cried out with his dried-up throat, but the girl, not hearing him, happened playfully to poke the anthill, pricking Cyavana's eye with a thorn. The angry hermit then caused the king's armed escort to suffer constipation, which somehow the king quickly discovered was Cyavana's reprisal for his daughter's misdeed. He then righted the wrong by giving his daughter to the hermit. Cayavana thereby became serene, the "fair-faced woman quickly ingratiated herself with him," and harmony was restored.[25]

Note that the tale both parodies selfish solitude and implies a solution: worldly compromise. Eremitic lechery aside, the most profound form of such compromise is *karma yoga,* the yoga of action, which makes its first appearance in the Bhagavadgita, probably in the last half of the first millennium B.C., and in the Mahayana philosophy of Buddhism, which likely appeared about the same time. (Because such philosophies deserve more detailed attention, I discuss them in a separate section below: "Solitude in Society.")

Another common form of worldly-spiritual compromise in Hindu culture is simply to defer yearning for ascetic solitude until later in life. There is ample precedent in the fact that nearly all the major religious figures in India from Yajnavalkya to the Buddha enjoyed worldly wealth and family life before their retirements. The same compromise has long been an institution in Hindu life, as codified probably beginning in the first millennium B.C. in the *Laws of Manu*. After completing the first two phases of life (childhood and parenthood), the proper Hindu who follows those laws may retire to the forest when he sees gray hair on his head and the sons of his sons. He may not eat any cultivated food or trim any of the hair on his body, but he may take his wife along with him. This appears to serve as an agreeable transition to the fourth—or wandering ascetic—phase, when the aged Hindu has the luxury of giving up all worldly possessions and cares and meanders in silence and always alone in order to attain the "final liberation."[26]

At the same time, some skeptical storytellers cautioned that there is a difference between obeying the letter of Manu's laws and their spirit; for even conjugal hermits may take world renunciation too far. Here again, it is one of the perennial duties of the gods to remind humans that the hermit's antisocial meditations may actually disrupt the balance of the entire universe. In a tale from the Puranas, to prove the point, Siva appears to a venerable group of hermits known as the Pine Forest Sages to show them the proper balance.[27] The sages (including Visvamitra and Vasistha) are living on an auspicious peak in the Himalayas. Having finished their childbearing years, they have retired to the forest for a life of meditation and religious ritual. But apparently the sages were concentrating too much of their energies on asceticism, while neglecting their wives. According to the tale, "some ate nothing but moss; some lay down immersed in water; some had clouds as their only shelter; others stood on the tip of the big toe."[28]

So Siva—who is, by the way, god of both asceticism and eroticism—is moved to teach them a lesson by paying a visit to the sages' forest retreat in order to bewitch and seduce their wives. To enhance the effect, he again transforms himself into a naked hermit, this time one with disorderly hair, enormous pointed teeth, genitals red with chalk, the tip of his generously erect penis ornamented with black and white paint, laughing horribly, and bellowing like an ass. In disgust, the sages curse the divine hermit with all their ascetic powers until his *lingam* (penis) falls off. Immediately, the world went dark. After much confusion and the intervention of the god Brahma, the sages finally discover their error and are able to restore light to the world only by installing and worshipping images of the Siva's lingam in the hills and caves surrounding their hermitage, a practice that continues to the present day.

As a counterpoint around the same time, the antiworldly strain in Indian eremitism became even more sophisticated and exotic than it was during India's early epidemic of eremitism. Sometime during the seventh or eighth century, the monk Shantideva reiterated the Buddha's call for inner solitude in fresh, forceful language. "No distractions can touch the man who's alone both in his body and mind," he said. "Therefore renounce you the world, give up all thinking discursive!" Two evils meet when fools consort together, he adds: "Alone I'll live, in peace and with unblemished mind."[29]

There is obviously an added touch of bitterness in these phrases from Shantideva's *Guide to the Bodhisattva's Way of Life*. Nonetheless, the same guide is intended to help the reader become a *bodhisattva*—an "enlightenment being" who chooses to remain active in the world—by realizing the equality of self and other. Many such how-to guidebooks were highly complex and systematized; others were popularizations. But virtually all of them begin with the same advice: "Find a lonely spot." Such was the recommendation, for example, in the second-century work *Saundarananda*, by the Buddhist poet Ashvagosha:

> Then, my friend, you should find yourself a living-place which, to be suitable for Yoga, must be without noise and

> without people. First the body must be placed in seclusion; then detachment of mind is easy to attain.[30]

Ashvagosha warns that "those who do not like to live in solitude, because their hearts are not at peace and because they are full of greed, will hurt themselves there, like someone who walks on very thorny ground because he cannot find the proper road."[31] He warns, further, that for those who stand in the fairground of the sensory world, fascinated by its brilliance, it is no easier to deny the urges of man than it is to restrain those of a bull grazing in a cornfield. Nevertheless, there are ways to do so if one follows the wisdom of the Buddha's teaching. If one is satisfied with living alone in an empty place, regarding the agents of defilement as bitter enemies, and content with his own company, then he may drink the "nectar of spiritual exultation" and enjoy "happiness greater than that of paradise."

It is a tribute to the Indian spirit of inclusiveness that the same work has a somewhat mellower side. Ashvagosha's advice is presented as a story about the Buddha's youngest stepbrother, a neophyte monk he refers to as "beautiful Nanda." Nanda remains attached to his wife and family after his entry into the monastery, but he is persuaded to forget them when the Buddha takes him to "Indra's pleasure grove," a hermit haven that is "free from exhaustion, drowsiness, disgust, grief, and disease." As a further boon, the pleasure grove allows uninhibited sex with resident *apsarases* (angels). Ashvagosha explains:

> They were ever young, ever busied in love alone and enjoyed jointly by those who have earned merit; celestial beings, union with them was no sin. In them centered the reward of austerities of the divine world.
>
> Some of them sang softly and proudly, some pulled lotuses to pieces for sport, others again danced because of their pleasure in each other with varied gesticulation, their pearl necklaces thrown into disorder by their breasts.[32]

As we will see, such assimilation of lovemaking with enlightenment is a common theme throughout the history of solitude. In every case, of course, including the tale of Nanda, the objective is to lead the seeker through a redirection of the passions to a higher degree of "pleasure" in immortality or God's grace.

Another common theme in the history of solitude—that of the enjoyment of worldly retirement and leisure as recommended by Petrarch—is virtually absent from India's eremitic literature of any era. The closest one comes to that theme appears in the descriptions of idyllic mountain hermitages and ashrams in the Mahabharata and various Puranas, or "ancient tales." According to one of them, "The Hermitage of Atri," King Purūvanas won his peerless kingdom of Madra through a twelve-night fast; but because he had oiled his limbs during his ordeal, he became so ugly that his people did not love him. To cure his ills, he went on foot to Atri's heavenly retreat high in the Himalayas

> where all desires are granted and whose trees drop fruit fit for the chief of gods. That supreme hermitage, where black bees are always buzzing, encircles the mountain like a necklace. Visited by the wives of the gods, it destroys all sins. There, heaps of snow, shining like the orb of the moon, are piled up here and there by playful monkeys. The hermitage is surrounded by valleys filled with snow and rocky caves always hidden from mankind.[33]

In a beautiful cave, where Atri had built a temple that shone luminous like the moonlight, the king performed tapas, worshiped the god Vishnu-Krishna without pause, and lived for some time "feeling no pain." When or if Purūvanas returned to his kingdom, the tale does not say.[34]

According to later tales, kings continued to be attracted to such a blissful, if antiworldly, life of solitude. According to the Jains, for instance, the great Maurya king Chandragupta vacated his throne in favor of his son in the third century to become a hermit. He retired to a life of ascetic purity in southern India, finally to commit ritual suicide in the Jain manner.[35]

Almost all Indian hermits that I have found after the first millennium B.C. likewise aim their sights beyond the worldly realm. The one refreshing anomaly is the seventh century statesman, poet, and grammarian, Bhartrihari. He does not write of nature's beauty nor of enlightenment in the world. Rather, he expresses an honest spirit of inner conflict between his worldly desires and his attraction to religious flights of spiritual solitude, which is the closest to that of Petrarch that I can find among the ancient Hindus. "Quivering looks" and "lusty breasts" figure prominently in his poems, particularly the "Passionate Encounters" section of his *Satakatraya*, a three-part collection of three hundred poems encompassing political wisdom, erotic love, and renunciation. In one poem, for instance, he warns the reader not to wander "in the forest of a woman's body," for there "in the mountains of her breasts lurks the robber god of love."[36] But in another poem in the series, he acknowledges that renunciation of worldly attachments is only the talk of garrulous scholars. "Who," he asks, "can really forsake the hips of beautiful women bound with girdles of ruby jewels?"[37]

It is not known whether Bhartrihari found some form of literary retreat in a Petrarchan mode, but in the section of his work titled "Refuge in the Forest," he tells us that he dwells "content in the hermit's dress of bark." And he sounds very much like a Hindu Horace when he contrasts his life with that of courtly men who "luxuriate in silken splendor." "My contentment is equal to yours," he tells the courtiers, stressing that outward appearances can be deceiving:

> Now let him be called a pauper
> Who bears an insatiable greed;
> When a mind rests content,
> What can it mean to be "wealthy" or "poor"?[38]

GREECE AND ROME

ON FIRST THOUGHT, one might reasonably assume that solitude would have played little or no role in the lives and culture of the ancient Greeks, the people of the polis, the agora, theater, war, trade, and dialogue.

True, many well-known references in classical literature emphasize the negative aspects of being alone. When the warrior Philoctetes was abandoned by Odysseus on a solitary coast of the island of Lemnos on his way to Troy, he lamented (as Sophocles tells the tale): "O wretched indeed that I am, O abhorred of heaven, that no word of this my plight should have won its way to my home or to any home of the Greeks!"[1]

Likewise, Aristotle proclaimed to his students at the Lyceum that "man is by nature a political animal," a social being whose life is best nurtured in the polis, or city-state community.[2] And the traditional reading of Ovid's tale of Narcissus has it that the youth died a pitiable death alone in the forest after he fell in love with his own mirror image in a pool and drowned as he tried to embrace the reflection, the result of his neurotic selfishness and a prophesy by the seer Tiresias that he would live to old age "only if he never comes to know himself."[3]

To Philoctetes solitude was indeed torture. But it would be wrong to conclude that all recognition of the value of being alone was absent from Greek culture. Far from it. If we examine Aristotle's works more carefully, particularly the tenth book of his *Nichomachian Ethics*, we find that he actually praises contemplation—thus solitude—as an "end in itself" and the highest realization of the good life in the polis.

"For contemplation," says Aristotle, is "the highest form of activity, since the intellect is the highest thing in us, and the objects that it apprehends are the highest things that can be known."[4] It is also the most continuous, because we are more capable of uninterrupted contemplation than we are of any practical activity. "The more people contemplate," he adds, “the happier they are,” because “happiness is a form of contemplation.”[5] The wise man, no less than anyone else, requires the necessities of life, which it is the role of the polis to provide, says Aristotle. But it is when the basic needs of life are met that “the wise man can practice contemplation by himself, and the wiser he is, the more he can do it.”[6]

There is likewise a redeeming facet to Narcissus' woeful legend. It is often forgotten that after Narcissus died, according to Ovid, he was transformed into a beautiful spring flower. There is a painting by Salvador Dali that illustrates this aspect of the tale to imply that there may be great creative power in “narcissistic” solitude. Titled “Metamorphosis of Narcissus,” the painting shows two figures in an apparent time sequence. One is a melancholy youth sitting alone, head drooping downward, in a pool amid a deserted moon-like landscape barren of all vegetation. The second figure sits in a similar position at the other end of the same pool. But this Narcissus is more vivid, and the surrounding land has sprouted new growth and strange creatures, while from a crack in his egg-shaped head a flower emerges: the narcissus.

AN AID TO THOUGHT

Moreover, solitude figures prominently in the lives of virtually all early Greek sages and philosophers as something of an aid to thought and prophecy. In part, Petrarch knew this. He notes in *The Life*, for instance, that Pythagoras “sought out not only agreeable seclusion but even vast and frightful wildernesses, and often went on toilsome journeys in deserted regions in his zeal for investigating the truth.”[7] And he points out that another ancient Greek philosopher, Democritus, was so enamored of solitude that he “tore out his eyes in order to see the truth and avoid seeing the mob, which is the enemy of truth.”[8]

Here, too, though, Petrarch left out quite a few illustrious Friends. Thales, for example, widely recognized in ancient Greece as the “first philosopher,” spent a great deal of time wandering and contemplating alone out in the countryside. Nor does Petrarch mention that King Minos and his brother Radamanthus acquired their wisdom of lawmaking living in solitude in the cave of Ida, or that Epimenides gained powers of prophesy by "sleeping" in the same cave.

Petrarch applauds Hyperboreans of the Far North, who he speculates were "unacquainted with strife, always enjoying peaceful leisure amid groves and solitudes."[9] But he fails to mention reports that many ancient Greek sages and prophets visited the Far North or that their powers, both occult and philosophical, seem to have been enhanced by contact with traditions of solitude and mystic flights associated with shamanism.

One such report relates to Aristeas of Prokonnesos, who is said to have visited Hyperborea in a state of possession. According to Herodotus, Aristeas made the trip after he "fell down dead" one day in a shop in his home town, then disappeared. After seven years, he returned with a poem titled the "Arimaspeia," which relates how he visited a northern land where "griffins guard the gold." Some 240 years later, he is said to have reappeared in Italy, proclaiming that he was the reincarnation of Apollo, the god of prophecy, music, and law who is also associated with the Far North. The first-century Roman naturalist Pliny the Elder reports that Aristeas' soul had been seen flying out of his mouth in the form of a raven, a probable association with northern shamans.[10]

The legendary prophet Abaris may also have been influenced by northern shamanism. Herodotus says that he came from the land of the Hyperboreans; and many ancient Greeks believed that he lived without food, and traveled all over the world as a wandering missionary like Aristeas bearing a golden arrow, the symbol of the god Apollo.

Among ancient Greek soloists more clearly identified as philosophers, Hermotimus of Kalzomenai is said to have gone on shaman-like psychic journeys for a look inward to what the classicist E.R. Dodds calls "an occult power innate in man himself."[11] Pliny reports that Hermotimus used to go off alone, where he would "leave his body and roam abroad, and in his wanderings report to himself from a distance many things that only one present at them could know of, his body in the meantime being only half-conscious."[12] Such wanderings, whether figurative or actual, must have borne philosophical rewards: Aristotle credits Hermotimus with the first assertion in Greek philosophy that the essence of the cosmos is *psyche* (mind).

The link between shamanism and philosophy was still more prominent in the writings of Parmenides of Elea in the sixth century B.C. Little is known about the philosopher's private life, but his single remaining work—a didactic poem known variously as "On Nature," or the "Prologue"—presents his philosophy of "true Being" as having been taught to him on a mental journey which, says W.K.C. Guthrie, has the general character of the "shamanistic" strain in early Greek philosophy.[13] In the poem, the philosopher is carried in a chariot pulled by a team of steeds through "the gates of the paths of Night and Day," where the goddess of "avenging Justice" welcomed him graciously and taught him the marks of true Being, the immortal essence of all things. As important, she taught him the method of correct thinking—that is, logic. The dialogue marks the first appearance of logical argument in Greek philosophy.

Using that powerful tool, the goddess explains that Being must be the only entity that exists, because it is the only thing that did not "come into being." For if Being came into being in the past or will do so in the future, then "it is not." But since Being does exist, says the goddess, it must be "unborn and imperishable, whole, unique, immovable, and without end." She even asserted that Being has a shape: "It is complete on every side, like the mass of a well-rounded sphere."

Plato and Socrates in the fourth century B.C. clearly knew of Parmenides' philosophy of spherical Being. There is a Platonic dialogue, the *Parmenides*, in which Socrates discusses it with him, albeit somewhat skeptically. Socrates may also have been influenced by Parmenides' psychic journey, because it is well attested in antiquity that he spent long periods of time in intense meditation. One such "fit of abstraction" occurred near a camp at Potidaea, when Socrates was serving in the Athenian military. One morning at sunrise, it is said that he "got some notion into his head, and there he stood in one spot from dawn, thinking, and when it did not come out, he would not give in but still stood pondering." After dinner, some soldiers came to make their beds nearby and to see if he would stand all night, which he did. Then at dawn, as the sun rose, "he offered a prayer to the sun and walked away."[14]

Later, on his way to the homo-erotic drinking party recounted in the *Symposium*, Plato says that Socrates fell into a similar fit and remained there standing on a porch. The party's host, Agathon, ordered a servant boy to go and fetch Socrates, but one of the guests said, "Don't do that, leave him alone. He often goes off and stands anywhere." In this case, Socrates completed his reflections "sooner than usual" and joined the symposium.[15]

In the course of the evening, several of the guests delivered speeches on the nature of Eros (Love). When Socrates' turn came, he told a story of what he learned about the highest metaphysical mysteries of Eros in an encounter with Diotima, a legendary priestess of Mantinea. She explained how one may rise on the wings of Eros through several interrelated stages toward a kind of enlightenment: first, by directing one's love to other bodies; then by transforming that love into a meditation on the "beauty in souls"; then by turning one's mind to "the great ocean of beauty, and in contemplation of it give birth to many beautiful and magnificent speeches and thoughts in the abundance of philosophy." Finally, at the highest level, one may contemplate "being by itself always in simplicity." "Therein," said Diotima, "is life worth living." For he who comprehends "Beauty itself" will be "the friend of God, and immortal if any man ever is."[16]

It is tempting to speculate that this pedagogical session with Diotima occurred to Socrates as he was standing alone on the porch or in another of his fits of contemplation. In any case, both Parmenides and Socrates imply that the way to understanding the transcendent world of Being or the imminent worlds of Truth and Beauty is through a mental journey of some kind. That reading is reinforced in Plato's *Republic*, where Socrates calls forth the image that living in the world as we see it is like being chained to the walls of a cave in which we are only aware of the underlying reality of things as flickering shadows. The way to wisdom is to climb figuratively out of the cave into the sunlight of Truth, or what he calls the world of Form. The image is commonly known as "Plato's cave"; but it may more appropriately be labeled a "Socratic journey" out of the cave of ordinary life in the world of illusion—which journey, we may infer, would be accomplished by solitary fits of meditation assisted by Eros and the logic of dialectical reasoning.

HERACLITUS

Another eremitic Greek philosopher, the fifth-century B.C. Heraclitus of Ephesus, took a very different path to truth.[17] Like other philosophers before him, he sought wisdom by looking inward, but he did not find gods or mystic spirits there. "I went in search of myself," he said, by way of offering an explanation as to why he chose to retire to the elegant Temple of Artemis, the Artemisium, known in ancient times as one of the Seven Wonders of the World.

Heraclitus earned a reputation as the "weeping philosopher," mainly because of his hard-nosed philosophy. The overt cause of his misanthropy, and the event that seems to have prompted his philosophical retreat, was his countrymen's mistreatment of his friend Hermodorus. This is abundantly clear in one of his surviving fragments:

> What the Ephesians deserve is to be hanged to the last man, every one of them, and leave the city to the boys, since they drove out their best man, Hermodorus, saying "Let no one be the best among us; if he is, let him be so elsewhere and among others."

Heraclitus is thus one of the grumpiest of curmudgeonly hermit-philosophers in the history of solitude. As one would expect, his residence in the temple as a kind of priestly sage must have aroused public feelings of both awe and derision. Many, according to Diogenes Laertius, looked on him as a mad philosopher, saying that he retired to the temple to "play knuckle-bones with the boys." When the citizens of Ephesus asked him what he was doing, he said, "Why you rascals…Are you astonished? Is it not better to do this than to take part in your civil life?"

Not only did Heraclitus stay away from politics, unlike other Greek philosophers, he formed no school, gave no speeches, and had no students. Instead, he chose to impart his wisdom in a book, *On Nature*, which he "deposited" in the Artemisium. The fragmentary portions of his work that have come down to us—such as "Nature loves to hide" or "Thinking is shared by all"—read like cryptic reports from solitude. Even Socrates said he had difficulty deciphering Heraclitus' "riddles."

Those who purported to understand found in Heraclitus a welcome, pragmatic-minded antidote to the idealist philosophy of Parmenides and Plato. Like most pre-Socratic philosophers, he spent a good deal of time speculating as to the underlying constituent of Nature. He called it *logos*, the hidden "story" or measure of things. But unlike Hermotimus' psyche or Parmenides' spherical Being, Heraclitus conceived the logos not as an abstract entity but as an attunement of conflicting elements, a tension—in other words, fire. His famous precept that all the world is change is another expression of that philosophy, as he states it in this fragment from *On Nature*:

> One cannot step twice into the same river, nor can one grasp any mortal substance in stable condition, but it scatters and again gathers; it forms and dissolves, and approaches and departs.

In another fragment Heraclitus posits that "the thunderbolt pilots all things." And using still another metaphor, he likens the fiery logos to the tension required in the strings of a bow or a lyre. Without tension and change there would be nothing, and no self-understanding. As to what is the ultimate nature of Nature, Heraclitus warns that we will never know—"so deep is its logos."

The essence of the cosmos, then, is a fiery if unplumbable attunement of opposites; in the inner world of each individual it is the soul, which also has its fiery aspects. For Heraclitus, it follows that one may get closest to an understanding of the essence of all things—the mysteries of life and death, as well as the workings of nature—by cultivating a dry soul. "A gleam of light is the dry soul," he says, adding that "for souls it is death to become water." One should, in other words, steer clear of the watery element (drunkenness, weepy passions, the mob) and face the truths of existence squarely, without the supporting hope of a loving divinity.

That may sound harsh. So be it, says Heraclitus: "It belongs to all men to know themselves and to think well." Of all the accounts of the cosmos, he adds, "none has gone so far as this: to recognize what is wise, set apart from all."

LONELY PLEASURE

It wasn't until around the fourth century B.C. that the history of solitude in the West finally sprouted another branch, one which would later figure prominently in the eremitic literature—personal enjoyment of being alone. It is impossible, of course, to tell who first enjoyed solitude. But it was Democritus, known since antiquity as the "laughing philosopher," to whom we owe the honor of being the first to espouse the worldly pleasures of solitude.

After a tour reminiscent of Pythagoras' journey to philosophical stations around the Mediterranean, Democritus (460–370 B.C.) returned to his native Abdera on the Bosporus, where he "cut off a little room in the garden round the house and shut himself up there." Thus aided by solitude, his powers of concentration were so great that he failed to notice when his father sacrificed an ox in the same garden.[18] According to the philosopher Antisthenes, Democritus "would train himself…by a variety of means to test his sense-impressions by going at times into solitude and frequenting tombs."[19]

In the three hundred or so works that he produced in his seclusion, the most prominent theme is an apologia for a philosophical life of moderation. The objective of moderation and "the end of all action," says Democritus, is *euthymia*, which may be translated as "cheerfulness," "well-being," or "contentment." Moderation, in turn, is best practiced through *apatheia*. The term is the root of our modern word "apathy," which is typically assumed to be synonymous with indifference and irresponsibility; but in ancient Greek it stood more for equanimity, tranquillity, and a wise retirement from social turmoil. Says Democritus:

> The man who wishes to have serenity of spirit should not engage in many activities, either private or public, nor choose activities beyond his power and natural capacity. He must guard against this, so that when good fortune strikes him and leads him on to excess by means of (false) seeming, he must rate it low, and not attempt things beyond his powers. A reasonable fullness is better than overfullness.[20]

Interestingly, the atomic theory for which Democritus is now best known may have been the basis for his philosophy of contentment. To account for the motion and change that is so apparent in the world, he postulated that everything is discontinuous, made up of invisible atomic units that are able to move because they float freely in the void. It follows that one can find happiness by avoiding agitation—for "souls which are stirred by great divergences," says Democritus, "are neither stable nor cheerful."[21]

This worldly philosophy nurtured in Democritus' garden had a strong influence on Western culture, among his most notable eremitic heirs in Greece being Aristotle and Epicurus; in Rome, Horace, Seneca, and Marcus Aurelius; and, much later, Michel de Montaigne and Robert Burton, who dubbed himself "Democritus, Jr."

Democritus must also have influenced another prominent soloist of the classical world: Diogenes the Cynic (382–322 B.C.). Whereas Democritus maintained that contentment will grow as one is satisfied with less, Diogenes lived and demonstrated that precept in Athens. A contemporary of Plato and Aristotle, he made his home in a tub, clothed himself in rags, and rejected all social graces and amenities. Like Heraclitus, he shunned idealist philosophy, but he did so with a mixture of in-your-face humility and democratic wit. His famous aphorisms are a rejection of all high-flying philosophical pretense and idealism, particularly that of Plato. According to his namesake, Diogenes Laertius,

> Plato had defined Man as an animal, biped and featherless, and was applauded. Diogenes plucked a fowl and brought it into the lecture-room with the words, "Here is Plato's man."[22]

Diogenes' nose-thumbing Cynicism and advocacy for a simple life served as both a comic relief and an example to Stoics and Epicureans for the next thousand years. And it must be said that whereas Athenians accused Socrates of corrupting the youth, Diogenes was loved by them. When a youngster broke up Diogenes' tub, Athenians gave the boy a flogging and presented the philosopher with another. His tombstone read as follows:

> Even brass becomes worn out in time, but never will future ages detract from your fame, Diogenes. For you alone showed the

> splendor of a frugal and moderate existence. You show the easiest path to the happiness of mortals.[23]

In the next century, Epicurus further developed this outlook on life, but in a far less posturing way. He lived and taught his philosophy of moderation, isolation, and worldly well-being not in a tub but in an enclosed garden in Athens. As his name now implies, he was a hedonist, which, according to a prominent strain in the ethical philosophy of ancient Greece, meant that he believed pleasure to be the principal source of happiness and proper aim of the good life. But it is important to note that his emphasis on pleasure was the opposite of self-indulgence or libertinism, for he viewed it not as excess, but as the absence of pain and anxiety.

Epicurus taught that in the long run such things as political office, striving in the world, sex, and fine food may often be more trouble than they are worth—they only "stir up the tides of grief and woe." Here Epicurus comes close to the world rejection so prevalent in Indian philosophy; but he stops far short of complete renunciation. Instead, he offers worldly hope. The world may sling outrageous fortunes, but Epicurus offers a way to keep things from bothering you. "Withdrawal into obscurity is the best form of security," he said, adding that

> The simplest means of procuring protection from other men (which is also gained to a certain extent by deterrent force) is the security of quiet solitude.[24]

Lethe bios (live the obscure life) became a popular saying among Epicureans; and it was partly this approach to life that made Epicurus a near religious figure in post-Alexandrine Greece, a model of the true secret of happiness. Lucretius called him

> ...the first to raise
> the shining light out of tremendous dark
> illuminating the blessings of our life.[25]

ROMAN RETIREMENT

As the Greek world subsided and the Roman Empire rose to take its place, the eremitism and moderation of Epicurus took a new aesthetic turn in the life and writings of Quintus Horatius Flaccus (Horace, 65–8 B.C.).

Horace's father was a freed slave but managed to become sufficiently wealthy as an auctioneer and tax collector to send his son to the best schools in Rome and Athens. In Greece, Horace joined Brutus' army of freedom fighters but was on the losing side against Octavian and Mark Antony and soon lost his family property. Back in Rome, he was granted amnesty and worked as a clerk in the Roman treasury but hoped to live by the pen. He soon published a few poems, befriended poets including Virgil, and was introduced to Maecenas, a powerful statesman and patron of the arts. Maecenas must have sensed Horace's exceptional talents and he must have sympathized with the poet's love for the country, because in 35 B.C. he presented him with a farm in the Sabine Hills, twenty-seven miles northeast of Rome. "Oh this, this is what I prayed for!" Horace wrote in one of his early *Satires*, and he made this prayer to Mercury, god of Luck:

> O make my flocks fat and all else that I possess, except my wits, and please continue to be my best guardian!
>
> Now that I have left Rome for my castle in the hills, what should I praise in Satires on my prosaic Muse, sooner than my farm?[26]

Horace lived and wrote at his farm for the remainder of his life in a happy, thoughtful, appreciative retirement that was as productive as that of Petrarch. He may have had reason to dislike the treacheries of war and politics or the "ignoble strife" of Rome. But what makes Horace among the most appealing of all the Friends of Solitude, at least those of a secular bent, is that he did not retire to his relative solitude with a chip on his shoulder anything like that of Petrarch or Chinese hermit-poets. Born in the country, he simply liked the tranquil, earthy life and the natural surroundings there. "I'm alive, royally alive, when free of all you adore and rise up as high as heaven," he wrote to his city-loving friend Fuscus.[27] It is good to leave the Senate to Senators and rich men alone in their houses, counting up power, he wrote in another poem:

It's good to marry tall poplars with climbing vines,
Or watch cattle grazing in your fields, wandering in far-off valleys,
Or trim woods that bear nothing and splice on fruit-bearing branches,
Or pour clean honey in deep clean jars,
Or shear fat soft sheep—[28]

In fact, Horace found country life so enjoyable that he often thought whimsically of returning to the city to write undistracted. Like Petrarch, he loved to receive friends and wrote many of his poems as letters of entreaty to his Sabine farm. In one of his *Epistles* he wrote to his friend Tibullus, commending his preference for rural realms. "What are you doing now?" he asked: "Walking peaceful, silent, in those healthful/Woods, meditating as a good man, a wise man, meditates?" Then he finished with this offer:

And when it's laughter you're looking for, come this way: you'd find me
Fat and happy, like a hog in Epicurus' herd!"[29]

Horace was not Epicurean in the Sybaritic sense, nor was he in any sense puritanical. He was a bachelor, but there was no Laura in his life. His loves seem to have been requited. He begins another *Epistle* inviting his lady friend Phyllis to his retreat by saying that he has a jar of nine-year-old wine, a ripe garden for weaving garlands, and ivy there "just right for your lovely hair, and to make you still lovelier." And he ends with a romantic appeal that might seem out of place for a Friend of Solitude:

Come, last love of my life—
How could I burn for any other woman?—
And learn to sing, use that lovely voice.
Songs can drive off sorrow, singing can help.[30]

Horace's poems are, for the most part, Epicurean moralizing—told with wit, art, urbanity, modest self-irony. He extols the rural life away from the crowd and the treachery of the Forum—but he says, nevertheless, that "each of us should do what he understands best."[31]

In a sense, Horace was a hermit on his Sabine farm. But he is a new type of soloist. He is the West's first eremitic poet, though not the world's first. As we will see, recluse poets of China beat him to that honor by several hundred years. Horace was not "religious." Nor, though he drank from their wells, was he a philosopher along the lines of his close cousins Democritus or Epicurus. He practiced moderation, but he was in no way an ascetic or a grandstander like Diogenes. He championed the peace and quiet of rural retreat, but not with the aim of becoming an immortal or to perfect worldly powers; rather, because he believed it made him more healthy, happy, contented, moral—and probably because it helped his poetry.

It is not surprising, therefore, that Horace plays a central role in Petrarch's history of solitude. From the *Epistles* he quotes lines that were written to Horace's friends but could just as well be taken as guiding lights for Petrarch's own life of solitude more than a millennium later:

> Give me a country life and leave me free,
> I would not choose the wealth of Araby.

And

> Go now; abstract yourself from outer things,
> And hearken what the inner spirit sings.[32]

A generation after Horace, Seneca—philosopher, playwright, and adviser to Roman emperors—likewise espoused moderate, gentlemanly retirement. He did not spend long stretches of time alone, except when Messalina had him exiled to Corsica in 41. Then in 62 Seneca offered his fortune to Nero and retired to southern Italy, where he wrote his *Letters to Lucilius*. Whether in the country or the city, he advised Epicurean obscurity to promote "internal peace." "You ask me to say what you should consider it particularly important to avoid. My answer is this:" he wrote to the young Lucilius, "a mass crowd. It is something to which you cannot entrust yourself yet without risk."[33]

"The wise man is content with himself," Seneca continues in another letter. Not that a man of wisdom should stand aside from all contact with the world and shut himself up inside his own skin; rather, all he needs for happiness, according to Seneca, is "a rational and elevated spirit that treats fortune with disdain."

> Self-contented as he is, then, he does need friends—and wants as many of them as possible—but not to enable him to lead a happy life; this he will have even without friends. The supreme ideal does not call for any external aids. It is home-grown, wholly self-developed. Once it starts looking outside itself or any part of itself it is on the way to being dominated by fortune.[34]

No one can say that Seneca did not practice what he preached about the acceptance of fate. In 65, after an unsuccessful coup, he was ordered to commit suicide—which he did. A paradoxical figure, Seneca was rich, yet he espoused Stoic frugality; he fought for freedom, yet he tutored Nero; he advised even-mindedness, yet was himself sickly, melancholy, and passionate. But in these respects, his temperament is similar to that of many other quirky secular hermits from Heraclitus to Petrarch. None were saints, but all were honest (if prickly) human beings, living in the world as it is.

Subsequently, the joys of secular retirement as advocated by Horace and Seneca seem to have been widely acknowledged by Roman patricians. Living on *latifundia*, or country retreats, became a tradition, as exemplified by Emperor Diocletian's estate in Dalmatia and the estates of Servilius Vatia and Theocritus. And many patrician homes, as recommended by Seneca, were equipped with "ascetic rooms" to which their owners would retire periodically for a salutary dose of "poverty" and to escape the psychic toils and trammels of Roman society.

Nor is it surprising that Petrarch found a way to show that even Julius Caesar (100–44 B.C.) was attracted to a life of leisure. Caesar, writes Petrarch, was "a very young man when he decided to withdraw from the struggles of public life to the peaceful atmosphere of Rhodes and devote himself to literature." Unfortunately, says Petrarch, he "was prevented at that time by attacks of pirates and later by the storms of domestic and foreign wars, and was unable to attain to the object of his wishes."[35]

In the second century, emperor Marcus Aurelius (121–180) found Seneca's Stoic philosophy of inner solitude useful during the thirteen years he spent, beginning in 167, "alone at his post of duty" with his armies on the Danube, "holding back the onrushing tide of barbarism." There he consoled his hours of loneliness and exile by penning a philosophical work that he called *To Himself* (now titled *Meditations*). Like most western Friends of Solitude before him, Marcus did not revel in solitudes of nature; rather he echoed Seneca in espousing an inner spirit of tranquillity regardless of the location:

> Men seek seclusion in the wilderness, by the seashore, or in the mountains—a dream you have cherished for yourself. But such fancies are wholly unworthy of a philosopher, since at any moment you choose you can retire within yourself.[36]

OTHERWORLDLY DIRECTIONS

As Stoicism and Epicurean philosophies of solitude were influencing Roman patricians, two more intense, antiworldly directions were reemerging: one was an extension of the mystic idealism of Plato, the other of the nose-thumbing asceticism of Diogenes. Both would help to pave the way to Christian spirituality.

The ultimate example of the ascetic direction in Rome is Peregrinus Proteus (circa 100–165). Peregrinus—whose name means, roughly, "Enflamed Wanderer"—took the way of Diogenes to its limit, in a showy self-immolation just after the Olympic games of 165. The Greek satirist Lucian portrays Peregrinus' stunt as sheer crowd-thrilling idiocy, calling him a man who "never fixed his gaze on the verities, but always did and said everything with a view to glory and the praise of the multitude, even to the extent of leaping into the fire, when he was sure not to enjoy the praise because he could not hear it."[37]

Nevertheless, Peregrinus was a man of his era. Suspected of murdering his father, he had earlier moved to Palestine to avoid scandal and there became a Christian, after which he studied ascetic training in Egypt under the philosopher Agathobulus. He then became a wandering preacher in the Cynic mode. He probably got the idea of burning himself alive from reports by Alexander's historian Arrian, whose story of the Indian ascetic Calamus' unflinching self-immolation was widely known in the Roman world. According to Lucian, however, Peregrinus said that he wished "to benefit mankind by showing them the way in which one should despise death." "I am through with the earth," he proclaimed from his funereal pyre, "to Olympus I fare"[38]—a position that was not entirely out of line with the Christian thought of the time. He, and his observers, might well have thought that his suicide would take him to a kind of Greek heaven. Christian martyrs never spoke of suicide, of course, but they were thought to attain immediate salvation following their heroic self-sacrifice.

Peregrinus was only one of many itinerant philosopher-preachers, such as the Christian Dion Chrysostum who underwent a "conversion" to Cynic philosophy in 82, after which he led a wandering life of poverty and preaching with a mission to enlighten the submerged masses as to the virtue and soul-saving power of world renunciation. The sage Apollonius of Tyana (purportedly from Cappadocia in present-day Turkey) likewise took Stoic apathy to the point of antiworldliness, while combining Cynic virtue with the magical powers of a shaman-like sage. Among many influences on his philosophy, he refers to Indian yogis and Egyptian sages, as well as Pythagorean wisdom.

Meanwhile, the intellectual, idealist potential in solitude continued to be developed by philosophers such as the Alexandrine Jew Philo (25 B.C.–50) and Neoplatonists such as the Syrian Numenius of Apamea (second century) and the Roman Plotinus (203–270).

Philo represents the culmination of a long tradition of Jewish Hellenism in Alexandria, which espoused that the people of Sodom and Gomorrah were the same as those described in *The Republic* of the "most holy Plato" as living unenlightened in a shadowy cave. Like Plato, Philo believed that the role of the philosopher is to show men the way out of the cave by laying bare the divine nature of their own souls, a process which is enhanced by solitude and silence. Philo visited members of the Jewish contemplative sect known as the Therapeutae near Alexandria and wrote enthusiastically about their love of rural tranquillity away from the "tumult and indescribable disturbances" of city life. Instead of living in towns, writes Philo in *The Contemplative Life*, "they spend their time outside the walls pursuing solitude in gardens or solitary places, not from having cultivated a cruel hatred of men, but because they know that intercourse with persons of dissimilar character is unprofitable and injurious."[39]

Like the Therapeutae, Philo's man of virtue does not love solitude out of misanthropy. He is rather a lover of men who spends his time in an out-of-the-way place to avoid the vices of the multitude. In solitude, Philo continues, sounding like an early Petrarch, the man of virtue finds "greater pleasure in having as his companions the cream of the human race, whose bodies time has dissolved but the fame of whose virtues has been quickened by the writings they have left behind in prose or verse, by which the soul is naturally improved."[40]

Accordingly, Philo entreats his readers (quoting Deuteronomy 27:9) to "be silent and hear." That is "an excellent precept!" he writes, "for ignorance is exceedingly rash and garrulous; and its first remedy is silence, the second to give attention to those who present something worth hearing."[41]

Like Philo, Numenius was a Platonic idealist who advocated that the only way to grasp the truth of things is to be like "a one-man skiff all alone, bobbing amid the waves." To know the truth, one should be

> far from the things of sense, and consort solitarily with the Good in its solitude, where there is neither man nor another living thing, nor anybody great or small, but some unspeakable and truly indescribable wondrous solitude, where are the accustomed places, the haunts and pleasances of the Good, and in itself in peace, in benevolence, in its tranquillity, in its sovereignty, riding upon the surface of Being.[42]

A generation later, Plotinus espoused the same sort of antiworldly philosophical idealism, first in Alexandria, then in Persia on an expedition with the Roman emperor Gordian III, and finally in Rome, where he set up his own school and frequented a school composed of prominent patricians. Plotinus planned to found a city of philosophers that was to have been run according to a Platonic model and called Platonopolis. But in 268 he became ill and retired to an estate in Campania. "It was a solitary life he lived now, but he had always been a man of solitude," writes J.M. Rist in his book *Plotinus: The Road to Reality*. The catch phrase by which Plotinus has since been known, "alone with the Alone," was not a cliché says Rist, "but a summation of his knowledge that ultimately there is no substitute for facing oneself and no avoidance of it."[43]

Porphyry, one of Plotinus' students, reports that the philosopher achieved union with the divine twice in his lifetime. To rise to that spiritual vision of inaccessible beauty, Plotinus advised:

> Withdraw into yourself and look. And if you do not find yourself beautiful yet, act as does the creator of a statue that is to be made beautiful; he cuts away here, he smoothes there, he makes this line lighter, this other purer, until a lovely face has grown upon his work. So do you also: cut away all that is excessive, straighten all that is crooked, bring light to all that is overcast, labor to make all one glow of beauty and never cease chiseling your statue until there shall shine from it the godlike splendor of virtue, until you shall see the perfect Goodness established in the stainless shrine.[44]

The objective, precisely in line with Indian uses of solitude a thousand or more years before, is to rise through mystic contemplation above the pains and flaws of this world to an ideal world of perfection, where "the essential man outgrows Being, becomes identical with the Transcendent Being." In his mystic-philosophic isolation, such an ardent Friend of Solitude rises, says Plotinus, from "image to archetype." Like Mahavira at the tip of the universe, or Buddha in nirvana, he may arrive at the final, glorious destination of the universe. Says Plotinus:

> This is the life of the gods and of godlike and blessed men,—liberation from the alien that besets us here, a life taking no pleasure in the things of earth—a flight of the alone to the Alone.[45]

Ancient China

Like much else in Chinese culture, the long history of solitude in China is one of balance and worldly practicality. For the most part, Chinese Friends of Solitude were not extreme ascetics. But with that exception, they explored all of the other major directions in solitude that we have discussed so far—most notably the creative employment of solitude and silence to foster worldly powers; intense inner solitudes to enhance mystical understanding of the world; and the secular solitudes in which one enjoys time alone, often with an aesthetic flourish. Each of these appeared in China from earliest times, often simultaneously, and rarely with any feeling that they could not coexist in the same noble soul.

This is best illustrated in a story told by the Taoist philosopher Chuang Tzu concerning the wisdom and powers of Master Kuang Ch'eng. He is supposed to have lived during the reign of the Yellow Emperor, dated by Chinese tradition in the twenty-sixth century B.C., which would make him the earliest Friend identified by more than name of any I have come across. That date may be questioned, given the fact that we know little about Master Kuang other than what Chuang Tzu says about him by way of philosophical instruction in the fourth century B.C. Nevertheless, the story elucidates a tradition that is very old.[1]

According to Chuang, the Yellow Emperor—the archetype of virtuous rulers in China—went to visit Master Kuang in his hermitage on the Mountain of Emptiness. Unsatisfied with his reign, the emperor asked what he might do to improve it. "I can't tell you," said Kuang. "No wonder your kingdom is in disarray. You have the disordered mind of a prattling knave!"

The emperor followed the Master's advice to leave his throne and retire to a solitary hut to calm the chaos in his mind. After three months there, he returned, crawling in supplication on his hands and knees to ask once again for the key to the "Perfect Way." Apparently believing that the emperor was now prepared to grasp his profundities, the Master responded with the subtle, enigmatic advice that is common across all the history of solitude, particularly in China. Stop your thinking, he said. Destroy your concepts. Think without "thinking." The text reads:

> Let there be no seeing, no hearing; enfold the spirit in quietude and the body will right itself. Be still, be pure, do not labor your body, do not churn up your essence…When the eye does not see, the ear does not hear, and the mind does not know, then your spirit will protect the body, and the body will enjoy long life.[2]

The emperor thanked Master Kuang, saying "you have been as a Heaven to me," thus implying that not only did he order his own mind to achieve a sense of personal equanimity but that he went on to improve his rule. That linkage between a ruler who understands and lives the true Way (*Tao*) and the welfare of his kingdom has long since been the ideal for Chinese statecraft. Many Taoists regard the Yellow Emperor as the founder of Taoism and he is said to have achieved immortality following his reign—although some say that he only lived 1,200 years.

THE "BEST MEN"

Master Kuang is associated with a long line of hermits known as *hsien*, alternatively translated as "immortals" or "best men," most of whom lived away from society in the mountains or on the magical Isles of the Blest off the Shandong coast in the Eastern Ocean. As was the case in ancient India and Greece, these shadowy characters possessed attributes and occult powers—including an ability to go on spirit flights—that indicate borrowings from shamanism. Those powers were also much sought after by kings and emperors. Among the earliest hsien is a "Pure One" named Fu Yue. He was once a convict laborer, but after the Shang king Wu Ding saw him in a dream, the king appointed him to be his counselor. When he died to the earthly world, Fu Yue is said to have mounted into the sky to take his place among the stars. Another is Han Zhong, who was sent by his emperor to look for the herb of immortality; but Han never reported back and many believe that he found what he was looking for in a remote place and kept it for himself.

It could have been that such hsien were relegated to solitude by mythological necessity; being both unseen and immortal (or exceptionally long-lived), they had to reside somewhere. But there are many indications that the hsiens' remote quietude, coupled with various ascetic practices and meditation techniques, was an important source of their powers. The most commonly quoted description of their practices comes from another of Chuang Tzu's philosophical tales concerning a hermit who lived on Ku-she Mountain. He has "skin like ice or snow" and is "gentle and shy like a young girl," says one of Chuang's characters. He doesn't eat the "five grains" and "drinks the dew," meaning that he follows an ascetic diet. He also "sucks the wind," referring to breathing practices intended to build inner powers. And he "climbs up on the clouds and mist, rides a flying dragon, and wanders beyond the four seas." Most notably, "by concentrating his spirit he can protect creatures from sickness and plague and make the harvest plentiful."[3]

The English poet Arthur Waley—who translated the *Tao Te Ching* of Lao Tzu in *The Way and Its Power*—argues that this later practice of inner concentration was borrowed from a form of shamanism peculiar to China: the *shih* ritual, in which an adept would make himself or herself as quiet as a corpse in order to communicate with the dead. Waley suggests that this ritual was likely internalized, as ancestor worship was discredited sometime around the middle of the first millennium B.C., when the introduction of iron among other social and political developments led to a period of philosophical questioning and speculation as to the nature of the world and proper government. That, in turn, helped to spawn another group of recluses who retired to lives of solitude and simplicity in order to escape what they saw as unjust and iniquitous regimes.[4]

In many cases, these secular soloists found justification for their retirement in the philosophies of men such as Lao Tzu, who reasoned that the perfection of the community will require similarly perfect individuals adept at the arts of stilling the mind to achieve equanimity and a grounded understanding of the true Way of the world. "Let each man perfect himself," they argued, according to Waley. "If the state asks from him one single act that interferes with this process of self-perfection, he should refuse, not merely on his own account, but out of regard for the community, which corporately suffers in as far as one of its members is imperfect."[5]

The archetypal instance of such high-minded withdrawal is that of the brothers Po Yi and Shu Ch'i. Sons of a king in western China, the brothers abdicated their rights to kingship when their kingdom was attacked by King Wu, who thereby founded the Chou Kingdom in 1027 B.C. They took issue with the violent manner in which the kingdom was formed and retreated to seclusion, living in a cave and nourishing themselves on herbs and fruits of the forest. Their retirement is typically presented as a form of protest, which even the civic-minded Confucius acknowledges in the *Analects* as the proper thing to do under certain circumstances. "Do not enter into a state which is in danger," he said. "Do not stay in a state which is in disorder. When the empire possesses the Way, be seen. When the empire does not possess the Way, hide."[6]

This tenet of political participation became so widely acknowledged in early Chinese culture that one of the first orders of business for a new regime was to call retreating scholar-statesmen back to support the state. Their pleas, however, were typically unsuccessful. According to the *Lieh-Nü Chuan* (*Traditions of Exemplary Women*), the king of Ch'u once sent two four-horse carriages bearing one hundred measures of gold to a man named Chieh Yü, The Madman of Ch'u. The king hoped that he could entice the hermit to administer the province of Huai-nan. But the Madman's wife did not have much trouble convincing him of the right thing to do. "To comply and still be opposed is unrighteousness. It is better to go away," she said. So, according to the tale, "the husband carried the cooking pots on his back, the wife her loom on her head. They changed their names and moved far away; no one knew where they went."[7]

That the Madman and his wife fled to complete obscurity is telling. Early on, practical-minded Chinese were skeptical of any association with government, as in this poem from the *Book of Songs,* collected around the year 600 B.C.:

> Don't escort the big chariot;
> You will only make yourself dusty.
> Don't think about the sorrows of the world;
> You will only make yourself wretched.[8]

Later, the *Songs of the South*, dating back as early as the fourth century B.C., are filled with poems by men who fled corrupt regimes. As one Ch'u king is said to have cut up and pickled his ministers, it is easy to sympathize with them. But unfortunately, they almost invariably depict themselves as living in miserable isolation. And their laments became a distinct genre in poems with titles such as "Oppressed by Grief" and "Mourning My Lot." In a poem titled "Reckless Remonstrance," for instance, one political refugee resolves to make his home in a mountain cave and end his days in silence. But he complains that he doesn't even have the energy to do that:

> So, alone, I nurse my anger and store up my bitterness,
> And the darkness of my sorrow remains with me, unending...
> I lay on my bed of sickness, consumed by constant sorrow;
> My true feelings are submerged and may not be expressed.[9]

In another poem, "Disgust with the World," a reclusive poet seriously contemplates suicide:

> The world is sunk and foul and undiscriminating,
> Its way irregular as jagged rocks...
> Better to throw myself in the river's waters
> And set myself hurrying across the swift currents.[10]

At the same time, like Petrarch, the poets found ways of easing their grief through poetry. "I tell my thoughts in song, thinking to ease my sorrow," writes the poet of "The Outpouring of Sad Thoughts." And even more than Petrarch, many found psychological compensation in poetry that is charged with an awareness of the beauty of nature. A poem titled "Nine Changes," for example, depicts a squire who has lost his office and "rests with never a friend on his long journey." He is melancholy and he "nurses a private sorrow." Yet in the next lines we are treated to a subtle description of the natural surroundings of his rest stop.

> The fluttering swallows leave on their homeward journey;
> The forlorn cicada makes no sound;
> The wild geese call as they travel southwards;
> The partridge chatters with a mournful cry.[11]

This, says the English translator David Hawkes, is perhaps the first appearance in a developed sense of "the pathos of natural objects, which was to become the theme of so much Chinese poetry throughout the ages."

Many such recluse poets sought further compensation for their woes by emulating the spirit flights and methods of inner concentration of the hsien. In "On Encountering Trouble," the poet has rejected public service and is living alone and near starvation, but he reasons that "If only my mind can be beautiful, it matters nothing that I often faint for famine." So he resolves to brush away his tears and follow the lifestyle of Peng Xian, the "Shaman Ancestor." The poet tells us that he drank dew from the magnolia tree, ate chrysanthemum petals, and made a coat of water-chestnut leaves and a skirt of lotus petals. Then suddenly, smelling the fragrance of a bouquet of flowers, he sees himself as a kind of shamanic aesthete:

> With me the love of beauty is a constant joy.
> I could not change this, even if my body were dismembered;
> For how could dismemberment ever hurt my mind?[12]

So prepared, he lets his eyes wander, yokes a team of jade dragons to a phoenix-figured car, and waits for the wind to take him on a journey worthy of the ecstatic French poet Arthur Rimbaud. The whirlwinds gather to meet his glittering train; he waters his dragons at the Pool of Heaven; and the Bird of Heaven heralds his arrival at various heavenly realms, where he follows his natural bent to please himself and wander in search of a lady. He finds many such ladies, but his courtships fail. Finally, after he has tasted the splendor of all the heavens, he catches a glimpse of his old home and cries: "Enough!" His dragons refuse to move any further and he returns to real life, where he contemplates suicide.

Working in the same genre, the second-century B.C. poet of "Far-off Journey" was apparently more successful in his ecstatic flights. He, too, is grieved by the state of the world's affairs and wants to "float up and away from it" in leisurely enjoyment, but his leisure is powered by philosophy. When he recalls how the ancient hsien Red Pine "washed the world's dust off," he takes that as a model for living. Honoring the "wondrous powers of the Pure Ones," he sups on the Eight Essences, drinks the Night Dew, savors the Morning Brightness, and travels to a realm where the hsien Wang Qiao tells him the way to the Door of Power. "Keep your soul from confusion, and it will come naturally," says Wang:

> Await in emptiness, before even inaction.
> All other things proceed from this...

As he wanders freely in the blue sky, the poet has his doubts as he glimpses his old home below and pictures his dear ones in his imagination. But he brushes his tears away and decides to fly even higher—"suppressing these willful thoughts, in control once more." Finally, he flies so high that the earth is invisible and even the sky cannot be seen in the vastness above:

> When I looked, my startled eyes saw nothing;
> When I listened, no sound met my amazed ear.
> Transcending Inaction, I came to Purity,
> And entered the neighborhood of the Great Beginning.[13]

TAOIST PHILOSOPHERS

It is clear that the poet of "Far-off Journey" was listening to more than the tales of the immortals. David Hawkes believes that he was a member of a small group influenced by Taoist philosophers who wrote several centuries earlier. Among the first of these was Master Kuan Cheng who probably wrote a portion of a work now known as the *Kuan Tzu* some time in the fourth century B.C. In it we hear almost nothing of the special diets, magical potions, or spirit flights of the Pure Ones, and nothing of immortality. Instead, Kuan concentrates his readers' attention on a rational, albeit mystically charged, explanation of what it was about the quietude of the men of old that gave them such powers. Nor does Kuan say anything about the need to live in the mountains away from society. In fact, he severely criticizes men who "withdraw to quiet places and hide away in caves or on mountains, there to rail at the prevailing government...and sneer at those in authority."[14] He speaks rather of inner solitude.

Like most Taoist philosophers, Kuan begins with this premise: "It is ever so that the essence of things is what gives them life." That essence—the

Tao—is silent, compact, and obscure, with no fixed place. The supreme quality for men, therefore, is also quiescence. It is "never to be summoned by one's call," and it "cannot be expressed by the mouth." But "it may be made welcome by the intellect"—and when that happens the results are of practical worldly value:

> When a man is capable of being correct and quiescent,
> His flesh is full, his ears and eyes sharp and clear,
> His muscles taut, and his bones sturdy…
> He is respectful and cautious and makes no miscalculations.
> He daily renews his Power, universally understands the world,
> Explores the four extremities of the universe, and respectfully develops his own fullness.
> This is called the inner attainment.[15]

Sounding very like a contemporary self-help guru on public television, Kuan adds:

> Do not pull! Do not push!
> Well being will then arrive of itself.
> You may count upon the Way coming of itself.
> If quiescent, you will then obtain it.
> If hasty, you will then lose it.[16]

The most explicit renderings of these uses of quiescence and inner solitude, both for personal equanimity and the welfare of the state, appear in the works of Lao Tzu and Chuang Tzu. The former, according to tradition, was a curator of the royal library in the Kingdom of Chou around the middle of the sixth century B.C. and was a contemporary of Confucius. When the two met, Confucius was reputedly impressed by Lao Tzu's practical insights. He asked Lao about the essence and importance of the ancestral rites, to which Lao reportedly replied that they are of little significance but memory: "The bones of those of whom you speak have long since turned to dust; only their words have been preserved for us."

Seeing the decay of the Chou dynasty, Lao Tzu fled, although some say he simply retreated behind a disguise of anonymity, as is implied later in the same dialogue with Confucius. "If time and fortune favor a person, he will travel to court in a carriage," Lao explained. "If they do not favor him he will roam about in unpretentious attire…A noble person with sufficient inner virtue may give the appearance of a fool. Therefore, give up your high-handed manner, your desires, your vanity, and your zeal—for they are of no use to you."

Taken aback, Confucius withdrew and later told his students that he had met a sage who could fly like a bird and swim like a fish. But whereas such animals can be trapped, said Confucius, Lao Tzu is like a dragon that cannot be limited by such clever snares. Rather, he "wings towards Heaven on wind and clouds."[17]

Others say that Lao traveled to India where he taught the wisdom of emptiness to Shakyamuni, or somehow reappeared there *as* the Buddha. The most prevalent tradition has it that he did flee the kingdom and that as he ran off a warden in the Chungnan Mountains by the name of Yin Hsi asked him to leave some of his wisdom behind in the form of a book. The result was the *Tao Te Ching*. In its way, the work advocates a life of simplicity that recalls that of the Stoics and Epicureans: "When you have little, you'll attain much," he wrote. "With much you'll be confused." Lao's advice to mankind also echoes that of Master Kuan:

> As the heavy must be the foundation of the light,
> So quietness is lord and master of activity.[18]

According to Chuang Tzu, Lao's personal devotion to quietude was consistent with his writings. On another day, as Chuang tells the story, Confucius happened upon Lao Tzu (a.k.a., Lao Tan) in the midst of his meditation, whereupon the sage exclaimed:

> Did my eyes play tricks on me, or was that really true? A moment ago, Sir, your form and body seemed stiff as an old tree, as though you had forgotten things, taken leave of men, and were standing in solitude itself! Lao Tan said, "I was letting my mind wander in the Beginning of things."[19]

Indeed, in the *Tao Te Ching*, Lao advises that he who is able to "Take emptiness to the limit" and "Maintain tranquillity in the center" may be able to live for more than a thousand years. His life will be filled with virtue and contentment. He will also be adept at statecraft, knowing when to remove himself from a corrupt chaotic regime and how, under the right circumstances, to foster peace and prosperity in a kingdom. The secret lies with understanding—or, more precisely, feeling, absorbing, and living in "the true essence of things."

Master Chuang lived a couple of centuries later, but he repeats essentially the same wisdom that we hear from Lao and Kuan in "goblet words"—that is, in a myriad of Sufi-like tales that do not over-explain but rather point the way to freedom, happiness, and perfection in unexpected quarters. Chuang himself appears to have been a courtly philosopher. An ancient Chinese historian maintains that he was married and served as an official in the lacquer garden of the state of Ch'i-yüan during the period of Warring States, an era of social oppression, war, and skepticism.

Thus Chuang was probably not a hermit residing in a mountain cave. Yet, if his own story concerning his refusal to rule ("I prefer to continue dragging my tail in the mud") is to be believed, he did reject worldly power. Was it because he thought striving for political power is futile and harmful to one's well-being, or was it that he viewed power mongering as an inefficient, dangerous way to run a state? Like Lao, he seems to have believed both. Like Yajnavalkya, he may have been a living paradox: a courtly recluse.

Building on tradition—but now with a greater sense of humor—Chuang's philosophy is directed at the individual: Free yourself from the world, he advises again and again, discard the baggage of conventional values. The result is *wu wei*, a course of action—more precisely, inaction or waylessness—not founded on purposeful motives.

One of my favorite takes on this perennial subject is what Chuang Tzu's Woman Crookback (old in years but with the complexion of a child) tells a gentleman named Nan-po Tzu-k'uei about the secret of her longevity and contentment. The first step, she explains, is to put the world outside yourself...then to put things outside yourself...then to put life outside yourself, at which point you will be able to achieve the "brightness of dawn" and to "see your aloneness." At that point, she says, one can "do away with past and present" and "enter a place where there is no life or death."[20]

The trick, then, if we can properly call it that, is not only to withdraw for a time from society but literally to isolate oneself from oneself—from all the excess baggage of one's painful memories, rigid habits, and learned feelings. The result may be more than long life. In another story, Chuang tells of the woodworker Ch'ing who, before he began his best work would fast to still his mind. After several days, he was so still that he forgot his body and the world. In that state his "skill is concentrated and all outside distractions fade away." His woodworking, then, was merely a matter of "matching up Heaven with Heaven." That is probably the reason, said Ch'ing, that "people wonder if the results were not made by spirits."[21]

Ironically, Chuang Tzu has Confucius, the arbiter of Chinese propriety, expound a similar strategy for statecraft. When his pupil Yen Hui decided to go to the chaotic kingdom of Wei with the aim of improving it, he asked Confucius how he should proceed, suggesting that if he is empty-hearted, diligent, single-minded, and follows the examples of antiquity, "won't that do?" "No!" said Confucius, you must also be "a companion of Heaven." "You have too many policies and plans and you haven't seen what is needed...You are still making mind your teacher." Instead, "you must fast!" said Confucius.

> Don't listen with your ears, listen with your mind. No, don't listen with your mind, but listen with your spirit. Listening stops with the ears, the mind stops with recognition, but spirit is empty and waits on all things. The Way gathers in emptiness alone...
>
> You have heard of flying with wings, but you have never heard of flying without wings. You have heard of the knowledge that knows, but you have never heard of the knowledge that does not know. Look into that closed room, the empty chamber where brightness is born! Fortune and blessing gather where there is stillness.[22]

Thus the ancient Chinese hermits advocated a kind of worldly mysticism. For some reason, most of the Friends of Solitude in ancient China were not idealists; they were somehow less ashamed of the body and more optimistic about prospects of being happy in the world. Like their counterparts of the Indian subcontinent and the Mediterranean, they had plenty of wars, political chaos, and other reasons to flee the world. But when they retired from the world, they retired not from all things worldly but from social life to nature or to an inward life of what may be termed "retirement in the world." As happened elsewhere, Chinese explorations in aloneness both mellowed and became more intensely ascetic over time. Through the next millennium or so, they will end up covering more of the stations in Lady Solitude's domain than I have been able to find in any other chapter of the long history of solitude.

We will save those later developments for a moment and turn back to the West. First I think it fitting to close this chapter with one of the most relevant quotes from China's literature of solitude. It, too, is recorded in the *Chuang Tzu*, where a man known as the Master from South of the Market pays a visit to the marquis of the state of Lu. The marquis complains that he has studied the way of former kings but still cannot seem to avoid disaster. The Master says that he is being too superficial. He should be more like Emperor Yao, who neither possessed men nor allowed himself to be possessed by them. "So I ask you," says the Master, "to rid yourself of hardship, to cast off your cares, and to wander alone with the Way to the Land of Great Silence."

The Desert Fathers

With the gradual fall of the Roman Empire, dramatic developments were occurring in the field of eremitism. Suddenly, around the third century in Egypt, an epidemic of Christian solitude erupted that would rival that of ancient India and wipe away a millennium of philosophizing by secular soloists in Greece and Rome.

There were precedents in the Old Testament. Petrarch cites biblical Friends of Solitude such as Moses, noting that he was alone on a high mountain when he obtained the law from God and "he was in the wilderness when he forced the bitter waters to grow sweet." Petrarch also mentions Elijah: "hiding in the wilderness, he was fed by thoughtful ravens at the command of God while the people were perishing of hunger in the cities." Indeed, says Petrarch, "The Savior himself, the source of all salutary examples, though he was not in need of solitude or fearful of numbers, desiring to furnish forth his teaching with illustrations, went up to the mountain to pray, and prayed alone."[1]

The Christian hermits also emerged amid a soup of philosophical influences already long brewing in the Roman Empire, including the Neoplatonism of Plotinus, the Jewish Hellenism of Philo, the Stoicism of Seneca and Marcus, the Cynicism of Peregrinus, and religious sects from Mithraism to Gnostic Christianity. In the second century, for example, a Syrian Christian with the interesting name Narcissus seems to have been influenced by such philosophy. Although Petrarch does not mention him, he is the first Christian hermit that I have been able to find in church history. According to the fourth-century historian Eusebius, Narcissus "could not endure a slander against him," so he fled sometime around the year 190. "He escaped the whole company of the church, and spent many years secretly in deserts and obscure places," says Eusebius, adding that Narcissus had already followed "a philosophic life for a long time."[2] In

Syria, he explains, that meant ascetic training in a philosophical "wrestling school," something like a Greek gymnasium turned spiritual and mystical.

Around the same time, we hear the influence of Stoic philosophy in one of the Gnostic gospels attributed to a preacher named Silvanus. "Abolish every childish time of life," he says:

> My son, throw every robber out of your gates. Guard all your gates with torches which are the words, and you will acquire all these things for a quiet life. But he who will not guard these things will become like a city which is desolate since it has been captured, and all kinds of wild beasts have trampled upon it.[3]

Another gospel, *The Gospel of Thomas*, is more explicit in its praise of solitude. Jesus, according to Thomas, said, "Blessed are the solitary…"[4] He also said that "only those who are solitary will enter the bridal chamber."[5] The gospel does not explain what will happen in the bridal chamber, but it is clearly an enclosure for solitude; and becoming a "bride of Christ," as we will see, was a common metaphor in medieval Christianity for union with the divine. The Gnostic gospels were deemed heretical by the early church fathers and ordered destroyed, mainly because they take the position that everyone has a spark of the divine within which can, through proper understanding of the words of Jesus, be nourished to bring forth enlightenment. The implication is that it can be done without the help of church, thus infringing on the central role of the church. When a disciple asked Jesus "when will the new world come?" he replied, according to Thomas, "What you look forward to has already come, but you do not recognize it."[6] "That which you have will save you," Jesus explained on another occasion, "if you bring it forth from yourselves."[7]

PAUL AND ANTHONY

The Gnostic Christians spoke of solitude, but it was only with Saint Paul the First Hermit and most definitely with Saint Anthony that Christians began to make a clean break with Roman civilization to take up a life of solitude in the desert, which became revered as an ideal, first in Egypt and eventually across Europe.

Paul, according to Jerome, was only fifteen when he "took flight to the mountains" shortly after his parents had died. He probably sought to escape a storm of persecution against Christians during the reign of Decius (249–251). He may also have been motivated by his study of both philosophy and theology. Jerome stresses that the "far sighted" boy was "excellently versed alike in Greek and Egyptian letters, of a gentle spirit, and a strong lover of God." Once in the desert, Paul chose a remarkably well appointed retreat—a huge cave with "a spacious courtyard open to the sky, roofed by the wide-spreading branches of an ancient palm, and with a spring of clear shining water." There, for 113 years, "the Blessed Paul lived the life of heaven upon earth," his palm tree providing him both food and clothing.[8]

A few decades later, after his parents had also passed away, Anthony heeded these words of Christ: "If you would be perfect, go, sell what you possess and give to the poor and you will have treasure in heaven and come and follow me" (Matthew 19:21). Like many another Friend, he went to live in the desert at age thirty-five, first in an ancient Egyptian tomb and then in a deserted fortress. Living on a delivery of bread every six months, Anthony resided in the fortress for twenty years, during which time he prayed to God, held all-night vigils, battled his inner demons, and learned the value of silence, humility, and spiritual alertness.

His biographer, Athanasius, reports that Anthony's retreat was conducive both to his spiritual and physical health. After two decades of pious seclusion, when a group of Anthony's friends came to his fortress to see how he was faring, they heard noises from within which sounded as though he was fighting with monsters. But when they peeked through the keyhole they saw him sitting in serene contemplation. When they then broke down his door, Athanasius writes that "Anthony came forth as though from some shrine, having been led into divine mysteries and inspired by God." The curious well-wishers were amazed to see that his body had maintained its former condition. It was

> neither fat from lack of exercise, nor emaciated from fasting and combat with demons, but was just as they had known him prior to his withdrawal. The state of his soul was one of purity, for it was not constricted by grief, nor relaxed by pleasure, nor affected

> by either laughter or dejection. Moreover, when he saw the crowd, he was not annoyed any more than he was elated at being embraced by so many people. He maintained utter equilibrium.[9]

Anthony had gained a number of occult powers in his retirement, including the ability to control animals. Later, for instance, when a party of brethren wished to cross a canal filled with crocodiles, he simply prayed, after which he and his company passed without harm. Anthony was also clairvoyant. Frequently, while sitting or walking with visitors, he was "struck dumb," during which time he witnessed spectacles and saw things that took place throughout Egypt.

The hermit finally tired of the crowds of followers surrounding his fortress and retreated farther into the desert to his "Inner Mountain." There he experienced a revelation that "there was deep in the desert another far better than he, and that he must make haste to visit him." As the day broke, Anthony set out in the scorching sun to find this Christian super-hermit (who turned out to be Paul).

Shortly, a centaur—half man, half horse, with bristling jaws, but a speech that was at once gnashing and barbarous and gentle—appeared to point the way, and then disappeared. After some time, and this is a telling sidelight, Anthony happened upon another desert creature—"a dwarfish figure of no great size, its nostrils joined together, and its forehead bristling with horns: the lower part of its body ended in goat's feet." Seeing Anthony, the humanoid beast wept and spoke on behalf of his freakish tribe to "entreat for us our common God who did come, we know, for the world's salvation." Jerome, who tells this story in *The Life of Saint Paul the First Hermit*, goes to great lengths to demonstrate that such creatures were real, having seen one preserved in salt in Alexandria. Anthony's reaction, significantly, is to pity those who place their faith in such worldly demons when they themselves acknowledge the supremacy of Christ: "Woe to thee, Alexandria," he cried, "who dost worship monsters in room of God."

When Anthony finally reached Paul's retreat, the hermit bolted his door. But when Anthony prayed and told Paul that he would sooner die than leave, Paul finally recognized who had come and welcomed him warmly. As the two hermits embraced, a crow is said to have delivered a loaf of bread to help celebrate the occasion. Paul then realized that the time had come for him "to be dissolved and to be with Christ" and that Anthony had been "sent by God to shelter his body in the ground." A few days later, Anthony saw Paul's soul "climbing the steps of heaven, and shining white as snow." Two lions then appeared to help him bury the body, in return for Anthony's blessing.[10]

Unlike Paul, Anthony was not particularly literate; and unlike Jerome, who later took a large library to his hermitage in a Syrian desert, Anthony possessed no books, not even the Bible. But his spoken words were very persuasive. To prove the point, Athanasius writes that when Greek philosophers visited Anthony in the desert he easily bested them in philosophical dialogues proving that faith in Christ had value far greater than that of their lascivious gods or their sophistic word battles. To offer evidence, Anthony argued:

> Among you the apparitions of the idols are being abolished, but our faith is spreading everywhere...Tell us, then, where are your oracles now?[11]

Athanasius adds that Anthony used his powers of persuasion to induce so many Egyptians—including both Greeks and indigenous Coptics—to take up the sweet life of solitude that "the desert became a city of monks, who left their own people and registered themselves for the citizenship in the heavens."[12] By the end of the third century it is said that half of the population of the Thebaid and Scete in Egypt consisted of hermits and monks.

But there was much more than rhetoric underpinning this new rush to religious solitude in the West. As happened in India and China, it is no coincidence that the flight to the desert coincided with a period of dramatic socio-economic change and associated questioning of traditional values. With the fall of Rome, particularly the fall of Antonine Rome in the third century, says Peter Brown in *The Making of Late Antiquity*, the oracles in the temples of Roman cities "fell silent" and Romans looked elsewhere for spiritual substitutes.

They had many to choose from. But those which in the end attracted the greatest following were Christian hermits that Brown calls "friends of god," who rejected all the trappings of Roman culture and went off into desolate places to reestablish spiritual connection with the divine essence of things through their own direct experience. The likes of Paul and Anthony provided new hope that Romans could reclaim a purity of heart and nearness to the divine that was presumed to exist before the disappointments and confusion of a dissolving civilization.

DESERT WISDOM

The spiritual investigations of Christian hermits in and around the Nile Valley—known subsequently as the Desert Fathers—lasted some four hundred years, from the days of Paul and Anthony to those of Saint John Climacus, who died near Mount Sinai sometime in the middle of the seventh century. There are so many sayings attributed to one or another of these men and women that to quote any particular utterances will necessarily give a distorted picture of their contribution to the history of solitude. With that in mind, we will confine ourselves here to a sampling of sayings that characterize their particular approach to solitude and their state of mind.

Arsenius, a Roman courtier turned hermit, was prompted into his withdrawal, it is said, while he was living and working in the king's palace in Constantinople. There he heard the word of God, who whispered to him from on high:

> Arsenius, flee from men, and thou shalt be saved.[13]

After he arrived in the Egyptian desert, another voice came to him saying:

> Arsenius, fly, be silent, rest in prayer: these are the roots of not sinning.[14]

The escape to solitude was, of course, an essential feature of the desert life. "A man who lives apart," said the reformed Ethiopian robber Abba Moses, "is like a ripe grape. And a man who lives in the company of others is a sour grape."[15] (The title Abba is Aramaic for Abbot, but it did not signify an elected superior, rather a monk or hermit who had been tried by years in the desert and proved himself a servant of God.)

It is generally assumed that the hermits' solitudes were always accompanied by ardent asceticism, but their recorded sayings paint a different picture. When an aspiring hermit came to Abba Ammonas wearing a hairshirt, for example, he said, "That thing won't do you a bit of good." Ammonas advised instead that the neophyte should go to his cell, eat little every day, and always keep in mind the words, "Lord have mercy on me."[16]

Above all, the way to salvation in the desert was to seek purity of heart by cultivating one's "inner man." Another Father, Abba Pastor, advised one of his followers that "Any trial whatever that comes to you can be conquered by silence."[17] Abba Hor confirmed that independent-minded observation when he admonished his disciple to "take care that you never bring into this cell the words of another."[18] But a different elder warned:

> If you see a young monk by his own will climbing up to heaven, take him by the foot and throw him to the ground, because what he is doing is not good for him.[19]

Such humility before God, as well as men, was another important hallmark of desert spirituality. The hermits were so intensely introspective and attuned to simple morality that even sitting in their remote caves or hastily constructed anchorages they tried not to project themselves as superior beings but rather as humble, hospitable souls, as in the story of a "certain solitary" who welcomed a desert brother with words of kindness. "Forgive me Father, for I have broken your Rule," the brother said. But the hermit replied, "My Rule is to receive you with hospitality and to let you go in peace."[20]

Not all hermits placed such emphasis on hospitality. Evagrius, the highly educated Roman classicist who withdrew to the desert after a failed love affair, focused more attention on a harsh life of renunciation. Using the Greek philosophical term, he called it apatheia, which he defined, simply, as "the health of the soul." Accordingly, in his didactic work *On Asceticism and Stillness*, he advises:

> If you cannot attain stillness where you now live, consider living in exile…Be like an astute businessman: make stillness your criterion for testing the value of everything, and choose always what contributes to it.[21]

Evagrius never became a saint, probably because of his intellectualism and links with traditional philosophy, which may not have sat well with the later Church Fathers. He advised neophyte hermits to "concentrate your intellect." Sounding like a Roman Stoic, he advised further that when a hermit is in his cell he should "remember the day of death, visualize the dying of your body, reflect on this calamity, experience the pain, reject the vanity of this world, its compromises and crazes, so that you may continue in the way of stillness and not weaken."[22]

Evagrius' emphasis on self-awakening may also have been viewed as somewhat heretical by the Church. The proof of having achieved a state of apatheia will come, says Evagrius, "when the spirit begins to see its own light, when it remains in a state of tranquillity in the presence of images it has during sleep and when it maintains its calm as it beholds the affairs of life."[23]

Saint Anthony never spoke of seeing his inner light, at least according to Athanasius, but he seems to have advocated the stern discipline associated with Stoicism. One day, to help Ammonas advance yet further in the fear of God, it is said that Anthony showed him a stone and directed him to insult it and beat it without ceasing. After the hermit obliged, Anthony asked him if the stone answered back. When Ammonas said it had not, Anthony replied: "You too must reach the point where you no longer take offense at anything."[24]

More than a rule for behavior, that lesson may have been intended as a goad to help Ammonas change his perspective. For alongside their humility, the Desert Fathers emphasized a moderate or contingent approach to virtue, which they called discernment. On another occasion, for example, a hermit asked Arsenius whether it is best to have nothing in one's cell that gives pleasure, citing the example of a brother who had a little wildflower come up in his hermitage and pulled it out by the roots.

> Well, said Abba Arsenius, that is all right. But each man should act according to his own spiritual way. And if one were not able to get along without the flower, he should plant it again.[25]

The same sense of discernment is evident in the Desert Fathers' attitude toward work. On the one hand, they recommended that a hermit aspiring to God's grace in solitude should avoid leaving his cell to work in the fields, where it is easy to forget the work of quieting one's inner self. On the other hand, their sense of humility suggested that each hermit should provide his own way in the desert, which was generally done by cultivating gardens and weaving baskets for sale to visitors.

This practical-minded recognition that there are many ways to achieve purity of heart may have been promoted by the experience of the desert itself. Denuded of foliage, the desert demonstrates the vastness of creation and the vulnerability of existence. At the same time, it teaches the watchfulness, say, of a Bedouin vigilant of mirages or a desert mouse always alert for a predatory hawk in the sky. Perhaps as a result of this—coupled with the underlying residual of classical philosophy and the example of Jesus' forty-days in the desert—the Desert Fathers came up with a philosophy of solitude that differed from anything in the eremitic explorations of India or China. They too discovered the spiritual and even occult powers latent in the universal experience of quietude and self-renunciation; but their emphasis was on humility before God's creation, coupled with a discerning recognition that the true life of solitude is beyond mortal understanding.

In fact, it was the latter-day Father, Climacus, who was first to suggest that there might be value in formulating a philosophy of solitude. "There are not many outstanding experts in worldly philosophy," he said. "But I would claim that rarer still are those who are truly expert in the philosophy of stillness."[26]

SUFI SOLOISTS

AFTER MUHAMMAD BECAME KNOWN as the Messenger of God in the seventh century, Islam quickly gained the upper hand in the Middle East and North Africa, where the Desert Fathers and their successors had long been the spiritual elite. What I find fascinating is that the dry, cave-spun philosophy of the Christian hermits had an influence on the Sufi sects of Islam and, we have reason to believe, on the Messenger himself.

At the age of twelve, according to several Muslim sources, Muhammad (570–632) accompanied his uncle Abu Talib on a commercial caravan through the Syrian desert. There he met a Christian hermit (in Arabic, a *rahib*) who prophesied that one day he would be a great spiritual leader. Many times thereafter Muhammad followed similar caravans to the north of Arabia where he would have had many opportunities to meet other pious rahibs and to draw spiritual nourishment from those encounters. From the time of his marriage at age 25 to his call to be the Messenger, Muhammad lived a quiet life in Mecca, devoting an increasing amount of time to meditation, typically in one of the many caves in the surrounding desert. According to his second wife, Aisha, "solitude became dear to him and he would go to a cave on Mount Hira to engage in meditation for a number of nights."[1]

It was there, during the month of Ramadan in 610, that a voice from heaven revealed to him that he was the Messenger of God and bid him to "Read!" (or recite) what was to become the holy book of the Quran. As Muhammad tells it, the voice emanated from a giant figure in the shape of a man whom he saw striding the horizon. Some say the figure was Allah Himself, others that he was the angel Gabriel. In any case, the Prophet experienced many subsequent contacts with the divine, typically off alone in the desert or sequestered in bed while enwrapped in blankets.

Later, as Muslim forces were spreading the religion of Allah, they frequently came upon Christian hermits. In a campaign in Syria, Abu Bakr is said to have given his soldiers a simple order as to how to treat them:

> You will find people who have shut themselves up in cells. Leave them alone; it is for the sake of God they have shut themselves in. You will also find others, whom Satan has branded on the tops of their heads. Cut their heads off.[2]

Those who lost their heads in this way were probably hermits who lacked the determination to remain in their cells or those who gathered in monasteries (and whose heads may have been "branded" with tonsures). Those who remained in their cells were deemed authentic rahibs, who followed the original way of Christ or were otherwise revered for their spiritual fortitude regardless of their religion.

There are many such references to the spiritual value of solitude in the early sayings of the Sufis; and the question-and-answer pattern of most Sufi anecdotes recalls that of the sayings of the Desert Fathers. Dialogues with rahibs are common in those recorded sayings. For instance, a Sufi ascetic of the ninth century said that he once questioned a rahib about the nature of his solitude and received the following replies:

> *Do you ever fear solitude?*
>
> If you had tasted the delight of solitude, you would long for it, away from your self. Solitude is the beginning of the worship of God.
>
> *What is the first thing you find in solitude?*
>
> Peace far from human intercourse and safety far from the evils which accompany it.
>
> *When may the servant taste the bliss of intimacy with God?*
>
> When his love for God becomes pure and he communes with him with a sincere heart.
>
> *When is his love pure?*
>
> When all his desires are concentrated in one: to obey God.[3]

Malik ibn Dinar (who was himself known as the rahib of the Arabs) reports a similar conference with a rahib whose position is just what you would expect a Christian hermit to hold. Dinar said that he once saw a rahib on a mountain and asked him to teach him something which will help him to abandon the world. "If you are capable of erecting an iron wall between yourself and your desires, then do it," said the rahib.[4]

It is not surprising that the purported sayings of Jewish and Christian prophets likewise appear in Sufi literature. Typically they espouse eremitism:

> God said to Moses: "Be like a solitary bird who eats what grows in the treetops and drinks the clear water. When dusk falls, it seeks refuge in some cave, intimately close to me and far from the disobedient."[5]

Jesus makes a particularly prominent appearance in the early Sufi sayings, where he is revered not as the son of god (which, of course, would run counter to Muslim belief) but as an ideal saint who is liberated from earthly cares, wanders about, and sleeps in the open with a stone for a pillow. For Jesus, according to the tenth-century Sufi Abu Talib al-Makki, humility was the supreme virtue.

> He said to the children of Israel: "Where does the grain grow?"
> "In the dust."
> "Verily I say unto you: Wisdom can only grow in a heart that has become like dust."[6]

Many of the early Sufis took the Desert Fathers' withdrawal from society very much to heart. According to the twelfth-century al-Jauzi, lovers of God should be asocial on principle. "Shun people," he advised, "as you would flee from a lion."[7] In the eleventh century, al-Sulami advised that "the people who know God are the wild beasts of god on the earth. They show no affection for any human being." The eighth-century saint Ibrahim ibn Adham was still more irritated with worldly life: "Humans have disappeared, apes remain."[8]

Adham represents one of the most dramatic cases of world renunciation among Sufis. Of pure Arab descent, he was born a prince in Balkh, now a small town in Afghanistan but revered by the Arabs before its destruction in 1220 by Genghiz Khan as "the mother of all cities." As king of Balkh, according to Sufi hagiography, "a whole world was under his command; forty gold swords and forty maces were carried before and behind him." But one day while sitting on his thrown a mirror was held up before him and when he looked into it he became disgusted with his kingdom. He saw that his lodging was a tomb with no familiar friend, that he had a long journey ahead with no provisions, and that he faced a judge with no defense.

Like the Buddha and King Visvamitra long before him, Adham renounced his royal status entirely to take up the life of a wandering ascetic. Traveling westward he met various Sufis, made a pilgrimage to Mecca, and earned his bread by honest toil until his death in Syria in 782. It is even said that when his son found him in Mecca, Adham embraced him but heard a voice that questioned how he could love both God and his son. He prayed to God that either he or his son should die, whereupon his son perished in his arms.[9]

It should be emphasized, however, that over time the Sufis tended to reject this sort of misanthropic asceticism. The eleventh-century Sufi philosopher al-Ghazali, for example, makes a point of saying that

> Serving God through asceticism—that is like breathing vinegar
> and mustard.
> Possessing divine knowledge—that is like the scent of musk and
> ambergris.[10]

The resolution to this apparent contradiction is implicit in al-Ghazali's statement. For many Sufis are not against asceticism, self-renunciation, or solitude as paths to divine knowledge. Rather they warn that any of these can become obstacles to the higher object of gathering divine knowledge from direct communion with God. This is best illustrated in a story of the ninth-century Persian Sufi Bayezid Bestami, who boasted that his ascetic phase lasted only three days. On the first day, he renounced this world. On the second, he renounced the Otherworld. And on the third, "he renounced everything save God." Thereafter, his true self was at one with the Infinite, so he had nothing more to either renounce or desire.[11]

That is probably why we do not find Sufi hermits living off in caves or mountain retreats like their Christian counterparts. They are more likely to build cellars in their homes for periodic spiritual retreat while living in the world. The roof, which in arid Arabia is a terrace, was also a favored place for spiritual retreat, as in a well-known anecdote concerning the eighth-century Sufi of Baghdad, Dawud al-Ta'i. One moonlit night, when Dawud went up on his roof and gazed at the sky, he began meditating on the splendor of God's kingdom and wept until he was beside himself—so much so that he fell off onto the roof of his neighbor. Thinking that a thief was on his roof, the neighbor rushed up with a sword. But when he saw Dawud there, he took him by the hand and asked: "Who threw you down here?" "I do not know," Dawud replied. "I was beside myself. I have no idea at all."[12]

THE TAVERN OF RUIN

Dawud could not find the words for it, but many other Sufis did find ways to express the inexpressible through language typically intended to shock the hearer into a higher order of thinking and which, to say the least, often sounds religiously incorrect. Over time, that expression centered on one thing—a complete absorption in love, love of man for God and God for man, in an ecstatic annihilation of the self that came to be known as "the tavern of ruin."

The first to place a strong emphasis on love above asceticism was the female Sufi saint Rabi'a, who lived in the eighth century just a hundred years after Muhammad. Having lost her family at an early age, she was sold into slavery. When freed shortly thereafter, it is said that she went to live in a desert hermitage where she "served god for a while."[13] She then returned to society, in a way, supporting herself by playing her flute. But her main aim in life was not to make a worldly living at all, rather to devote her entire being to love of God and nothing else. That aim sometimes took a classically ascetic turn:

> If all the tortures of all the circles of Hell
> Were put into one needle;
> And if my right eye were lined with many such needles, all stuck
>   in a row;

If my left eye twitched only once, and disturbed my prayer—
I would tear it out of its socket.[14]

At the same time, she delighted in using worldly imagery to convey her spiritual wisdom. Other verses attributed to Rabi'a, for example, replace a feeling of ascetic torture with that of equally intense sensual love:

Peace, brothers, is my aloneness
Because my Beloved is alone with me there—always.
I've found nothing to equal His love,
That Love which harrows the sands of my desert.[15]

Rabi'a seems to have taken as a starting point the Quranic statement that God's love precedes that of man: "He loves them and they love Him" (Sura 5:59). She then went much further than would be expected from a casual reading of that verse to direct all of her love to God, without exception. It is said that when she once saw Mohammad in a dream he asked her, "Do you love me?"—to which she replied, "O Prophet of God, who is there who does not love you? But my love of God has so possessed me that no space is left for loving—or hating—any but him."[16]

According to another story, a serving girl, proclaiming, "It's Spring, Rabi'a," once bid her to "come outside, and look at all the beauty that God has made!" Rabi'a answered simply:

Why not come inside instead, serving girl
And see the One who made it all—
Naked, without veil.[17]

Her reference to seeing God naked is already pointing to the use of potentially risqué metaphors to express divine love, a practice that occurs throughout Sufism. Rabi'a is also thought to be the first to refer to drinking of wine as a symbol of the joyful ecstasy of divine union:

Cup, Wine, and Friend make three:
And I, thirsty with love, am Four…
The Cupbearer hands to each, one after another
The cup of unending joy:

If I look, it's Him I am looking for;
And if I arrive, then He is my eyes.[18]

It is always difficult to tell whether the Sufi poet who employs such earthly references is doing so purely for spiritual effect or whether he or she has somehow found a shrewd compromise between spiritual and worldly affairs. The ninth-century Sufi Dho 'l-Nun al-Masri seems to take the latter approach as he rhapsodizes in this prayer on the beauties of nature:

> O God, I never hearken to the voices of the beasts or the rustle of the trees, the splashing of the waters or the song of birds, the whistling of the wind or the rumble of the thunder, but I sense in them a testimony to Thy Unity, and a proof of Thy incomparability, that Thou art the All-Pervading, the All-Knowing, the All-True.[19]

It should be kept in mind, though, that Dho 'l-Nun maintained a positive attitude toward the world because, as he says, he took everything to be a manifestation of God. That may help to explain why it is said that after he died, birds flocked above his coffin to give it shade.

Years later, in his *Divine Flashes*, the thirteenth century poet Fakhruddin 'Iraqi could take the admixture of worldliness and spiritual aims to a higher level of sophistication. But there is always the suggestion that his inebriation derives from spiritual wine.

"If my words seem to smell of drunkenness, forgive me," he writes in his Twenty-Eighth Flash concerning "the arrival of the lover at the Station of Articulation." His words are tipsy, he says, because they "flow of themselves."

I drain a cup
    In every subtle meaning
And by every voice in the universe
    I am filled with delight.[20]

'Iraqi's guide to mystic flashes begins in a "cell of seclusion." But as his heart tugs him to the tavern of ruin, he finds he can no longer seclude himself from anything and wonders how he can remain with pious hermits. He realizes that his worthiness in the eyes of God depends not on worldly solitude but on "his own being a lover." At that point, as 'Iraqi puts it, he is "at the level of being-the-Beloved," where the distinction between worldliness and divinity tend to dissolve and "only God remains."

The main things in much Sufi spirituality, then, are love and the perennial eremitic admonition to annihilate the self. It is only by renouncing all desire in both its worldly and outwardly "spiritual" forms that one can achieve one's true desire: love of the Infinite. The secret seems to lie back in 'Iraqi's Twenty-First Flash:

> What you get by wanting is only as big as your capacity for desire. Give up desire therefore, think that whatever you get is what you want, and in this acceptance find ease and joy.
>
> Renounce desire
> A hundred times
> Or else not once
> Will you embrace your Desire.[21]

That, I think, is the wonderful standpoint from which one of the greatest Sufi poet-mystics, the thirteenth-century Jalaluddin Rumi (1207–73), lived, taught, and composed his monumental beehive and ocean of mystic rambling, the *Mathnawi* and *The Works of Shams of Tabriz*. He, too, lived in a "tavern of ruin." The poems, which amount to tens of thousands of verses, were mainly dictated in a state of ecstasy. Rumi's work is so vast that interpreters can generally find in them whatever they wish, from the orthodox to the pantheistic. Prominent in his verses, though, is an insistence that true understanding emanates from inner experience, along with a spontaneous, open-minded recognition that all things are divine things, as in this passage as translated by Coleman Barks from the *Mathnawi*:

> Jesus was lost in his love for God.
> His donkey was drunk with barley.
>
> Drink from this presence of saints,
> Not from those other jars.

Every object, every being,
Is a jar full of delight.[22]

Continuing the alcoholic metaphor he makes it clear that the Sufi's drunkenness is a matter of getting high in a spiritual sense on both the nearness of God and life:

The wine we really drink is our own blood.
Our bodies ferment in these barrels.
We give everything for a glass of this.
We give our minds for a sip.[23]

Rumi was not really a hermit, you could say. But in a sense all "Perfect Beings" of Sufism are Friends of Solitude, as well as Friends of God, when they are with the Beloved. A contemporary Sufi, Dr. Javad Nurbakhsh explains that although the Sufi lives outwardly among people, inwardly he is constantly with God: "Externally he is congenial with everyone. Inwardly, he is a stranger to all. He is at peace with all people, yet within himself tranquillity is to be found only in Divine Love."[24] Rumi was certainly a hermit in that sense.

Muhammad proclaimed that Muslims should not live in monastic retreats, and that is probably why the Sufi "monastery" is more of a mystic-poetic secret society, hidden from the clamor of the world. Rumi was the head of such an order in Konya, Anatolia (now Turkey). In Rumi's verses we hear nothing of the solitude of the desert hermit. Rather, we hear of the ecstasy of union with the One: "I am so drunk in this world," he says in a poem to his friend Shams of Tabriz, "that except for drunkenness and revelry I have no tale to tell."[25] We also get a strong message that nothing he writes is the real thing, that the wisdom he points to can only be understood, truly heard, and evoked in the silence and emptiness of one's own heart, as he tells us in this verse from *The Works of Shams of Tabriz* on love in quietness:

Inside this new love, die.
Your way begins on the other side.
Becomes the sky.
Take an ax to the prison wall.
Escape.

Walk out like someone suddenly born into color.
Do it now.
You're covered with a thick cloud.
Slide out the side. Die,
And be quiet. Quietness is the surest sign
That you've died.
Your old life was a frantic running
From silence.

The speechless full moon
Comes out Now. [26]

Similes aside, many Sufis did seek physical isolation from society. In his autobiographic tale, *Deliverance from Error,* the twelfth-century philosopher al-Ghazali tells us that, around the age of forty, when he was a renowned writer and "professor of religious sciences" in Baghdad, it became clear to him that his hope of attaining beatitude in the afterlife could only be achieved, not through study, but rather through direct (i.e., mystic) experience. "How great a difference there is," he said, "between your *knowing* the definitions and causes and conditions of health and satiety and your *being* healthy and sated." Accordingly, he sold most of his belongings and retired to a life of solitude and poverty. There, in a manner similar to that described by the later French philosopher René Descartes in his *Meditations*, he sought to put aside all distractions in order to discover that which can be known with certainty in this life of dreams.

Al-Ghazali's time alone was productive. Things "innumerable and unfathomable" were revealed to him and, unlike Descartes, he found the greatest certainty in mystic transport: "I knew with certainty that the Sufis are those who uniquely follow the way to God Most High, their mode of life is the best of all, their way the most direct, and their ethic the purest." Indeed, he continues, were one to attempt to combine the insights of the intellectuals, the wisdom of the wise, and the knowledge of the scholars, it would remain impossible to improve their conduct. For the motions and the quiescence of the mystics, says a-Ghazali, "are learned from the light of the niche of prophecy." And beyond that there is "no other light on earth from which illumination can be obtained."[27]

After ten years, a religious leader persuaded al-Ghazali to bring his inner solitude back into society to solve a heretical problem in an Iraqi province, after which he lived the remainder of his days as a mystic philosopher in the world. The degree to which Sufis have interacted with society varies greatly, but it is significant that Mohammad himself was married and espoused family life and many who founded mystical fraternities had large families. The Sufi Ahma-I Jam, for instance, is said to have sired forty-two children.[28]

A much later Friend, the fourteenth-century contemporary of Petrarch, Hafiz of Shiraz, took the Sufi's cheerful mixture of the worldly with the spiritual a step further than al-Ghazali or even Rumi by writing love poetry that seems—on the surface, at least—to be patently in the world. Perhaps this is not surprising since his "refuge" was the courts of caliphs, who appreciated his earthly imagery and protected him from the theologians who branded him a heretic. Compare the following selection from his verses with those of Rumi on the subject of love:

Rumi:

This is Love: to fly heavenward,
To rend, every instant, a hundred veils.
The first moment, to renounce life;
The last step, to fare without feet
To regard this world as invisible,
Not to see what appears to one's self.[29]

Hafiz:

Her hair in disarray, lips laughing;
Drunk in the sweat of revelry
Singing of love, she came, flask in hand.

Disheveled and her clothes rent
Last midnight by my bed she bent;
Her lips curved in regret…

Find no fault, anchorite, with the drinker of dregs,
For on the day of the Covenent
We were given no other gift.

We lift our lips
Whatever he pours into the wine bowl,
The wine of Paradise or the cup of Hell.[30]

It may be hard for a westerner in the twenty-first century to avoid thinking that Hafiz is expressing worldly love, at least in part. But the contemporary Sufi commentator Idris Shaw insists that those who would see blasphemy or even pornography in Hafiz's poetry are simply ill-equipped to understand him, because there is no similar tradition the West. Hafiz, says Shaw, is filling that gap between the profane and divine in a manner characteristic of the Sufi School of Naqshbandiyya (The Designers), with which tradition associates him. "The phenomenal is the Bridge to the Real," is a favorite Naqshbandiyya aphorism expressing that approach. And the masters of that school, Shaw explains, have always been marked by their adherence to the outward norms of the communities in which they work and the use of common images from those communities as raw material for higher mystical teachings.[31]

That certainly squares with the Sufi admonition that to arrive at higher mystic truths through direct, spontaneous contact with the indefinable Infinite, one must rise above all things worldly, including asceticism and preprogrammed concepts of Heaven. It only stands to reason, therefore, that no images are inherently bad; any of them may provide concrete material to build a joyful spiritual bridge or tools to break out of the prison of ordinary life. I find a great sense of optimism in that approach. But it naturally comes with worldly risk.

In whatever century, Sufis seem to recognize that the esoteric and ecstatic reaches of their mystical explorations place them in danger of being seen as heretics. Throughout the Sufi literature one gets the impression that beyond the clever use of words to shock and surprise there is also a practical-minded effort to conceal mystical, sometimes free-thinking meaning from orthodoxy. Ibn Adham, for example, said that he saw God one-hundred-twenty times and asked him seventy questions, the answers to only four of which he mentioned to people and they disapproved.[32] The others he kept secret. Hafiz, by contrast, is often called by another name: "The Tongue of the Hidden."[33]

MEDIEVAL EUROPE

THE DESERT FATHERS HAD A VERY STRONG INFLUENCE on the course of Christianity. Without them, the West might never have turned medieval and we might have had a precocious Renaissance of a sort, returning to secular humanism a millennium or so earlier than was the case. But that did not happen. Instead, the humble, mystically charged religious retirement of the hermits of Egypt became a revered institution. As it developed in the later Middle Ages, the same emphasis on love and use of worldly imagery that we hear in Sufi mysticism began to make an ever stronger appearance in the solitudes of Christian hermits.

In Western Christendom, John Cassian's *Conferences*, based on interviews with Egyptian hermits in the early fifth century, animated the spread of monasticism. Saint Benedict read them and incorporated the sentiments and experience therein into his rules for monks; and he made the regular reading of the work one of his instructions for harmonious monastic life. During the same period eremitism spread east, where grandstanding solitudes of the likes of Saint Simeon Stylites continued to promote the notion that the hermit possessed special spiritual insights and constituted a worldly link to the divine. Simeon, you may recall, remained for many years on top of a column exposed to the weather, the better to be nearer to God and, apparently, to demonstrate his holiness.

Throughout the Christian world, monasteries sprang up around the hermits' cells to provide discipline and spiritual guidance for the less-than-saintly portion of the population for whom eremitism was viewed as too spiritually hazardous. The monastery also provided a refuge from a chaotic world and served as an anchor for medieval European towns. Nevertheless, the life of independent solitude continued to be recognized throughout the Middle Ages as a higher, more adventurous calling.

As the ideal of desert spirituality spread northward, many sought to emulate Saint Anthony in the holy intensity of their retreats. The Venerable Bede recounts that in seventh-century England Saint Cuthbert retreated to a secluded place near his monastery at Lindisfarne off the coast of Northumberland. There he "gained victory over our invisible enemy by prayer and fasting." He then sought a more remote battlefield a few miles out to sea on Farne Island. According to Bede:

> The island was haunted by devils; Cuthbert was the first man brave enough to live there alone. At the entry of our soldier of Christ armed with "the helmet of salvation, the shield of faith and the sword of the spirit which is the word of God" the devil fled and his host of allies with him. Cuthbert, having routed the enemy, became monarch of the place.[1]

Like Anthony, Cuthbert was a miracle worker. Following the example of the Desert Fathers, he decided to live by his own hands on the inhospitable island, where he was able to grow barley with the help of God. When birds came to devour his crop, Cuthbert shooed them away, just as the Egyptian saint was able to keep wild asses from trampling his little garden in the desert by words alone. On another occasion, Cuthbert was able to restrain ravens from tearing the straw from his guest house by admonishing them sharply, after which the contrite birds returned with what Bede terms a "fitting gift"—a lump of pig's lard, which Cuthbert "would often show his guests, inviting them to grease their shoes with it."[2]

At the same time, hermits in Celtic Ireland seem to have been in love with both God and His creation. There are many poems by or about Irish hermits in the following few centuries that portray them as nature lovers on the order of Wordsworth or Thoreau. In one, "The Hermit's Hut," the poet tells us that he has a modest hut in the wood, which no one knows but God. It is surrounded by ash and hazel trees and a "she-bird in its dress of blackbird color sings a melodious strain from its gable."[3]

Perhaps it is the chutzpah of the Irish poet, but according to another Celtic verse, even the spiritually dedicated Saint Colomba would have appreciated the natural surroundings of his hermitage on an island off the

Irish coast: "Delightful I think it to be in the bosom of an isle, on the peak of a rock, that I might often see there the calm of the sea," he says, in the poet's imagination. From there, the saint can see "heavy waves over the littering ocean, as they chant a melody to their Father on their eternal course." It would be delightful on the island to "meditate upon the Kingdom of Heaven," he continues, while in his cell, fishing, giving food to the poor, or "at labor not too heavy."[4]

As in every other culture where eremitism became an institution, European nobles were also attracted to the recluse's tranquil and morally upright solitude. This is illustrated in the early French tale-in-verse titled, "How William Became a Hermit."[5] Troubled by his worldly sins, appalled by robbers' attacks on hermits in the forest, and "going the way that God leads him," King William of Orange spends a week alone in the forest until he finally finds a hermit. At first, the hermit bars the door and flees, fearing that William is another robber, even larger and more fearsome than the others. But, after William's sincere entreaties, the hermit finally welcomes him as warmly as Paul received Anthony. No raven intervened, but the holy eremite proffered a relatively sumptuous offering of water boiled with a little flour, rye bread, cider, apples, beech nuts, and ripe medlars.

"God," said William, "what a good life this is! I would rather have this food than a swan, peacock, or crane, or capon or fowl, stag from the moor or bear or roebuck or doe." Hearing those words, the hermit realizes that William is a nobleman, then confesses that he too is a noble who retreated to the forest twenty-four years earlier to flee the sorry world in which, he says, "I have committed so many mortal sins, I have killed so many men and burnt so many cities, laid waste lands and destroyed castles, until my sins make me dread lest I go to everlasting Hell." Soon thereafter, the two discover that they are indeed related, and William resolves to join his cousin in his forest retreat.

In the romantic age of knights of honor and damsels in distress, the hermit is ever a supporting character, says Rotha Mary Clay in her comprehensive history of English eremitism, *Hermits and Anchorites of England*. She cites, for instance, the Celtic *Quest for the Holy Grail*, in which the solitary plays a role that might fairly be described as that of a

Christian shaman: teacher, expounder of visions, confessor, counselor, healer, and host. Likewise, Knights of the Round Table, including Perceval, Lancelot, Galahad, Bors, and Lionel all consulted hermits or found beneficial refuges in hermitages during their careers. And it is generally revealed that the hermit is some noble knight who has forsaken the world for the life of spiritual solitude.

Thanks to Ms. Clay we have a catalogue of the grand variety of hermits from every social stratum that lived in England during medieval times—including forest hermits, island hermits, hillside hermits, cave hermits, wandering hermits, and light-keepers. Some were educated; some were not. Many performed useful worldly functions such as tending bridges or manning lighthouses; others produced works of spiritual direction and inspiration that were widely read—including books by Dame Julian of Norwich and Richard Rolle, Hermit of Hampole (about which we will hear a few pages on).

Most hermits, but not all, were celibate. After taking the hermit's vow, one Adam Cressevill is said to have married a certain Margaret. The validity of the union was questioned, but the archbishop of the time judged it valid ruling that eremitic orders did not preclude a subsequent "contract of marriage which was instituted in Paradise."[6]

With such diversity, it is not surprising that the church often sought to control the hermits' independence, demanding that all solitaries be properly licensed and ordained. Church officials maintained that only those who were truly "called" and prepared for the solo life could attempt it without danger to themselves. But there was also a fear that freelance hermits would spread heresy. For instance, Clay reports that a runaway monk named William Stapleton took up the hermit life to further his interest in the "science" of necromancy. His activities in solitude were deemed inappropriate, but since the proper authorities had approved William's retirement, he was allowed to continue. An apostate friar by the name of Ranulf was not so lucky; he found himself excommunicated from the Church on the charge that he was "a heretic in the habit of a hermit."[7]

Rather than living entirely on their own, medieval hermits were often persuaded to live within the monastery grounds or in loose, albeit supervised, groupings called *lauras*. Female hermits were typically enclosed in "anchorages," cells attached directly to churches, from which, through openings in the wall, they could both witness the services within and broadcast their holiness into the mystic space of the church. Such anchorites of either gender were often obliged to begin their enclosure with a special ceremony in which they appeared bareheaded before a bishop, received a new set of clothes, and were required to sign a deed of profession. The written guidelines for one such agreement, "The Office for the Enclosing of Anchorites," state specify that the anchorite is not to think highly of himself, but rather that he is being enclosed so as not to fall further into sin:

> Let him therefore think that he is convicted to his sins and committed to solitary confinement as to a prison, and that on account of his own weakness he is unworthy of the fellowship of mankind.[8]

It should be noted, however, that many eremitic guidelines of the day were not so strict, emphasizing the spirit over the letter of their instructions. The twelfth-century *Ancren Wisse* advises that an anchoress should obey an "inward rule" above all else and may on occasion leave the confines of her anchorage, read religious literature, and even keep a cat. The spiritual guidebook states that, "The outward rule may be changed and varied according to every one's state and circumstance…It is only a slave to help the lady to rule the heart."[9]

RETURN OF PLATO

With the beginning of the High Middle Ages in the eleventh century, Europe was on the ascendance in line with technical developments such as the control of flood lands in Northern Europe, increasing emphasis on trade, challenges to religious institutions, and growing literacy and education of the laity. These developments seem to have had an uplifting effect on matters both material and spiritual. Across Europe, there was a new emphasis on mystical exploration, along with an emphasis on the power of love for mystic transports that recalls Socrates' dialogue with Diotima.

Petrarch seems to have been adverse to mystically oriented solitudes. He fails, for instance, to mention Plotinus' flights to the Alone or those of any of the Christian Friends I mention below. Perhaps he feared that their spiritual explorations in solitude came too close to self-induced ecstasy and might too readily be interpreted as heresy by his conservative readers (he was already treading heretical ground in his advocacy of secular solitude).

The Desert Fathers, too, had been careful not to portray themselves as mystic travelers; nevertheless, the heritage of solitude, humility, and self-renunciation that they bequeathed helped to spawn a rich mystic tradition that also drew from Plato, Philo, and Plotinus. We will follow a sampling of the late medieval Friends of Solitude who best typify these traditions.

The most prominent link between the Neoplatonists of Rome and late medieval mysticism was Dionysius the Areopagite, a Christian who lived in the early sixth century, probably in the vicinity of Syria. There is no specific evidence that he lived as a hermit, even according to my liberal definition. But I include him here because of his advocacy of what is known in the West as the apophatic *via negativa*, the "negative way" to mystic union with God. In his famous letter to his friend Timothy, "The Mystical Theology," he advises that to traverse these mystic heights one must leave the senses and "all things in this world of nothingness." He opens the letter with this prayer to the heavenly wisdom of the Trinity:

> Guide us to that topmost height of mystic lore which exceedeth light and more than exceedeth knowledge, where the simple, absolute and unchangeable mysteries of heavenly Truth lie hidden in the dazzling obscurity of the secret Silence, outshining all brilliance with the intensity of their darkness, and surcharging our blinded intellects with the utterly impalpable and invisible fairness of glories which exceed all beauty![10]

I include Dionysius, too, because his philosophy embodies the perennial eremitic notion that essential spiritual truths can only be "known" literally by "not thinking" or "unknowing." That avenue to truth was further explored by the first English translator of "The Mystical Theology," who is also thought to have been the anonymous author of the fourteenth-century work *The Cloud of Unknowing*. His admonition to Christian mystics is this:

> See to it that there is nothing at work in your mind or will but only God. Try to suppress all knowledge and feeling of anything less than God, and trample it down deep under the cloud of forgetting.[11]

One might think that such a cloud would fog one's spirit and push one further away from God. The *Cloud* author insists, however, that it is the *absence* of a cloud that has that effect. He acknowledges that no one who expects to advance along the spiritual way will get very far without first "having meditated often on his own sinfulness, the Passion of Christ, and the kindness, goodness, and dignity of God." But a person who has long pondered these things must eventually leave all that behind:

> Every time I say "all creatures," I refer not only to every created thing but also to all their circumstances and activities. I make no exception. You are to concern yourself with no creature whether material or spiritual nor with their situation or doings whether good or ill.[12]

The *Cloud* author was thus opposed to any method or visualization in spiritual contemplation other than freeing the mind and spirit of all conceptions whatever in favor of direct experience. The contemplative should fix his mind on the "naked existence" of God. If his thoughts ask "Who is this God?" tell them, says the author, that "You are powerless to grasp him. Be Still." How? The author recommends focusing the mind on a single word, such as "love" or "God." And, he says, "If your mind continues to intellectualize over the meaning and connotations of this little word, remind yourself that its value lies in its simplicity. Do this and I assure you these thoughts will vanish."[13]

A century earlier, the German preacher Meister Eckhart (1260–1327) made about the same point in one of his sermons. True possession of God cannot be gained through "steady contemplation by a given method," he said. Rather, the mystic should recognize that any conception we may have about the deity or how to arrive at union with Him is likely to be wrong:

> We ought not to have or let ourselves be satisfied with the God we have thought of, for when the thought slips the mind, that god slips with it. What we want rather is the reality of God, exalted far above any human thought or creature.[14]

A TUMULT OF LOVE

Perhaps it is the final secret of Lady Solitude's domain that the Truth will appear as nothing…and somehow we will understand it. Christian hermits who wrote down their thoughts and offered guidance were inevitably the same sort of mystic. But over time, their brand of *via negativa* tended to become more emotional and highly charged with love for God. It is notable, for example, that the *Cloud* author emphasizes that the dark cloud of unknowing confusion may only be pierced by a "dart of love." And another German luminary, the nun Mechthild of Magdeburg (1210–1297) had already stressed a century earlier that love and emptiness in solitude could work together.

Like many Sufis of the same time, she was not afraid to use the imagery of courtly love poetry to enhance the impact of her serious-minded spiritual desires. In the first book of her work *The Flowing Light of the Godhead,* she says she wants to "drink undiluted wine" and come to her divine lover as "a full-grown bride." In the same place, she says that the Lord invited her to "take off your clothes," so that "not the slightest thing can be between you and me." "Lord, now I am a naked soul," she answers, "and you in yourself are a well-adorned God," after which a "blessed stillness over comes both of them." It is clear, however, that Mechthild is not speaking of worldly passion any more than was Rabi'a in her romantic moments with God. For she emphasizes throughout that any divine union she may have experienced in the bridal chamber was the result of a complete abandonment of self, with no certainty whatever that her spiritual desire would be fulfilled. Among the twelve prerequisites for living in the "true desert," she says, are to love nothingness, to flee somethingness, to stand alone, and to "drink the water of suffering."[15]

Though many railed against any methodology or effort to explain, the urge to communicate the path to union with the divine was great. A contemporary of the *Cloud* author, Jan van Ruysbroek (1293–1381), went to great lengths to lay out the "why and the wherefore" and the way by which a right-minded individual may achieve union as a bride of Christ. In the process, he managed to touch on all the main elements of mystic transcendence in flowery, ecstatic prose, while steering clear of being declared a heretic by church leaders.

Saint Ruysbroek spent most of his worldly life as a preacher in a small town near Brussels. At age fifty, he and a few companions fled the distractions of city life by retiring to the nearby forest of Soignes, where Ruysbroek spent the next thirty-eight years until his death in 1381. In his *The Adornment of the Spiritual Marriage* he begins by holding out the joyful hope that "the second coming of Christ our Bridegroom takes place every day within good men; often and many times, with new graces and gifts, in all those who make themselves ready for it, each according to his power."[16]

Like so many other hermits, Ruysbroek recommends that the first step toward becoming a bride of Christ (a state that may be attained equally by men or women) is renunciation of self and the world to the point of complete emptiness and lowliness. One should become like a valley between two mountains awaiting the radiance of the sun (i.e., Christ) as it rises to noontide. Says Ruysbroek:

> When a good man takes his stand upon his own littleness, in the most lowly part of himself, and confesses and knows that he has nothing, and is nothing, and can nothing of himself neither stand still nor go on, and when he sees how often he fails in virtues and good works: then he confesses his poverty and his helplessness, then he makes a valley of humility.[17]

At that point, the Savior, from his position at the highest part of the firmament, "shines into the bottom of the humble heart." For Christ is always moved, says Ruysbroek, "by helplessness, whenever a man complains of it and lays it before Him with humility." Unfortunately (but it is the nature of the cosmos) the desires of such an open heart and the shining of the divine rays cause perpetual pain in the soul of the bride. As he "considers the place of exile in which he has been imprisoned, and from which he cannot escape; then tears of sadness and misery gush forth."

Living in this "fierce tumult of love" the bride should not contemplate suicide nor "follow strange paths or singular ways." Rather, like an ant, he or she should work during the summer of life to gather the fruits of virtue in preparation for the winter of eternity. With sufficient virtue, one may even get a taste of that joyous winter while on earth, before the snow falls. This is accomplished through a mystic groping with God Himself:

> In this storm of love two spirits strive together: the spirit of God and our own spirit. God, through the Holy Ghost, inclines Himself towards us; and, thereby, we are touched in love. And our spirit, by God's working and by the power of love, presses and inclines itself into God: and, thereby God is touched.[18]

Each spirit is deeply wounded in this ardent encounter, says Ruysbroek. Each sparkles and shines into the other and shows the other its face. In the "flux and reflux," the fountain of love brims over to such a degree that the touch of God becomes one with the mystic's spiritual craving. In the process, the bride must forget both himself and God, and realize that he can do nothing but love. "Thereby," says Ruysbroek, "the spirit is burned up in the fire of love."[19]

In addition to preparation through renunciation of self and a buildup of the fire of love, it is important to note that Ruysbroek also recommends essentially the same strategy of unknowing that we hear from the likes of Dionysius and the *Cloud* author. Says Ruysbroek of the hermit aspiring to union with the Infinite:

> He must have lost himself in a Waylessness and in a Darkness, in which all contemplative men wander in fruition and wherein they never again can find themselves in a creaturely way. In the abyss of this darkness, in which the loving spirit has died to itself, there begin the manifestation of God and eternal life. For in this darkness there shines and is born an incomprehensible Light, which is the Son of God, in whom we behold eternal life.[20]

One may wonder how it is possible to be completely wayless while also following Ruysbroek's advice and staying within the bounds of orthodoxy, but that too may be beyond understanding. The more the religious hermit—or any Friend of Solitude—attempts clear explanation of his deepest mental explorations, the more he is suspect and open to critique, particularly by those with an orthodox bent and without the creative wit to follow him in his empty wanderings.

So it was with Richard Rolle (1300–1349), who can best be characterized as the Henry Thoreau of fourteenth-century Christian spirituality. He was born to a rich family in Yorkshire and schooled for several years at Oxford, although he did not complete his master's degree. Instead, he decided to return to Yorkshire, where he ran away from his father's home to become a hermit. Like his American counterpart half a millennium later, Rolle wrote constantly, even automatically, in his solitude.

The most famous of his many works, *Incendium Amoris* (*The Fire of Love*), is presented as a guide to the mystic raptures of the spiritual life. But Rolle's is a more personal account than that of Ruysbroek. Written mainly in first person, it is often autobiographical and includes discursive musings worthy of Montaigne. He begins with a report of his remarkable experience in solitude, a physical feeling of fire in his body that gives concrete meaning to Ruysbroek's image of the spirit "burned up by the fire of love."

> I cannot tell you how surprised I was the first time I felt my head begin to warm. It was real warmth too, not imaginary, and it felt as if it were actually on fire. I was astonished at the way the heat surged up, and how this new sensation brought great unexpected comfort. I had to keep feeling my breast to make sure there was no physical reason for it! But once I realized that it came entirely from within, that this fire of love had no cause, material or sinful, but was the gift of my Maker, I was absolutely delighted, and wanted my love to be even greater. And this longing was all the more urgent because of the delightful effect and the interior sweetness which this spiritual flame fed into my soul. Before the infusion of this comfort I had never thought that we exiles could possibly have known such warmth, so sweet was the devotion it kindled. It set my soul aglow as if a real fire was burning there.[21]

No other Christian hermit before Rolle wrote of world renunciation so journalistically, or with such worldly honestly. Perhaps that is why some portray him as the father of English literature. Like other literary soloists such as Horace or, much later, Kierkegaard, he could recommend the value of humor. For Rolle, it was a form of humility. God's saint, he says, "reveals himself to be a man neither too lighthearted nor too sad. There is a maturity about his cheerfulness."

> There are some who disapprove of laughter, and others who praise it. The laughter of a frivolous, silly mind can be reprehensible, but surely that which springs from a cheerful conscience and spiritual buoyancy is worth praising. The righteous have it, and they call it delighting in the love of God.[22]

THE DARK NIGHT

Meanwhile, in another part of England, just a year after Petrarch's death in the hills of Padua, a thirty-two-year-old nun now known as Julian of Norwich (1342–1416) had a life-shaking experience that confirmed her vocation as an anchoress and brought a new emphasis on the importance of suffering to mystic spirituality in the West.

It seems that Julian had fallen gravely ill. Having already been administered the last rights of the church, she resigned herself wholeheartedly to death. With the lower half of her body dead, she later recounted, death crept to claim the other half. Her breath became shorter and shorter; and, apart from the cross held by the priest administering the rights, "everything else seemed horrible as if it were occupied by fiends." Then suddenly, at about four o'clock in the morning, the pain was taken completely away and Julian was granted sixteen visions, or "showings," each instructive of God's overwhelming love for humanity.

She saw Christ himself, wearing the blessed crown of thorns—"red blood trickling down from under the garland, hot, fresh, and plentiful." She saw the passion of Christ and He brought the Godhead to her mind. She was "overwhelmed with wonder that he, so holy and awful, could be so friendly at once to a sinful creature." She saw the Virgin Mary as though she were physically present, and the Lord showed her that His love "clothes us, enfolds us and embraces us."

Then He showed her more:

> a little thing, the size of a hazelnut, on the palm of my hand, round like a ball. I looked at it thoughtfully and wondered, "What is this?" And the answer came, "It is all that is made." I marveled that it continued to exist and did not suddenly disintegrate; it was so small. And again my mind supplied the answer, "It exists, both now and forever, because God loves it." In short, everything owes existence to the love of God.[23]

In that "little thing"—something, perhaps, like the universe just before the Big Bang—Julian realized that until there is nothing between her and God she could never have the full rest of real happiness. "We have got to realize," she says, "the littleness of creation and to see it for the nothing that it is before we can love and possess God who is uncreated." We cannot seek our rest in trivial things which will not satisfy, she adds, very much in the spirit of the Rabi'a or Mechthild. Only union with the Uncreated will suffice: "He is true rest. It is his will that we should know him, and his pleasure that we should rest in him. Nothing less will satisfy us. No soul can rest until it is detached from all creation."[24]

Having learned that divinely inspired lesson, Julian resolved to spend the remainder of her seventy-one years in an anchorage attached to a church that bears her name, the Church of Saint Julian at Norwich. Her anchorage has not survived, but it is reported to have been somewhat atypical—a multi-room apartment of stone, with an opening into the church's alter and a door to the world. Julian's life there seems to have been comfortable. It is known that she had two servants and her residence may have been surrounded by a garden. Though she was by her own description uneducated, her visions and their meaning were written down with the help of a scribe in *Revelations of Divine Love*. She is thought to be the first woman to compose a book in English.

The call to spiritual solitude continued to be a relatively important part of religious culture in Europe for the next two centuries or so, culminating in the intense solitary experience of Saint John of the Cross

(1542–91). John has an important place in the history of solitude in the West, because what he termed his "Dark Night of the Soul" has since been recognized as something of an archetype for the kind of enlightening episodes born of suffering that occurred to Julian, as well as those we have heard described by Iglulik shamans.

John's mystic transformation came at the age of thirty-five, when he was imprisoned in a small (ten-by-ten foot) cell in Toledo, Spain, where he had already lived in solitary confinement for more than a year. A fervent exponent of the Counter Reformation, John advocated a return to the spirit of antiworldliness espoused throughout in the Middle Ages. He spent much of his early life as a monk in an active campaign against the growing urbanity in Christendom and in favor of the harsh monastic discipline of the Carmelite order, which he helped to found. As might be expected, John's idealism put him at odds with the Spanish establishment and was the main reason for his imprisonment.

That forced seclusion had its benefits, though, because something unexplainable happened there. One day a mysterious heavenly light appeared in the darkness of his cell. He began to compose a poem about the experience in his head, then back in his monastery after his release a few months later he penned "The Dark Night," his now famous tribute and invitation to an extremely rigorous detachment from created things.

"One dark night," says John, when he was fired with love's urgent longings and his spirit was stilled, he went out unseen into a "guiding night" that united "The Lover and His beloved."

> Upon my blooming breast,
> That is His and His alone,
> This is where He fell asleep,
> And I caressed Him there
> In the cedars' fanning breath.
>
> When the turrets' breezes
> Had parted His hair,
> He pierced my neck
> With his tender hand,
> And I lost all my senses.

As I lay self-abandoned,
My face on my Beloved,
All things ceased and left me
Carefree in safekeeping,
Forgotten among the lilies.[25]

Constantly in John's poetry we hear the world's beauty and the joy of solitude evoked in words intended to help the reader join him in passionate, supra-sensual heights of ecstasy. It is also notable that his poetic descriptions of his encounters with God combine both the sexually charged yearning for the divine of a Mechthild or a Rumi with unknowing of the *Cloud* author. In his "Stanzas Concerning an Ecstasy Experienced in High Contemplation," he recounts the following experience:

I knew not where I was,
Yet, when I saw myself,
Not knowing where I was,
I grasped great things;
I'll not say what I felt,
For I knew without knowing,
All knowledge transcending.

The greater the secret, the greater the understanding:

This unknowing knowing
Holds such enormous power,
That the sages' sly disputing
Will never overcome it;
For their wisdom cannot reach
Unknowing understanding,
All knowledge transcending.[26]

We can imagine that John would have spent the darkest of such exquisite nights in his prison cell. Thereafter, according to Kieran Kavanaugh, John continued to lead an active life as an abbot and leader of a monastic reform movement; but he also cherished the time he was able to spend alone in the countryside, at a favorite grotto near Seville, or reading the Bible in a corner of the monastery grounds. Later in life, he spent so much time in contemplation, even in the course of ordinary life, that he would frequently resort to rapping his knuckles on the stone wall of the monastery to bring himself back to the creaturely world.[27]

Scholars and Ch'an Masters

HAD THEY KNOWN OF THE RECLUSE SCHOLARS OF CHINA, Horace and Petrarch would have found much in common. As we have heard, it was the clever, practical-minded ancient Chinese hermits who seem to have invented the notion of combining religious solitudes with philosophical-poetic ones. This opened the way for a later gentrification of eremitism similar to that which developed in Rome before the rise of Christianity.

In the middle of the third century, when Paul the first Hermit was living in his cave in the Thebaid, Juan Chi, leader of a group of poets known as the Seven Sages of the Bamboo Grove, had a completely different take on retirement. It continued to be a time of political intrigue and instability in China; and following long-standing tradition, the sages' response was withdrawal from political life. Like the poets of the *Songs of the South,* Juan found refuge of a sort in melancholy lyric verse, which helped to mollify the pain of lost hopes or lost love. In one of his "Poems of My Heart," for example, he laments:

> Being sleepless at night,
> I rise to play the lute.
> The moon is visible through the curtains
> And a gentle breeze sways the cords of my robe.
> A lonely wild goose cries in the wilderness
> And is echoed by a bird in the woods.
> As it circles, it gazes
> At me, alone, imbued with sadness.[1]

This mix of honest regret with delight in the quiet subtleties of nature continues to be the hallmark of Chinese eremitic poetry, along with a love of freedom, moral principle, the simple life, books, music, painting, drink, and friends. All of these are present in the poetry of the gentleman hermit

T'ao Ch'ien (365–427). It was with him that the long Chinese line of recluse scholars found its most characteristic form, where the term "scholar" referred to their early education in the classics as a preparation for government service.

T'ao tried official life several times. He served as secretary to warlord generals in the last days of the chaotic Chin dynasty. But each time he soon returned with his family to "idle studies" on his farm in the country. In "Returning to the Farm to Dwell," T'ao admits that from his earliest days he was "at odds with the world" and that his "instinctive love is hills and mountains." It was only by mischance, he says, that he fell into the "dusty net" of government work, which took him away from home for a total of thirteen years. Then, like a migrant bird that longs for its native grove, he was able finally to return to his simple farm, which he describes with all the love and charming verse that Horace used to immortalize his Sabine retreat. His house had a thatched roof, five rooms, and trees for shade. It was "unsoiled by worldly dust" and its bare rooms gave him peace of mind: "Once I was prisoner in a cage," he says, "now I have my freedom."[2]

Like most secular soloists, T'ao also had a penchant for moral philosophy. "We have so little time in the world!" he says in "The Return," so it is best to "follow the inclinations the heart." He has no desire for riches, or expectation for heaven—but, rather, he is content to walk alone near his home, composing verses by a clear stream. "I'll accept my lot until the final homecoming," he says. "Rejoicing in the way of Heaven, what is there to doubt?"[3]

In the tradition of the hermit poets of the *Songs of the South*, there is a melancholy loneliness in T'ao's poetry, seasoned with an appreciation for the beauties of nature, which Horace did not emphasize. He also speaks of the notion (which we hear in the *Bhagavadgita*, from Petrarch, and many other sources) that with the right mental attitude of equanimity, one may find the joys of solitude even in the city. I think T'ao picked it up from the Taoist philosophy he loved to read. He expressed it in this insightful poem, one of twenty which he says he wrote after drinking some excellent wine:

> I built my hut beside a traveled road
> Yet hear no noise of passing carts and horses.
> Would you like to know how it is done?

With the mind detached, my place is remote.
Picking mums by the eastern hedge
I catch sight of distant southern hills:
The mountain air is lovely as the sun sets
And flocks of flying birds return together.
In these things is a fundamental truth
I would like to tell, but lack the words.[4]

Perhaps words failed him because he was tipsy. Or maybe he sensed, with his mind detached, one of those deeper caves of insight that Nietzsche speaks of which can only be ruined by trying to express them. I think the latter.

Among the many subsequent Chinese recluse poets one could quote, the most famous—and most interesting—is Wang Wei (699–761), who wrote about three centuries later during the Tang Dynasty. He lived the Chinese ideal of gentlemanly retirement in style on his sizable Wang River estate. He had served as assistant secretary of music under Emperor Hsuan-tsung in the early eighth century, then was demoted to administrator of granaries in Shantung Province in the far western part of China. He went into retirement at age thirty after the death of his wife, but he also traveled and studied Taoism and Buddhism, the latter under the Ch'an master Tao-kuang. He was, and is, revered in China as both a poet and an artist.

Wang's poems are like meditations on the subtle transience of the world, intended to be mulled, savored, seen through…as though to evoke the essential emptiness of life and the world (*sunyata* in Buddhist philosophy), but still with the frank melancholy of the secular recluse. His "Back to Wang River" is a good example:

A bell sounds in the valley's mouth
As woodsmen and fishermen return.
Evening comes to the distant mountains
And I head home to the white clouds.
Strands of water chestnut rustle delicately
While willow catkins take to the air
And the marsh shows its colors of spring:
In sadness, I close my brushwood gate.[5]

The "white clouds" are a Tang poetic convention referring to the enlightenment or transcendental bliss that one might be most likely to achieve in lonely meditation up in the mountains, which in China are typically shrouded with clouds. Wang found great solace in the rest of nature, too. In fact, whereas T'ao could make his mind remote to evoke a positive-minded solitude, Wang found a similar blessing in a contemplation of landscape. This poem, "Heading Down to Pa Pass," might have been written when he was off in Shantung Province, where he felt alien to the people, but not to nature:

I set out at dawn for Pa Pass
Taking spring with me out of the capital
A woman washes in the glistening river
As birds sing to the morning sun
Markets on boats in a land of water
Mountain bridges amid the treetops
My climb reveals a hundred villages
And two rivers shining in the distance
People here speak an unknown tongue
But orioles sound a familiar song
Luckily, I understand landscape
And that erases my loneliness.[6]

Unlike most earlier recluse scholars, Wang was a wealthy landowner. If not drifting on a lonely lake or meditating in idyllic mountain scenes that have since become staples of Chinese art, we envision him sitting in a scholar's chair, wearing flowing robes, a brush and inkwell on his fine wooden desk, the sound of a cricket filling the room from its cage, his study overlooking on one side a pond with goldfish, on the other a rock garden containing a single large stone with odd pockmarks that would suggest a meteorite. This, as depicted in the scholar's retreat in the New York Metropolitan Museum of Art, is the traditional image that has come down to us of the recluse scholar.

Unfortunately, that ideal was erased from Chinese culture by the vicious rigors of Maoist communism. Only a few reminders remain in often misinterpreted passages in Chinese literature or finely robed scholars ruminating in idyllic mountain retreats, as depicted in the delicate, wistful paintings that can be seen in the Palace Museum in Taipei, the Fogg Museum at Harvard, and in the wonderful twelve-story painting inside the Shangri-La hotel in Hong Kong, with its winding paths up steep mountainsides that can be viewed from a glass elevator that runs as high as the painting. The work represents a hermit or two meditating with apparently faraway looks in their eyes, but grounded, I'm sure, in the scene before them, in fact an integral part of it. That had long been a stylistic element in Chinese art and the ideal of the recluse scholar had been an institution for more than a millennium. Perhaps with the advent of the free market economy, the Internet, and the laptop computer in China, that sane and comforting ideal will soon be restored.

BODHIDHARMA

There is another auspicious sign that eremitic traditions will again take their place in Chinese culture. Recently, I read Bill Porter's fascinating book *Road to Heaven*: *Encounters with Chinese Hermits* to find, much to my surprise and delight, that there are still hermits in China. Many were extracted from their hermitages and turned to other lines of activity during the Cultural Revolution of the 1960s; but others, following long-standing tradition, moved further into the mountains to escape Mao's turbulent regime.

Porter, a American translator and Friend of Solitude, dropped out of graduate school in the early 1970s, then spent what turned out to be two decades in Taiwan, first as a monk in a Buddhist monastery, then as a freelance hermit on a farm, where he devoted his time to study and translation of Buddhist and Taoist poetry and religious texts, most of which had been written by hermits. In the late eighties, as mainland China began to open to foreign visitors, he decided to go looking for contemporary hermits there.

At first, nearly everyone he spoke with believed his search would prove fruitless. Indeed, as Porter traveled closer to the homeland of eremitism in the Chungnan Mountains of Central China, he discovered that many temples and hermitages had been destroyed or allowed to fall into ruins. Nevertheless, he was able to find something on the order of one hundred hermits living mainly in remote caves and huts. As the early fanaticism of Maoism had worn off, the bureaucracy had also become more friendly to religion. Temples were being rebuilt, monastic orders reestablished, and the "no-mind" meditation practice common to both Buddhists and Taoists reinvigorated.

Porter did not encounter poets or recluse scholars, but his findings do suggest that the place of the religious hermit in Chinese culture continues to be deeply ingrained. It is from those hermits, who, in some sense, hold the lamp of creativity in their lonely contemplations, from which a rich cultural and religious heritage that goes back several millennia may reemerge.

A similar process of reinvigoration seems to have occurred in the middle of the first millennium, when Buddhism was already well established in China but its fertile roots in solitude had been neglected. Around the year 520, an Indian prince known as Bodhidharma (470–532) brought a highly philosophical and intensely meditative form of Buddhism to China, which soon combined with congenial elements of Taoism to create a new strain known as *Ch'an* (*Zen*, in Japanese). Taoism, as we have heard, has similar characteristics; but Bodhidharma took religious practice in China to heights of spiritual exploration into the essence of things that were characteristic of the early epidemic of Indian eremitism.

The famous story of his meeting with the Buddhist emperor Wu illustrates what a shock and disappointment Bodhidharma's view of things must have been to the early Buddhists of China. The emperor spoke of his lavish temple building and many other good works, then asked the Indian hermit what merit he had earned. "No merit at all!" replied Bodhidharma.

Taken aback, Emperor Wu asked: "Then what is the sacred doctrine's first principle?" The sage replied with the answer that had already been implicit in Taoist teaching for more than a thousand years but needed to be reapplied to the Chinese understanding of the Buddha's central teaching. "It's just empty," he said. "Nothing is holy."

The Chinese character he used to refer to the mystery of "emptiness" was *ku*, which means absence or void. But as Peter Matthiessen aptly points out, it "also signifies the clear blue firmament, without north or south, future or past, without boundaries or dimension." It is like an empty mirror on which all things pass, leaving no trace, says Matthiessen, but the emptiness is also fullness, containing all forms and phenomena above and below Heaven: "In this universal or absolute reality, there is no holiness (nor any non-holiness), only the immediacy of sky *as-it-is* in this present moment."[7]

"In that case," the emperor then asked, "who are you to stand before us?" And the sage replied simply, "I don't know." It could have been, I suppose, that Bodhidharma was simply being dismissive of the emperor to illustrate his spiritual superiority. But these are essentially the same points that we hear across the history of solitude—from the likes of Yajnavalkya, who said that the divine nature is "not this, not that"; in the *Cloud* author's anti-concept to "unknowing"; and, of course, from the Buddha, whose wisdom Bodhidharma sought to "transmit" to his followers. It seems to appear most prominently when religious spirituality becomes distorted by words and ritual and may profit from a wake-up call pointing back to direct, personal experience in solitude. Bodhidharma's strong position seems to have had that effect in China, because he is widely regarded as the founder, or patriarch, of Ch'an Buddhism.

There are many other stories indicating that Bodhidharma was received in China as an enigmatic spiritual superman. When he arrived, it is said that he rode on a single reed to cross the Yangtze River. He learned Chinese and many scholars came to question him. But he soon realized that they were not capable of listening. When he met scholars and religious men, they merely babbled about books, he said. He wasn't interested in their wisdom.

So Bodhidharma retired to the mountains, specifically to Mount Sung, in Honan Province. The key thing which he felt the scholars lacked was correct practice, by which he meant a highly disciplined, yet mindless, form of meditation which he called *pei-kuan,* or "wall gazing." Partly by way of illustration, Bodhidharma is said to have sat for nine years meditating before a high cliff on the mountain, which is another reason why he is often called the "wall-gazer." It is also said that he cut out his eyelids, presumably to assure the wakefulness of his meditations, perhaps to demonstrate their intensity.

Despite his critique of books, he also brought along the *Lankavatara Sutra*. This Mahayana Buddhist text is replete with complicated esoteric concepts that must have given the scholars Bodhidharma criticizes much to ponder. But its central conceptions took hold with many followers—notably that the world is "mind-only" and that a state of "not craving" should be the object of true meditation and attentive living. When Bodhidharma transmitted this teaching by direct insight to two young monks, he acknowledged that study of scripture and practice of meditation may go together. Thereby, one may "come to have a deep faith in the True Nature which is common to all sentient beings." When one abides in pei-kuan with singleness of thought, said the sage, "he finds that there is neither self nor other, that the masses and the worthies are of one essence…He will not then be a slave to words, for he is in silent communion with the principle itself, free from conceptual discrimination, serene and not-acting."[8] In that state, Bodhidharma further explained, "there is neither yourself nor the other; secular and sacred are one and the same."

After the two monks received these and other words conducive to direct enlightenment, a similar process—known as the Transmission of the Lamp—continued in an unbroken chain beginning with the Buddha and stretching via spiritual masters mainly in China and Japan down to the present day. This transmission must have influenced Wang Wei through his Buddhist teachers, and, more profoundly a generation later, another scholar poet—Han Shan, "Cold Mountain."

Though not quite a wall-gazer, Han combined Ch'an influences stemming from Bodhidharma with the melancholy simplicity of life, the self-renunciation, and the poetry of the recluse scholar. Cold Mountain, from which Han Shan gets his poetic name, is located in the Tiantai prefecture of Zhejiang province. There is a mountain there named Tiantai, which Han Shan refers to, but according to local tradition Cold Mountain is actually more of a canyon several miles from the mountain itself. Its two steep granite walls form a V-shaped valley reminiscent of The Fountain of Vaucluse, including a spring-fed stream and a dramatic cave lit by a single opening to the sky several hundred feet above the cave's floor. Today it is home to a remote grouping of Buddhist temples and a monastery tended mainly by nuns.

Han Shan, so the nuns told me on a visit there in the fall of 2002, lived in one of the caves in the rocky cliffs, on which he brushed many of his poems, about three hundred of which are now extant. In one poem he implies that he brought his wife and son with him into retirement, in another that he and other scholars in nearby hermitages lived lives of poverty, out of work, and in extremes of cold and hunger. Scribbling poems, he says, was their only pleasure, but apparently that, too, was not rewarding. "Who will read the work of us nobodys?" he laments, adding that even if they wrote their verses on gruel cakes, homeless dogs wouldn't bother to nibble at them. Of course, his sense of humor and humility belies any sense of sadness. And elsewhere he tells us that he loves the stillness and the "joy of solitude" at Cold Mountain, where he remains a "man beyond."[9]

Han's poetry also has some of Wang's appreciation of nature in it, along with honest moral advice in a Horatian vein, and always a love for the freedom of retirement—which makes up for a lot. He lives as an idle man, he says in another poem, wandering in the mountains amid a thousand clouds and ten thousand streams, sleeping at night by a cliff. As the seasons pass, he is at peace with his unburdened self: "happy clinging to nothing/still like a river in fall."[10]

Han always implies that he and his fellows are in the right place, wrapped, as he says in several poems, in white clouds. Many of his poems are enticements to his secluded spot, far from the "dust" of city life. "If you're looking for a place to rest," he says, "Cold Mountain is good for a long stay." There you would find a white-haired man mumbling over Taoist texts. After ten years, he has forgotten the way home. Yet somehow we know he is home and that he has found the Way.[11]

The poet-recluse wants to entice the reader to the "everyday mind" of Cold Mountain, where one's existence is "free and clear of clamor." But he also wants to make it clear that Cold Mountain is remote from the world. The path there is winding and difficult, along a "road that never ends." And should you arrive, he warns that you may find him to be a screwball, which is why he is recognized in Japanese tradition as something of a laughing Ch'an master in hobo disguise:

> When people see Han Shan
> they think he's nuts

nothing to look at
just a buffoon in rags.
They don't get me
I speak another language.
But I invite them anyway—
Try Cold Mountain sometime![12]

ZEN SOLOISTS

By Petrarch's day in the fourteenth century, the recluse scholar tradition in China seems to have lost some of its original creative energy. But that of Ch'an masters following Bodhidharma continued. For example, using his pen name Red Pine, Bill Porter has translated the poems and talks of a master called Stonehouse, who retired in 1312, at age forty, to a hut he built on Hsiamu mountain near Hangzhou in the same province where Han Shan lived several hundred years earlier.

Stonehouse lived there for twenty years, writing, meditating, and just living. With characteristic humility, he writes that he was a Ch'an monk who didn't know Ch'an. So he went to live out his remaining years in the woods, wearing a patched robe and a belt of braided bamboo. There, he says, mountain shades and the light from streams explain to him Bodhidharma's meaning, as "flower smiles and bird songs reveal the hidden key."[13]

Bodhidharma's transmissions also had a strong influence on Buddhism in Japan, where they nourished the healthy Zen line of poetry that mirrors the subtle moods of Wang Wei. In 1223, the Buddhist monk Dogen Zenji traveled to China, where he studied for a decade and is said to have achieved enlightenment while studying under several masters, particularly in Zhejiang Province. Master Dogen returned to Japan bringing what became the Soto School of Zen, which features *chi-kuan* meditation that aims at freeing the mind, but with an important caveat.

In general, Zen can be described as a means for practicing *zazen*, or "sitting in absorption" so as to eschew any thought-form. Dogen emphasizes, however, that zazen should be construed not as meditation in the discursive philosophical sense nor as contemplation intended to empty consciousness completely (which he thought to be impossible). Instead, he advises to "think not thinking"—a "nonconcept" to which we will return in a discussion of the psychology of solitude below.

Of course, one wouldn't want to try to "understand" zazen, but rather practice it. That effort can be enhanced in a mental environment of tranquillity, the need for which, after ten years amid the political intrigues of the imperial city of Kyoto, prompted Dogen to escape along with a few followers to a hermitage in a remote, mountainous region today known as Fukui province. It was there that Dogen composed this thought in mountain solitude—"I won't even stop at the brook in the valley," he wrote, "for fear my shadow will flow back into the world."[14]

Dogen liked to say that personal enlightenment (of the selfless self) can occur in the same way as one can see the universe in a dewdrop on a moonlit night. This tradition of subtle spiritual-poetic eremitism may have waned in China, but in the middle of the seventeenth century one of Japan's greatest haiku poets, Matsuo Basho (1644-94), was clearly a Friend of Solitude along the lines of Han Shan.

Basho's father died when he was only nine years old and in the service of a wealthy family, where he was the close friend and study-mate of their son. For a period of fifteen years after his friend died, Basho was depressed; but he continued studying in Kyoto under the greatest poets of the day and became well known throughout Japan for his spare, elegant writings. When Basho was thirty-six, one of his admirers built a hut for him in a secluded spot near the river Sumida. There he spent his time meditating and studying periodically under the guidance of a local Zen priest. But when his house burned to the ground two years later and his mother died soon thereafter, Basho became something of a vagabond poet, writing haiku verse interspersed in travel diaries published under titles such as *The Records of a Travel-Worn Satchel* and *The Narrow Road to the Deep North*. Basho's writings include "everything under the sun." They can be read as the record of a man aiming, in the style of a sort of peripatetic zazen, to free himself from the self.

It is not known whether Basho actually achieved enlightenment in the Buddhist sense. Like Han Shan, he admitted that he always maintained "one foot in both worlds," the everyday and the spiritual. But it stands to reason that he did achieve enlightenment, because according to Dogen and many other Buddhists, seen deeply, the two worlds are the same.

What is perhaps his most famous haiku captures the spirit of his life and tells why he was a Friend of Solitude. The poem was published in a 1686 anthology titled *Frog Contests*:

> Splash—
> A frog leaps
> Into an ancient pond—
> Deep resonance.[15]

"It is only he who has dug deep into the mystery of the universe," commented one of Basho's disciples, "who can chose a phrase like this."

Modern Recluses

PETRARCH MIGHT HAVE LIKED THE DEVELOPMENTS in the history of solitude in modern times, but only in part. He would probably have been happy to find that nearly all the truly interesting Friends of Solitude after his day turned out to be secular soloists, mainly poets and philosophers whose work and lives benefited greatly from the time they spent alone. Like Thoreau at Walden Pond, to name just one of many, they wrote extensively about their experiences and much to advocate the fruits of solitude to others.

Nevertheless, Petrarch would likely have found two problems in recent happenings. First, after the rapturous solitudes of Saint John of the Cross, the religious eremitism that was so essential throughout the medieval period entered its own dark night in the West. With very few exceptions, it has not reemerged. The use of isolation in shamanism persisted on the outskirts of civilization. And solitude continued to play its time-honored role in the religious traditions of India and Tibet, in parts of Eastern Christendom, in some sects of Islam, hidden in the mountains of China, and in the religious and poetic life of Japan. But even in these cultures there were few significant new developments beyond those already discussed.

Second, the important role that solitude played in fostering the creativity and the well-being of the modern Friends has generally been ignored or presented in an unfavorable light, often as a mysterious biographical detail. For the most part, the positive role of solitude in the lives of the post-Petrarchan Friends has remained "in the closet." There are so many such modern recluses whose solitudes deserve to be brought into the open that it would require another volume to do so. To round out our brief history, I will be content here to mention a few of them, particularly those whose experiences are cited in my attempt at a philosophy and psychology of solitude below.

The first notable example is the French essayist Michel de Montaigne (1533–1592). He is not generally thought of as a hermit or recluse. But in fact, after a worldly life of government service, most notably as mayor of his home town of Bordeaux, Montaigne retired at the age of thirty-five to his nearby family estate. There he spent most of his time reading and writing his worldly, meditative *Essais* in a three-story tower up on a hill (in French, *montaigne*) in a corner of his estate. In one essay, he tells us that he retired to the tower to spend his remaining years contemplating life:

> There is my throne. I try to make my authority over it absolute, and to withdraw this one corner from all society, conjugal, filial, and civil...Sorry the man, to my mind, who has not in his own home a place to be all by himself, to pay his court privately to himself, to hide![1]

In another essay, "On Solitude," Montaigne praises and defends the value of his retirement, saying: "My opinion is that we must lend ourselves to others and give ourselves only to ourselves. If my will happened to be prone to mortgage and attach itself, I would not last: I am too tender, both by nature and by practice—*fleeing affairs, and born in idle ease.*"[2] It is clear that Montaigne's seclusion fueled his voluminous literary output, and probably its leisurely common sense philosophy.

Just a few years later, René Descartes (1569–1650) made a similar exit from French society, in his case by going to live alone in a crowded city, Amsterdam, where, he says he was "able to live as solitary and withdrawn as I would in the most remote of deserts."[3] He spent much of his time there sitting in front of his fireplace, with his mind detached from his senses, meditating on a new philosophy of certainty:

> Now therefore, that my mind is free of all cares, and I have obtained for myself assured leisure in peaceful solitude, I shall apply myself seriously and freely to the general destruction of all my former opinions.[4]

The result, recounted in his *Meditations*, was his famous starting point: *cogito ergo sum,* "I think therefore I exist." From there he finds his way to a proof of the existence of God; and from there, he says, "I seem to discover a path that will lead us from the contemplation of the true God, in whom all treasures of knowledge and wisdom are contained, to the knowledge of the other things in the universe." Descartes acknowledged that it may take some time before such solitary meditations provide certain answers on how best to live. In the meantime, he recommended that one should live by the laws of one's country, be firm and resolute in one's actions, and manage desires in the manner of "those philosophers who in former times were able to escape the sway of Fortune and, in spite of suffering and poverty, to rival their gods in happiness."[5]

After Descartes, French poets and letter writers of the seventeenth century—from Madame de Sévigné to Antoine-Girard de Saint-Amant—praised solitude as a respite from the trials and tribulations of society. Meanwhile, the voluminous insights of the French philosopher Blaise Pascal (1623–1662), as recorded in his *Pensées*, suggest that they were fashioned in solitude, where he penned this famous statement on the harmful penchant of mankind for diversions from serious contemplation on the realities of life:

> Sometimes, when I think about the diverse activities of men, the dangers and troubles which they face in court, or in war, giving rise to so many quarrels and passions, daring and often wicked enterprises and so on, I have often said that all of man's unhappiness derives from one thing, which is not knowing how to rest quietly in a room.[6]

In England, Robert Burton (1577–1640) toiled in the Bodleian Library at Oxford to produce *The Anatomy of Melancholy*, in which he analyzed the nature of melancholy and the tentative value and the dangers of "voluntary solitariness." And English poets including Abraham Cowley and Charles Cotton lived the life of solitude for some time and praised it in works such as "On Solitude" and "The Retirement."

Then in eighteenth century France, Jean-Jacques Rousseau (1712–1778) reveled in solitude as a respite from the authorities who outlawed his writings. Later in life, he lived with his mistress in a residence outside Paris, which he called "The Hermitage" and where he wrote his wonderful analysis of time alone in *Reveries of a Solitary Walker.* We may find solitude profitable, he says, partly because it gives us the freedom to think with the emotions, which can provide "reason of a different stamp." In modern terms, Rousseau was something of an outsider, forced into solitude by a "society of wicked men which is nourished only by betrayals and hatred." Nevertheless, he declares that he was frequently "the happiest of men" when alone. To find that happiness, he says, it is necessary only to "love pleasure" and to give oneself up to the delicious sensations of devoting oneself to idleness. "What do we enjoy in such a situation?" he asks. It is nothing external to ourselves. Rather:

> The sentiment of existence, stripped of another emotion, is in itself a precious sentiment of contentment and of peace which alone would suffice to make this existence dear and sweet to anyone able to spurn all the sensual and earthly impressions which incessantly come to distract us from it and to trouble its sweetness here-below.[7]

The English poet William Wordsworth (1750–1850) was likewise a lover of what he called the "self-sufficing power of solitude." He lived much of his life in retirement at Grasmere in the Lake District, where he composed a large portion of his poetry. There, in the *Prelude*, he wrote of "a quiet independence of thought" in time spent alone, particularly in nature, deep in the "bosom of the wilderness"—

> When from our better selves we have too long
> Been parted by the hurrying world, and droop,
> Sick of its business, of its pleasures tired,
> How gracious, how benign, is Solitude…[8]

In nineteenth-century America, Ralph Waldo Emerson (1803–1882) wrote much for and against the life of solitude and loved to write and contemplate in the solitude of his study. "I shun father and mother and wife and brother when my genius calls me," he wrote in his essay "Self Reliance." "I would write on the lintels of the doorpost, *Whim*," he said. "I hope it is better than whim at last, but we cannot spend the whole day in explanation." Emerson also spoke highly of time spent alone outside in nature: "To go into solitude, a man needs to retire as much from his chamber as from society."

Emerson's "student" in Concord, Massachusetts, Henry David Thoreau (1817–1872), took the latter recommendation very much to heart. He was the first American recluse (aside from the indigenous Indians) to draw his main energy from the American landscape and is by far the most famous of all secular Friends of Solitude in modern times. Whereas Emerson's solitudes were in his chamber, with occasional forays into nature, Thoreau rejected that convenient sense of balance. He sought a harder, more adventurous life. He wanted to live, not only in solitude, but in *wild* solitudes. "I laugh," he said, "when you tell me of the danger of impoverishing myself by isolation. It is here that the walrus and the seal, and the white bear, and the eider ducks and auks on which I fatten, most abound."[9]

Walden Pond has its analogue in Petrarch's Fontaine de Vaucluse—without, of course, the yearning for a Laura. In all likelihood, Petrarch would have frowned on Thoreau's apology for solitude in *Walden* for its lack of emphasis on Christianity. Nevertheless, it is the second *De Vita Solitaria*, replacing Christianity and classical heroes with a kind of nature mysticism and commonsense reflections on life. Thoreau spent only two experimental years at Walden, but all of his writings were the product of time alone. And intimations of the divine, though not emphasized, are always present there, as in this excerpt from Thoreau's *Journals*:

> To be calm, to be serene! There is the calmness of the lake when there is not a breath of wind; there is the calmness of a stagnant ditch. So it is with us. Sometimes we are clarified and calmed healthily, as we were never before in our lives, not by an opiate, but by some obedience to the all-just laws, so that we become like a still lake of purest crystal and without an effort our depths are revealed to ourselves. All the world goes by us and is reflected in our deeps. Such clarity! obtained by such pure means! by simple living, by honesty of purpose. We live and rejoice. I awoke into a music which no one about me heard. Whom shall I thank for it? The luxury of wisdom! the luxury of virtue! Are there any intemperate in these things? I feel my Maker blessing me.[10]

Emily Dickinson (1830–1876), "Queen Recluse of Amherst," was influenced to a degree by Thoreau, and also by Emerson (who, she said, speaks from "where dreams come from"). She had a well-marked copy of *Walden* in her library, along with a copy of Emerson's "Solitude and Society." She is almost invariably viewed by literary critics as a spinster who chose, as a result of unrequited love, to live her life ferreted away in her upstairs bedroom in her family home at Amherst, Massachusetts. But a closer, more sympathetic reading of many of her poems shows that she enjoyed, reveled in, and profited by her solitude there, as evidenced by her line—"There is another Loneliness"—and by the fact that all her poetry seems to have been written in that Loneliness. Even the poems that are typically interpreted as evidence of the pain of her isolation—e.g., "I felt a funeral in my brain…"—are better read in a positive light as expressions of her secular "dark night" experiences.

It is not generally thought that the gregarious and exuberant Walt Whitman (1819–1892) was in any way a recluse, but he spent some of the happiest days of his life in later years living alone on a farm near Camden, New Jersey. There he produced *Specimen Days*: "Everyday, seclusion," he wrote, "everyday at least two or three hours of freedom, bathing, no talk, no bonds, no dress, no books, no manners."[11] The opening lines of Whitman's "Song of Myself" convey an impression of what he was feeling in that freedom:

> I loafe and invite my soul,
> I lean and loafe at my ease…observing a spear of summer grass.

Back in Europe, two major philosophers of the nineteenth century were stalwart Friends of Solitude—Søren Kierkegaard (1813–1855) and, of course, Nietzsche. Both fell in love with thought at an early age; both lived lives as isolated bachelors; and both were extremely productive and iconoclastic in their solitudes. Kierkegaard was a protestant Protestant, you might say, chiding his readers to a truer Christianity that does not hide itself in ritual but thinks its way to a higher honesty with God and life. His most original contributions to the literature of solitude appear in *Either/Or*, which he published pseudonymously under the name "Victor Eremita," and in *Fear and Trembling*, authored by "Johannes de Silentio."

In one sense, both works represent a critique of the hermit's withdrawal. At the same time, they applaud a renunciation of the world that is so complete that it also becomes an acceptance of the holiness of everything and brings one about-face back into a joyful and profound reacceptance of ordinary life in the world. The miraculous person who could live such a life he named "The Knight of Faith."

There are several European literary figures (poets and novelists) who were also Friends of Solitude. Gustave Flaubert (1821–1880), author of the worldly *Madame Bovery*, might at first thought appear to be the opposite of a hermit. But he lived the life of an anti-bourgeois bachelor and said that he often wished he were a monk, or a renegade, or an Indian brahmin. This would explain his strong interest in the life of Saint Anthony. In *The Temptation of Saint Anthony*, Flaubert portrays a sort of night-in-the-life of the saint in which he battles with demons of lust and glory and ponders the vast array of philosophies and religious sects that might have been at play in the volksgeist of fourth-century Egypt, including meditative dialogues with figures ranging from Apollonius of Tyana to the Buddha.

It is often thought that Flaubert wrote the book as a parody of Christian hermits and it can certainly be read that way, but a closer reading shows that he wanted to explore all the possible pathways in consciousness of Anthony's adventurous life of solitude. That interpretation is made clear by the fact that he has the saint end his all-night romp in the world of mysticism by achieving a kind of enlightenment. "O happiness! Happiness!" Flaubert's Anthony exclaims. "I have seen the birth of life, I have seen the beginning of movement. The blood in my veins is beating so hard that it will burst them." As the day dawns, the face of Jesus radiates in the desert sun and Anthony returns to his prayers.[12]

Paul Valéry (1871–1945), perhaps the greatest French poet of the twentieth century, was likewise a man of inner exploration. From his earliest years he began to make an island of his mind. "I increasingly kept a secret garden for myself," he writes in his journals (*Cahiers*), "where I cultivated the images that seemed entirely my own, could only belong to me."[13]

Throughout his life, Valéry was attracted both to society and a secret life of solitude. He married, maintained relations with literary figures in France and England, and worked as a journalist and administrator. But he continued his abstract, quasi-scientific adventures in lonely consciousness each morning, writing his poetry and in his journal over a period of half a century. That side of him is best typified in his writings about M. Edmond Teste, a character he conceived at a moment of profound change during his mid-twenties to facilitate his deepest explorations in aloneness: "I was strong in my infinite desire for clarity, in my contempt for beliefs and idols, my disgust for all that was easy, and my awareness of my limitations."[14]

Valéry says that Teste resembles him "as closely as a child." He calls Teste a "monster" who couldn't exist, an "experimental man," but he is also an "inner apostle of consciousness—to which faith he eternally exhorts himself."[15] Accordingly, Valéry speculates that Teste achieved a kind of modernist enlightenment in his solitude: "I am at home in MYSELF, I speak my own language, I hate extraordinary things," says Teste. "Only weak minds need them. Believe me literally: genius is *easy*, *divinity* is *easy*...I mean simply...that I know how it is to be conceived. It is easy."[16]

There must be something about a mind brought up in French culture that is attracted to abstract musings that are best fostered in solitude. The novelist Marcel Proust (1871–1927) spent much of his early life writing literary criticism and collecting material for a novel that never quite materialized. Things changed after both of his parents died and he retreated for good at age thirty-six to his famous cork-lined room in his Parisian apartment, a hermitage of sorts, so insulated to keep out all noise that would distract his meditations and his writing. It was there that he was able to get down to the business of recapturing past consciousness through a vast, almost symphonic, flow of words in his series of related novels, which he titled collectively *In Search of Lost Time*. Proust was as much an eremitic philosopher of time and consciousness as he was a novelist. In that effort he was, in a way, the opposite of a religious hermit in the desert purifying his soul. His only rule, he wrote to his friend Louis de Robert, was "to yield to one's demon, to one's thought, to write on everything to the point of exhaustion."[17]

In Europe at about the same time, the German writer Rainer Maria Rilke (1857–1926) lived the productive life of a lonely wandering poet. This can be heard in many of his poems that were nourished by his solitude: "I love the dark hours of my being/in which my senses drop into the deep" and "I am too alone in the world, and not alone enough/to make every minute holy."[18] His *Letters to a Young Poet* can be read as a paean to loneliness remade as a deep, positive-minded solitude. "What is necessary, after all, is only this," he writes to the poet, "solitude, vast inner solitude. To walk inside oneself and meet no one for hours—that is what you must be able to attain."[19]

In America during the twentieth century, there were many writers who were also what I would term inner apostles of consciousness. As I mentioned earlier, Wallace Stevens (1878–1955) worked as an insurance lawyer in Hartford, Connecticut, but also lived a life of inner solitude, which we find expressed in poems such as "Hermitage at the Center" and "A Quiet Normal Life." The English philosopher-novelist John Cowper Powys (1872–1963), accompanied by his tolerant lady friend, spent most of the Great Depression living in retirement in rural Dutchess County about a hundred miles north of New York City. There he wrote the only secular apology for solitude published in the twentieth century, *A Philosophy of Solitude*, which expounds both the value of solitude and that of a later-day stoic philosophy of life he called "elementalism."

The American poet Robinson Jeffers (1887–1962) lived and worked most of his mature life with his wife and family in a secluded home he built himself, Tor House, on the California beach at Big Sur, where he wrote poems including "Thebaid," "Oh, Lovely Rock," and "Rock and Hawk." Like that of so many other hermit-poets, Jeffers work has mystical overtones, but his are all the more striking—and easy to miss—because they are grounded in the most stoic, hard-boiled, anti-romantic view of the world that one can imagine. Overemphasis on the petty desires, aspirations, and violence of man, he maintained, is not sane. For sanity, he says, turn away from man to the enormous eternity of rock and to life attuned to that reality, as typified, for example, by a hawk.

Finally, the most famous of all Friends of Solitude in the twentieth century was not a secular littérateur or philosopher, but rather the untimely American monk Thomas Merton (1915–1968). Throughout his life, Merton was touched like the others with a strong desire to dig into the spiritual essence of things and to answer the unanswered questions of life. But after youthful explorations, notably with existentialism and Hindu philosophy, he soon came to the conclusion that the only way to discover real answers is through the help and love of a higher power—namely, Christ.

In his mid-twenties, Merton became a Roman Catholic and joined the Trappist order at Gethsemani Abbey in Kentucky. There he spent a good deal of his time pondering the nature of solitude and the way to salvation. He also spent time, through extensive study and contemplation of the heritage of Christian eremitism, justifying to his superiors the value of allowing him to live as a hermit, a wish that was eventually granted. "I must go into solitude to immobilize my life," he argued, "to reduce all things to a frozen concentration upon inner experience."[20]

Echoing the wisdom of the Desert Fathers, Merton seems to have believed that every effort must be made to preserve the essence of correct Christian thought in solitude—that is, prayer and devotion to God through the Christ. At the same time, he believed that ultimately there is no "correct" or definable Christian way of thinking apart from its source. The way to that source is through direct, loving experience of the living Christ, which experience can best (although perhaps not only) be obtained by profound, open, humble, completely empty contemplation alone.

Merton wrote a great deal about solitude, always from a Christian perspective; and he generally presents unbelieving secular soloists as pathetic, pantheistic half-mystics, rather like baseball teams who come out second in the World Series. Nevertheless, he continued to write and speak in a way that was informed by other religious traditions from Taoist to Islamic, as well as existential philosophy, which openness is one reason for his modern popularity.

Merton's views are expressed in an outpouring of writings, including *Thoughts in Solitude*, *Contemplative Prayer*, and "Notes for a Philosophy of Solitude." I will turn to those for further evidence in our investigations into the philosophy and psychology of solitude. But, like the views and experiences of all Friends of Solitude, no brief history of solitude can ever do them full justice. We must recognize, moreover, that the longest history of solitude could never do it justice. For every secret revealed, there are many more hidden in private experience.

ON CLOISTERPHOBIA

It is an awful satire, and an epigram on the materialism of our modern age, that nowadays the only use that can be made of solitude is imposing it as a penalty, as jail.

—Søren Kierkegaard, *Journals*, 1847

The Hermit Bashers

PETRARCH'S PRAISE OF LADY SOLITUDE at the Fountain of Vaucluse must stand out in history as one of the great examples of the law of unintended consequences. After he so eloquently defined her charms and so lovingly revealed her hidden virtues and snares, hardly anyone paid attention for more than six hundred years. Even if we take him at his word that *The Life of Solitude* is only intended to persuade the few, it was clearly a flop. Not one of the post-Petrarchan Friends I've mentioned so far refers to it even in passing. The literature of solitude continued in obscurity, but the modern Friends seem to have discovered the creative joys of time alone through their own experience.

In fact, *The Life* marks the beginning of a long period of "cloisterphobia" in the West that has persisted to the present day. In the twenty-first century, there are pockets of interest in various forms of mind-cleansing meditation and in tranquil walks in nature, while Christian and Buddhist monasteries are becoming more prominent on the fringes of Western culture. But generally solitude is feared and its value long since forgotten. As Kierkegaard lamented in the early nineteenth century, the only use that can now be made of solitude is "imposing it as a penalty, as jail." What a difference there is, he adds, "between those times when, no matter how secular materialism always was, man believed in the solitude of the convent, when, in other words, solitude was revered as the highest, as the destiny of Eternity—and the present when it is detested as a curse and is used only for the punishment of criminals. Alas, what a change."[1]

The greatest irony is that many of the key arguments that Petrarch advances in favor of solitude—his appeals to forgotten wisdom of the ancient Greeks and Romans; his advocacy of the secular; and his position that each man should choose the life most suited to himself—were the same points cited in a general rejection of the cloister as a vestige of medieval decadence. They helped to spur the rise of humanism in the Renaissance and initiated the long march in the West toward modernism, free-thinking philosophy, science, the downfall of religion, world exploration, and great material wealth. In that cultural milieu, the religious solitudes of the cloister had no place and the classical secular approach to solitude that Petrarch wanted to reestablish dropped out of the picture almost entirely.

Since *The Life* was not widely read, it seems unlikely that the work played any role in these developments. Nevertheless, Jacob Zeitlin, its American translator, believed otherwise. "In no moral treatise before this," he maintains, "do we find the writer's own experience and character made the ground of a plea for the human personality. It is a step in the liberation of the modern man from the bondage of an absolute moral code." In *The Life*, Zeitlin argues further, Petrarch comes closer than any of his contemporaries "to announcing the philosophical terms and principles which have governed the expansion of the human intelligence in Europe since his day."[2]

Petrarch is often referred to as the first Renaissance man, and it is more likely that his other works on classical heroes, and particularly the sonnets to Laura, played a stronger role in the onset of modernization in Europe. Regardless of the source, it is clear that the spirit of independent-mindedness that Petrarch and many others espoused also helped to spur a kind of modernization of religion—in other words, Protestantism. That, in turn, added more fuel to the fire of cloisterphobia, particularly in Western Europe.

In concept, one would think that Protestants would welcome solitude. Rather than depending on a priest to read and interpret the Bible and to dispense the benefices of the church, the Protestant Christian, beginning with Martin Luther, became what might be called a "do-it-yourself" clergyman responsible for the welfare of his own soul. He could read modern language translations of the Bible; and it was his responsibility to live in a manner at least as holy as monks dwelling sheepishly in their monasteries. It would seem appropriate, therefore, that the proper Protestant would also practice the solitude of Christ and the Desert Fathers at home. But that did not happen.

Although Luther himself spent his early religious life as a monk, he soon rejected the solitude of the cloister. "It is a perilous thing for a man to be alone," he wrote:

> Wherefore they that ordained that accursed, monkish, and solitary life gave occasion to many thousands to despair. If a monk should separate himself from the company of others for a day or two to be occupied in prayer (as we read of Christ that He sometimes went aside alone into the mountains and by night continued in prayer), there was no danger therein. But when they constrained men continually to live a solitary life, it was a device of the devil himself: for when a man is tempted and alone he is not able to raise himself up, no, not in the least temptation that can be.[3]

Luther does acknowledge that a temporary retirement might do no harm, but his critique of the solitude of the hermitage and the monastery was the viewpoint that took hold in Europe. Luther posted his famous ninety-five theses against the Catholic establishment in 1517; only two decades later (1536–9) the monasteries of England were dissolved by King Henry VIII and many monasteries and hermitages across Europe soon met the same fate. Silence continued to play a part in some Protestant sects, notably Quaker meetings, which begin in silence and remain so until any one of the attendees is moved to speak. But the medieval notion that the solitude of the hermit might be a nurturing source of deep religiosity or profound wisdom fell by the wayside in Protestantism and generally in Catholicism.

In the early twentieth century, the Englishman Herbert B. Workman, a Methodist minister, expressed the prevailing viewpoint in his history of Christian solitude, *The Evolution of the Monastic Ideal.* It is only grudgingly, with many disclaimers and professions of objectivity, that Workman can draw any positive lessons at all from Christianity's thousand-year love affair with solitude. The monks' aim of self-sacrifice and self-surrender, he concedes, was admirable; but on every page of his Protestant history of solitude one hears the patronizing voice of a latter-day cleric patiently examining the errant ways of the childhood of Christianity. "We stand on another shore," says Workman, "and watch the 'tired waves' of a different ocean gain here and there a 'painful inch.'"[4] The minister concludes that both monasticism and its individualistic brother eremitism are failed experiments which, from the point of view of right-minded Christian practice, should never have been conducted.

Cloisterphobia is so strong in the West that one senses it must derive from something more fundamental than Protestant critiques. For one thing, the fact that the monasteries were great hoarders of land and became centers for economic production as well as education was a key factor precipitating their dissolution and a secular "repatriation" of their wealth. But the historian Max Weber proposed another theory in *The Protestant Ethic and the Spirit of Capitalism*, which represents a still greater irony about the emergence of modern economic life. Essentially, Weber maintains that while Protestants denigrated the religious solitude of the cloister they adopted monkish discipline and turned it to secular purposes in what he calls "worldly asceticism."[5]

Rather than believing that religious contemplation might help to foster spiritual life, the Protestant, says Weber, places greater emphasis on a belief that selfless, worldly industry is the way to achieve God's grace. In its earliest formulations, this Protestant ethic demanded that one devote one's spiritual life entirely to Jesus; but at the same time, as symbolized by Luther's marriage, one should live responsibly in the world, accepting fate as a kind of worldly penance. Later Protestants took a somewhat different tack, according to Weber, particularly the Puritans of England and Holland, who had the strongest influence on the subsequent development of Northern European and American capitalism. They maintained not only that society should be tolerated, but that one should work diligently and selflessly in the world to accumulate goodness. Depending on one's calling, that ethic involved gathering of wealth on behalf of family, neighbors, God's creatures, whomever; but in all cases, Weber maintains, the accumulation was a sign of spiritual attainment.

In line with the Old Testament's emphasis on good works, the Protestant continued to view the selfish *pursuit* of wealth as immoral. But he found ways to view the *attainment* of wealth, provided it was the fruit of labor in a worldly calling, as a sign of God's blessing. Even more important, says Weber, the religious valuation of restless, continuous, systematic work became "the surest and most evident proof of rebirth and genuine faith." As such, he adds, work for profit "must have been the most powerful conceivable lever for the expansion of that attitude toward life which we have here called the spirit of capitalism."[6]

Taking this line of thinking to its logical conclusion, it is reasonable to surmise that the ascetic discipline of the monk and the hermit—the self-denial, the submission to authority, the dedicated industriousness for a greater good—was transformed into the worldly asceticism that is now the foundation of that most successful of modern institutions: the corporation. We might better term it the "capitalist monastery."

If you find this a frivolous equation, think of the systematic life in any modern day office. And listen to Thomas Merton's viewpoint, writing from that anomaly of American culture, a religious cloister:

> Compare our monastery and the General Electric plant in Louisville. Which one is the more serious and more "religious" institution? One might be tempted to say "the monastery," out of sheer habit. But, in fact, the religious seriousness of the monastery is like sandlot baseball compared with the big-league seriousness of General Electric. It may in fact occur to many, including the monks, to doubt the monastery and what it represents. Who doubts GE?[7]

"Today," says Weber, "the spirit of religious asceticism—whether finally, who knows?—has escaped from the cage. But victorious capitalism, since it rests on mechanical foundations, needs its support no longer." What is still more surprising to me is that the subtler, more worldly virtues of that other life of solitude—the contemplative, philosophical life of retired leisure in the style of Petrarch—has also wilted inside Weber's cage.

NO MANNER OF PURPOSE

As one might expect, cloisterphobia is not exclusively a modern phenomenon. Long before the Renaissance, Aristotle's dictum that man is by nature a "political animal" was widely quoted in debates about the virtues of social over solitary life. Aristotle goes on to say that "anyone who by his nature and not simply by ill luck has no state is either too bad or too good, either subhuman or superhuman—he is like the war-mad man condemned in Homer's words as having no family, no home. He is a 'non-cooperator' like an isolated piece in a game of draughts."[8] The Greek myth of Narcissus conveys a similar moral warning, as does Lucian's report on the self-immolation of Peregrinus.

Later, when Christian hermits showed their displeasure with current society by fleeing in droves to live spiritual lives in deserts and on desolate islands, the tenor of their critics' reactions turned from bemusement to disgust. The fifth-century Latin poet Rutilius Namatianus was astonished to find that so many of his youthful countrymen would choose intentionally to live an apparently painful, unhealthy, and stupid life of ascetic isolation:

> ...they dub themselves
> 'Monks,' with a Grecian name, because they wish
> To dwell alone, observed by none. They dread
> The gifts of Fortune, while her ills they fear.
> Who, to shirk pain, would choose a life of pain?
> What madness of a brain diseased so fond,
> As, fearing evil, to refuse all good?[9]

During the Middle Ages, when Christianity gained the field of Western culture, we hear few such critiques, but things changed after the worldly spirit of the Renaissance took hold. In the eighteenth century, for instance, the philosopher David Hume, in his *Treatise of Human Nature* (1739), looked with horror and amazement on the uselessness, not only of religious solitude but, apparently, of all solitude:

> Celibacy, fasting, penance, mortification, self-denial, humility, silence, solitude, and the whole train of monkish virtues; for what reason are they everywhere rejected by men of sense, but because they serve to no manner of purpose; neither advance a man's fortune in the world, nor render him a more valuable member of society, neither qualify him for the entertainment of company, nor increase his power of self-enjoyment? We observe,

> on the contrary, that they cross all these desirable ends; stupefy the understanding and harden the heart, obscure the fancy and sour the temper.[10]

Surveying the rise of Christianity from his vantage point in nineteenth-century England, Edward Gibbon took even stronger offense than did Rutilius at the Christian hermits' renunciation of the world:

> There is perhaps no phase in the moral history of mankind of a deeper and more painful interest than this ascetic epidemic. A hideous distorted and emaciated maniac without knowledge, without patriotism, without natural affection, spending his life in a long routine of useless and atrocious self-torture, and quailing before the ghastly phantoms of his delirious brain, had become the ideal of the nations which had known the writings of Plato and Cicero and the lives of Socrates and Cato.[11]

To Gibbon, the whiny, world-renouncing attitude of the hermit and the monk was one of the sickly roots that caused the fall of the Roman Empire. Somewhat surprisingly, Nietzsche is the most vehement modern critic of monkish asceticism, exceeding even Gibbon in heated rhetoric. He viewed religious asceticism and solitude as a wrong-headed yearning for an illusory spiritual absolute deriving from thoughtless, degenerate passion that is capable of destroying civilization. Is there anything more disgusting than the desert hermits of Egypt? he asked.

> Perhaps a whole Hell of criminals could not produce an effect so oppressive, poisonous to air and land, uncanny and protracted as is this noble little community of unruly, fantastic, half-crazy people of genius who cannot control themselves and can experience pleasure in themselves only when they have lost themselves.[12]

In the last century, Sir J.G. Frazer continued the Gibbonian-Nietzschean tradition by bemoaning the onslaught around the time of Christ of "Oriental religions which inculcated the communion of the soul with God and its eternal salvation as the only objects worth living for." Frazer denounced their "selfish and immoral doctrine," which, he believed, bred contempt for the present life and withdrew the devotee more and more from public service.

> The saint and the recluse, disdainful of earth and rapt in ecstatic contemplation of heaven, became in popular opinion the highest ideal of humanity, displacing the old ideal of the patriot and hero who, forgetful of self, lives and is bred to die for the good of his country. The earthly city seemed poor and contemptible to men whose eyes beheld the City of God coming in the clouds of heaven.[13]

Frazer argued for "saner, manlier views of the world," such as those he found in pagan mythology, in classical civilization more broadly, and in Western civilization since the Renaissance—when "the tide of the Oriental invasion had turned at last."

Given the influence of humanism and Protestantism in the modern world, this vitriol is to be expected in the West. But I was particularly surprised to learn that many of the same arguments against religious solitude are also to be heard in the East—specifically, in India, that fount of Oriental religion which produced the world's most intense, longest-lasting eremitic tradition.

Indian religious literature, as we have heard, is replete with anecdotes of sensational eremitic mortifications of the sort that Gibbon, Nietzsche, and Frazer detested. Yet in spiritually inclined India it is not generally the ardor or unhealthiness of these exercises that appalls the critical observer. The chief complaint, rather, is lodged against the hermit's flight from social responsibilities. A story is told in the Mahabharata that when King Janaka cast off wealth, family, and his entire kingdom to take up the life of a religious mendicant, one of his wives admonished him roundly:

> Having been a large and sacred lake unto all creatures, having been a mighty tree worthy of adoration and granting its shelter unto all, alas, how can you wait upon and worship others? If even an elephant desists from all work, carnivorous creatures coming in packs and innumerable worms would eat it up...If you can act up to your resolution of abandoning everything then who am I to you, who are you to me, and what good is your grace to me? If you would be inclined to grace, rule this Earth![14]

Nonreligious Friends such as Horace or T'ao Ch'ien tend by nature to be less open to critiques that they are antiworldly ascetics. But they are often criticized as being irresponsible, uncompromising, stupid, or mad, particularly in those few societies where secular eremitism became an institution. The philosopher Han Fei Tzu critiqued the recluse scholars, arguing that such "men of wisdom" refuse to make the compromises necessary for effective statecraft. As a result, "armies grow weaker and the government cannot escape disorder." Though praised by the people and honored by the ruler, such idealism, he added, will "lead to the ruin of the state."[15]

When the ideal of secular retirement to the quiet country life of solitude came into vogue in England around the middle of the seventeenth century, it likewise provoked criticism. The diarist John Evelyn probably penned the strongest—and most whimsically imaginative—diatribe in this regard, indicting both Lady Solitude's secular and religious manifestations in one fell swoop. Mincing no words in his "Public Employment and an Active Life Prefer'd to Solitude," Evelyn charges that

> Solitude produces ignorance, renders us barbarous, feeds revenge, disposes to envy, creates Witches, dispeoples the World, renders it a desart, and would soon dissolve it.[16]

MISSING THE GOOD THINGS

Another common jab in the annals of cloisterphobic critiques is the obvious argument that it is silly to retreat to solitude because one will miss the security and all the good things offered by life with others in a community. The hermit, it is argued, will miss the education, the benefits of culture, and the benefits of a productive economy, which provides food, wine, transportation, comfortable lodging, entertainment, and health care. And isn't solitude simply boring? Why sit in the forest reading a book or looking at the flowers when you could be enjoying yourself in the city?

Such appeals to the hermit's comfort make their most frequent appearance in Chinese literature. For example, the poet of "Summons for a Gentleman Who Became a Recluse" in the *Songs of Ch'u* warns the gentleman hermit that living alone in the mountains—where bears, tigers, and leopards prowl—is not just lonely; it's dangerous. "Oh prince, return!" the poet pleads: "In the mountains you cannot stay long."[17]

Implicit in that plea is the related critique that he who lives alone foregoes human sympathy and the support that is provided by a close community—or, better, a friend. It is an age-old view that figures prominently in the Old Testament. "Two are better than one; because they have a good reward for their labor," says the writer of Ecclesiastes (4:9–10), adding, "Woe to him that is alone when he falleth; for he hath not another to help him."

"Without friends," writes Francis Bacon (in "Of Friendship"), "the world is but a wilderness." Lack of friendship may also dull the mind, he says:

> Whosoever hath his mind fraught with many thoughts, his wits and understanding do clarify and break up in communicating and discoursing with another; he tosseth his thoughts more easily; he marshalleth them more orderly; he seeth how they look when they are turned into words; finally he waxeth wiser than himself; and that more by an hour's discourse than by a day's meditation.

A lonely cogitator distracted by his own thoughts may also face unexpected dangers, as Herman Melville warns readers of *Moby Dick*. "For nowadays," says his narrator Ishmael, "the whale fishery furnishes an asylum for many romantic, melancholy and absent-minded young men, disgusted with the carking cares of earth, and seeking sentiment in tar and blubber." These young philosophers are so given to unseasonable meditativeness that when it is their turn to stand solitary watch on the masthead, the vast prospect of the oceanic vista causes them to enter a mystic swoon, rendering them unable to spot the whales they are supposed to be looking out for. That, warns Ishmael, is both a false spiritualism, and perilous:

> lulled into such an opium-like listlessness of vacant, unconscious reverie is this absent-minded youth by the blending cadence of waves with thoughts, that at last he loses his identity; takes the mystic ocean at his feet for the visible image of that deep, blue, bottomless soul, pervading mankind and nature…
>
> But while this sleep, this dream is on ye, move your foot or hand an inch; slip your hold at all; and your identity comes back

> in horror. Over Descartian vortices you hover. And perhaps, at mid-day, in the fairest weather, with one half-throttled shriek you drop through that transparent air into the summer sea, no more to rise for ever. Heed it well, ye Pantheists![18]

This, too, is not a modern warning. For according to Diogenes Laertius, it was said in ancient Greece that the philosopher Thales spent so much time staring up at the heavens while walking in rapt contemplation that he accidentally stumbled into a well and died. But even if distracted meditation does not end in death, some warn of another danger that the secular Friend of Solitude enjoying spiritual, philosophical, or aesthetical flights is just wasting his time with worldly pleasures. To Thomas Merton, for instance, such "spirituality" is disappointing and inauthentic. In his "Notes for a Philosophy of Solitude" Merton—echoing Augustinus' discussion with Francesco in Petrarch's *Secretum*—bemoans "that noble security, that intelligent depth, that artistic finesse which the more academic contemplative seeks in his sedate respectability."[19]

To Merton, the secular philosopher-hermit is not sufficiently open and honest to the painful realities of human existence to truly feel the need for The Savior Jesus. The intrepid philosopher may indeed be exploring the depths of his soul, but he is missing the most profound adventure—that is, climbing a real spiritual ladder to God. His solitude, says Merton, is essentially a masquerade.

> True solitude is found in humility, which is infinitely rich. False solitude is the refuge of pride, and it is infinitely poor. The poverty of false solitude comes from an illusion which pretends, by adorning itself in things it can never possess, to distinguish one individual self from the mass of other men. True solitude is selfless.[20]

Merton hoped to find true solitude in a Christian hermitage; but Saint Jerome cautioned that the life of solitude will almost inevitably run afoul without the discipline and support to be found in a religious community. One of the worst stumbling blocks for hermits is that they are likely to commit the sin of pride, thinking that they will be able to rise to the enlightened state of grace on the wings of their personal meditations. In such a self-deluded state, it is likely, so this reasoning goes, that the hermit will fall away from the true path into a life of worldly pleasures or free-thinking philosophy—in other words, heresy and vainglory.

Jerome himself spent several early years living in a Syrian cave, amid, as Petrarch put it, "that vast wilderness which provided a savage dwelling place for monks." There, as later depicted in countless paintings, he felt lonely and agitated. Jerome later admitted that "my mind still surged with evil thoughts," not to mention lascivious ones:

> O how often, when I was living in the desert, in that lonely waste, scorched by the burning sun, that affords to hermits their primitive dwelling place, how often did I fancy myself surrounded by the pleasures of Rome...though in my fear of Hell, I had condemned myself to this prison house, where my only companions were scorpions and wild beasts, I often found myself surrounded by bands of dancing girls.[21]

Beset by such potent distractions and because of a strong bout with the psychic malady *acedia* (the hermit's blues), the young Jerome could not keep himself from reading the classical books he carried with him into his hermitage. Jerome says he was eventually able to fight off these demons. But he wrote that he had seen many others who were unable to do so and whose life of solitude was a mere sham. "Their renunciation consisted in a change of clothes and a verbal profession," he wrote to his young acquaintance Rusticus, "while their real life and their former habits have remained unchanged." They were tended by servants in their hermitages and many increased their property as they continued to practice their crafts and trades. Jerome's advice to Rusticus adds another concern:

> Some too there are who from the dampness of their cells and from the severity of their fasts, from their weariness of solitude and from excessive study have a singing in their ears day and night and turn melancholy mad.[22]

THE HERMIT'S MADNESS

That unfortunate barb, that the hermit must be mad, or will soon become so, is another common symptom of cloisterphobia. Aristotle's statement that a hermit is either a beast or a god acknowledges the possibility that the soloist may actually be a hero. But in every era there is a lingering suspicion—more accurately, an assumption—that only mental instability could account for the hermit's strange rejection of society. Buddha was accused of being a "hole-in-corner man" whose mental abilities declined because of his prolonged isolation from society. And, as we have heard, it was said that Heraclitus retired to the Temple of Artemis only to play "knuckle bones" with the children there.

There are also many tales of eremitic insanity in modern novels. Take for instance, this account by the narrator of Conrad's *Heart of Darkness* of the European trader turned jungle hermit, Kurtz:

> Believe me or not, his intelligence was perfectly clear…But his soul was mad. Being alone in the wilderness, it had looked within itself, and, by heavens! I tell you, it had gone mad.[23]

To modern ears, Kurtz's madness sounds the perennial warning against the Greek admonition at Delphi—"Know thyself," the same forewarning that the seer Tiresias issued to the young Narcissus. Narcissus died in a forest pool, Kurtz in an African jungle. No eloquence could have been so withering to one's belief in mankind, reports Conrad's narrator, than the final burst of sincerity that shown upon Kurtz's face at the moment of his death: "I saw the inconceivable mystery of the soul that knew no restraint, no faith, and no fear, yet struggling blindly with itself."[24]

Melville's tale, "Bartleby the Scrivener," embodies a similar warning. As with Kurtz, the case of poor Bartleby implies that the emptiness and blind materialism of modern society may (perhaps inevitably) push a sensitive soul into an oblivion of desperation—one that is doomed to pitiful, if oddly heroic, failure in madness. Bartleby is a lowly clerk on Wall Street who one day decides that he would "prefer not to do anything at all." Carrying out his plan he conjures the pity of his employer and us readers.

Eventually he dies in prison having achieved nothing by his steadfast adventure in immobility and isolation. Although Melville, to his credit, does not specify the reasons for Bartleby's preferring not to, he does speculate that Bartleby could have been pushed into his apparent state of schizophrenia and inert despair by the mechanical, alienating jobs at which he toiled: He worked as a scrivener, a kind of human copy machine, and before that in the dead-letter office of the postal bureau.

George Eliot's *Silas Marner* tells another tale of a pitiable solitary. A sensitive young man, Silas was prone to epileptic seizures that were taken by townsfolk in his out-of-the-way English village as signs of spiritual, perhaps demonic, capacities. Just as he was about to be married, Silas was falsely accused, apparently by a rival suitor, of theft. His faith in both man and God deeply shaken, he moved to another village, where he lived in mind-deadening despair and devoted all his time to weaving cloth in his solitary hut. The poor weaver has no other joy in his life than compulsively fondling the glittering pot of gold that contains the earnings from his weaving. There is no offsetting value to his solitude.

Some modern psychologists are prepared to go much further in the association of solitude with madness. J. Moussaieff Masson, for one, posits that "all ascetics suffered massive traumas in their childhood in one of three ways: they were sexually seduced, or they were the object of overt or covert aggression, or they lost those closest to them early in their lives."[25] In fact, Masson is at least partly correct—for it is possible to identify some unfortunate experience in the life of nearly every Friend, such as a loss of parents or a dear friend, or a failed love affair, which episode may have been the psychic trauma that kicked them into seclusion. But Masson seems to maintain that all ascetics, thus all solitaries, continue their psychotic ways after retreating to solitude, where they are "pervaded with sadness; their rituals, their obsessive gestures of every kind, are an attempt to recapture the lost childhood they never had."[26]

In such a state, they may gain a feeling of godlike omnipotence and power, a sense of oneness with the world, or, among other things, an exquisite sense of "physical" pleasure by conjuring delectable images of eating, sexual encounter, or worldly glory, all lived out only in the imagination. And so, says Masson, the melancholy hermit creates happiness for himself as a form of self-deception, a shadow-play with no real people enacted for his own pleasure or one directed at a specific if long-departed audience. If that were not bad enough, Masson warns further that "the ascetic's belief in psychic immunity is purchased at a high price: irreversible psychosis, self-destruction, or unbearable loneliness."[27]

This psychological view of things may have come to Masson via the work of Sigmund Freud. In *Civilization and Its Discontents*, Freud acknowledges that we cannot dispense with palliative measures designed to deflect our attention from the painful reality of life. One of these, he admits, is the wise advice of Voltaire's Candide to cultivate one's garden, but should the garden become a cave, Freud is concerned. In search of happiness, he writes, "the hermit turns his back on the world and will have no truck with it." The hermit will often do more than that, as he tries to re-create the world by building up another world of fantasy "in which its most unbearable features are eliminated and replaced by others that are in conformity with one's own wishes." "But whoever, in desperate defiance, sets out upon this path to happiness" warns Freud, "will as a rule attain nothing. Reality is too strong for him. He becomes a madman, who for the most part finds no one to help him in carrying through the delusion."[28]

In a less harsh but similar vein, Robert Burton concludes his epic analysis of melancholia with the warning that those so afflicted are simply not suited to the life of solitude and should steer clear of it altogether:

> As thou tenderest thine own welfare in this and all other melancholy, thy good health of body and mind, observe this short precept, give not way to solitariness or idleness. 'Be not solitary, be not idle.'[29]

Reply to Cloisterphobes

It is easy, especially in modern times, to criticize solitude. Perhaps the hermit bashers' eloquent invective strikes a chord with us because it appeals to the persistent work ethic in modern civilization, particularly in American culture, which makes us feel instinctively that there is something sinful about leisure for its own sake. Sometimes I think that just as there was an ingrained reverence for the solitude of the cloister and the hermitage in the Middle Ages, now there is an underlying fear that should solitude again become popular all the achievements since the Renaissance will be lost and the world would again plunge into medieval darkness.

Just how deep-seated that fear is lodged in us can be heard in Hamlet's soliloquy: "To be or not to be; that is the question..." Confronted with "slings and arrows of outrageous fortune," Hamlet considers only two options: continue to suffer his fortune or end it in suicide, with the help of "a bare bodkin." He does not consider a third option: the time-honored alternative of retreat to a life of solitude. He does order his fiancée, Ophelia, to "get thee to a nunnery." But in Shakespeare's England, a few years after the dissolution of the monasteries, "nunnery" was another term for "brothel."

If a retreat to solitude is now seen as in any way unmanly or a sin, there must be some misunderstanding. Hamlet's choice to continue fighting amid calamity may be seen as a kind of heroic acting out of fate, but it ended only in further calamity and death. Moreover, there are many forms of solitude, spiritual as well as secular, which do not entail a permanent withdrawal from society or responsibilities. As Petrarch reminds us, even the heroic Romans revered occasional retreat to gentlemanly leisure. And if we read the hermit bashers more carefully, we find that many spoke highly of solitude on occasion.

Aristotle, as we have heard, reasoned that contemplation is the highest achievement of life in the polis. As for Hume, in the same long essay in which he debunks time alone he concedes that the pleasure of solitary reflection is "the origin of my philosophy." Even Gibbon conceded that one may find value in solitude. Conversation enriches the understanding," he wrote in his magnum opus, *The Decline and Fall of the Roman Empire*, "but solitude is the school of genius." Gibbon was referring to what he called Muhammad's "addiction to religious contemplation."[30] In his memoirs, Gibbon further acknowledged his own ability to enjoy solitude, saying: "I was never less alone than when by myself."[31]

And surprisingly, John Donne, whose off-handed maxim, it seems, will forever remind English speakers that "no man is an island," demonstrated through his own experience that solitude can have a profoundly positive and joyful effect on one's life. Following an extended sickness, Donne writes in his essay "Devotions upon Emergent Occasions" that his return to society from the solitude of his hospital bed was a transformative occasion. "I have had three Births," he boasts, "One, Naturall, when I came into the World; One, Supernatural, when I entered into the Ministry; and now a preter-naturall Birth, in returning to Life, from this Sicknes."[32] He implies that it was his return that brought joy, while his sickness in solitude may have been a hell—but maybe not. Without the time he spent suffering alone he would not have experienced his life-enhancing third birth.

Among the most striking things about the critiques of the hermit bashers, then, is that nearly all of them are issued from the viewpoint of society at large rather than personal experience. And most are critiques of particular forms of aloneness: notably intense, world-renouncing solitude; psychic isolation that is caused by madness; or secular retirement. That leaves the implication that *all* forms of time spent alone are therefore useless and absurd. But as our brief history shows, there may be value in what the hermit bashers left out that far outweighs the social and personal dangers of solitude.

Secular critics, for instance, tend to ignore the fact that great, albeit unpredictable, social value may result when men or women retire to rethink the bases of their troubled lives and civilizations. That is precisely what the historian Arnold Toynbee asserts in his theory of "withdrawal and return," which posits that a flight into solitude is the first movement of a process of discovery and social influence that has been the mainspring of change throughout history. According to Toynbee, a soon-to-be-world-historical figure withdraws into solitude at a certain troubled time in his life, and at a crucial turning point in the development, more commonly the disintegration, of his civilization. Alone, he rethinks the predicaments in which he finds himself. Then, in a mysterious action of the soul, he produces new seeds of thought that may be capable, at one extreme, of altering the growth pattern of the entire civilization or, at the other, of destroying genius in madness.

Of the latter extreme, perhaps Nietzsche, Van Gogh, and Diogenes the Cynic are typical cases. Countless others are not known, having been completely destroyed in their withdrawal. Of the former, Toynbee cites the lives of mystics, saints, and statesmen, including several soloists already discussed above: Moses, Jesus, the Buddha, and Muhammad. Each of these superhuman creators spent his "forty days in the desert," and each returned with sufficient "power of spirit" to found religions or otherwise transform or enrich society, often for the better.

Petrarch's withdrawal to Vaucluse is neglected in Toynbee's analysis, but among secular-minded lovers of solitude he mentions the Italian philosopher-statesman Machiavelli, who was imprisoned, then "exiled," to a perpetual rustication on his farm in the Florentine countryside following the French occupation beginning in 1494. There, he devoted his days to humdrum social and sporting activities. Each night, he exchanged his mud-caked country clothes for courtly dress and entered, through his studies, "into the ancient mansions of the men of ancient days" and feasted himself on what he termed "that food which alone is my true nourishment." One product of that retreat was his famous book *The Prince*, which embodies an "Exhortation to Liberate Italy from the Barbarians." As a practical effort to free Italy, the book was a failure. Nevertheless, says Toynbee, Machiavelli rose above his vexation of spirit and "succeeded in transmuting his practical energies into a series of mighty intellectual works—*The Prince, The Discourses on Livy, The Art of War* and *The History of Florence*—which have been the seeds of our modern Western political philosophy."[33]

Toynbee also notes that the withdrawal-and-return motif is to be found in mythology, notably in foundling myths such as that of Zeus, whose father, Chronos, cast him away in infancy out of concern that the child would grow up to supplant him, but whose mother, Rhea, bore him secretly in the cave of Ida. When Zeus grew to manhood, he overthrew his father to take his place as the supreme god in the Greek pantheon.

In his book *The Hero with a Thousand Faces*, Joseph Campbell finds a similar consistency across world mythology relating to rites of passage, what he calls the "monomyth" of *separation—initiation—return.* In that mythic structure, says Campbell "A hero ventures forth from the world of common day into a region of supernatural wonder: fabulous forces are there encountered and a decisive victory is won: the hero comes back from this mysterious adventure with the power to bestow boons to his fellow men."[34]

Campbell, too, cites the withdrawal and return of the Buddha and Moses, along with Prometheus' ascent to the heavens to steal fire from the gods, and Jason's journey through crashing rocks and a sea of marvels to obtain the Golden Fleece, with its power to wrest his rightful throne from usurpers. Among many other examples, he also points to the shaman's descent to the underworld and flight to the spirit world where he or she receives wisdom and supernatural powers. In all these myths, some form of separation from society is a starting point. "Willed introversion," Campbell explains, "is one of the classic implements of creative genius."[35]

In his *A Study of History*, Toynbee explains how the process may work:

> The withdrawal makes it possible for the personality to realize powers within himself which might have remained dormant if he had not been released for the time being from his social toils and trammels. Such a withdrawal may be a voluntary action on his part or it may be forced upon him by circumstances beyond his control; in either case the withdrawal is an opportunity, and perhaps a necessary condition, for the anchorite's transfiguration.[36]

Toynbee finds a concise rendering of the value of that transformative adventure in a statement by the English social scientist Walter Bagehot:

"All the great nations have been prepared in privacy and in secret. They have been composed far away from all distraction."[37] John Cowper Powys extends the scope of that tribute even further when he muses that "all the nobler instincts of our race are born in solitude and suckled by silence."[38]

The contemporary psychologist Anthony Storr takes a similar position in *Solitude: A Return to the Self*, which to date is undoubtedly the most insightful analysis of solitude by any psychologist, ancient or modern. Storr argues that the creative "fantasy life" of thoughts and ideas provoked by suffering and cultivated in solitude are "part of man's biological endowment." Man's extraordinary success as a species, says Storr, "springs from his discontent, which compels him to employ his imagination. The type of modern man who exhibits more discontent than any other, Western man, has been the most successful."

It is imagination in the broadest sense that is ultimately responsible for that success, says Storr. "The human mind seems to be so constructed that the discovery, or perception, of order or unity in the external world is mirrored, transformed, and experienced as if it were a discovery of a new order and balance in the inner world of the psyche."[39] The best place to foster that creative imagination, Storr concludes, is in solitude, free from the distractions of social life. His position is not very far from that expressed metaphorically by Chuang Tzu, who maintained: "Emptiness, stillness, limpidity, silence, inaction are the root of the ten thousand things."[40]

Reading Toynbee, one might think that the creative powers of solitude would apply only to geniuses on the order of Buddha or Muhammad and that a creative withdrawal that does not finally return to society to promote great historical change may not be worthwhile. But Toynbee does manage to cite Machiavelli as a transformative creator, though his influence on history was subtle and not immediate. In the same way, few question the aesthetic or philosophical worth of Horace or Democritus or, more recently, Wang Wei, Rumi, Montaigne, Rousseau, Wordsworth, or Dickinson. They may not have pushed the course of history along radically new paths, but it is beyond doubt that their writings, conceived in solitude, were widely appreciated in their own day and still preserve rich, provocative food for the souls of subsequent generations.

Just as one need not be a genius to be a wise man, so the solitudes of many lesser figures may hold value. For if, as I will argue, the power of solitude stems from timeless qualities of human consciousness, then its creative potency is available to all. The shaman is capable of withdrawing at will into a solitary trance-state in order to dive into the underworld or fly like an angel to the haunts of the gods to bring back a boon for his or her tribe. Some shamans may be geniuses, surely not all. We may say the same for the creative productivity of countless writers, artists, philosophers, and scientists whose work is carried out alone.

At the same time, an obsessive focus on immediate action in the world may itself be dangerous, both for geniuses and us lesser mortals carried along by the tide of events. In this age of information explosions, mass democracy, and fast-paced economic competition, the harried citizen's natural tendency is to shoot from the hip and to either skip thinking altogether or confine thoughts to the shallowest of contemporary issues.

That is a shame, argues Louis Mumford in his book *The Conduct of Life*: "For every person who is lost so completely in reverie or abstract thought that he forfeits the capacity to act, there are now a hundred so closely committed to actions or routine that they have lost the capacity for rational insight and contemplative reconstruction."[41] As a result they have lost the very possibility of re-formation and self-direction through which life becomes meaningful and purposeful. Those who omit this act of recuperation and re-creation by oversubmission to the pressure of practical affairs will lose their hold over those affairs, says Mumford. In that light, reverie before action has value for living:

> Detachment: silence: innerness—these are the undervalued parts of our life, and only by their deliberate restoration, both in our personal habits and in our collective routines, can we establish a balanced regimen.[42]

When we isolate thought from its immediate obligation to action and from the anxious distractions of society, we may find that it is "new and improved." It is beyond doubt, as we see again and again in the history of solitude, that being alone for a while can add depth, clarity, and perspective to thought that might otherwise be drowned out in the clamor of social life. As an added benefit, quiet meditation may be therapeutic. Or it may be charged with inspiration, divine or otherwise.

I can find no reason, therefore, other than the most deeply ingrained social temperament or personal prejudice, why solitude might not be beneficial to anyone. Petrarch reminds us that the wilderness of solitude has neither porter nor watchman but is open to all. It certainly cannot be harmful when taken in moderation; for the prescription of being alone is a placebo in the purest sense of the term, the medicine that doesn't do anything but leave you alone.

ECONOMICS OF SOLITUDE

If we try to assess the social value of solitude through the lens of conventional economic analysis, there seems to be little to recommend it with certainty. If the life of solitude were taken up more widely, there is little reason to believe that geniuses would be any more productive, since solitude is already open to them or anyone, anyway. Nor is there any guarantee that such deliberations would lead to a higher Gross National Product, even over the long term. Major historical change may take decades or even centuries to develop and the ultimate results are uncertain. Likewise, while there is a reasonable likelihood that citizens who take more time to reflect will thereby make better decisions, there is no guarantee that will be the case. Skeptics will naturally assume that most of those who choose a life of retirement will spend their time only in unproductive leisure—in other words, "goofing off."

Nevertheless, there is another way to think about social value. Most economists would agree that the GNP cannot serve as a true measure of overall social welfare. To be more accurate, we would have to construct an index that might be termed the Refined National Product (RNP). Such a hypothetical measure would account for the happiness, not to mention the enlightenment that may be derived from either occasional or prolonged time away from society.

An added benefit both from an economic and a personal perspective is that the condition of solitude comes free of charge to every human being.

It is certainly not something that can be removed by any sort of social punishment, such as fines or jail. Short of psychological torture, it cannot be taken away even by forcing the solitary to work in a labor camp, as was the case with writers such as Alexander Solzhenitsyn, who continued to compose in his head while exiled to a Soviet gulag.

Aristotle came to about the same conclusion when he said that contemplation has value *in itself,* because it can be practiced alone, without dependence on others, and the more one can do it the happier he or she will be. Perhaps it is not surprising that most Christians of the Middle Ages would heartily concur. One of the most popular topics for debate during that supremely spiritual period pitted the champions of the contemplative life against advocates of the active life in the world. Such arguments were inevitably put to a close by a simple reference to the biblical story of Jesus, Mary, and Martha in Luke 10:40–2.

Martha, according to Luke, was working in a truly selfless and religious spirit, ministering to the needy, serving the Lord and his disciples. Her sister Mary, meanwhile, was sitting at Jesus' feet, which she had kissed and anointed, and was hanging upon every word of his spiritual teaching. Busy with serving, Martha saw that she could not minister to many people unaided, and asked for her sister's help. But Jesus replied:

> Martha, Martha, thou art anxious and troubled about many things: we need few things, or even one thing. Mary has chosen the good part, which shall not be taken from her.

Thinking along the same lines, is it not a vulgar sign of immaturity to think that every poem I read must prompt me to some crusade or other; or that every book must tell me how to fix a carburetor, mend a fence, or get rich quick; or that every spiritual thought on the nature of life and the divine must lead directly to measurable improvement of my life or stoke my missionary zeal to help others achieve the same enlightenment? "People are fools," says Democritus, "who live without enjoyment of life." Though Democritus may not have, I would take his words as applicable to the spiritual as well as the material aspects of the life of solitude.

In our calculations of the RNP, we must also weigh the indirect value to society of individual contentedness. If one who chooses solitude does nothing but enjoy himself, but thereby avoids stirring up all manner of nonsense in the world, I would consider that a great good. If more did so, would not the world be a calmer, more noble-minded place? They might direct their instinctual energies and inner resources less to the day-do-day battles in society and more to joy of living and creativity.

If only a few were thereby motivated to work in quiet time and thereby produced new thoughts and discoveries, that could more than pay in purely economic terms for the general indolence of others. And if more citizens were at home in themselves, if more were able to enjoy their present lives, society might well be the subtler for it, less harried, less weary, less restless, less violent, more thoughtful and dignified. If more of us spent time alone thinking through our own troubles and fears, less time and money might be spent on psychiatrists and psychotherapists.[43] Life itself might be less hated.

And perhaps more individuals would be less inclined to hate or envy others, more inclined to understand them. Friends as outwardly different as Merton and Rilke point out, for example, that it is in solitude—perhaps only in solitude—that one may learn to become truly social.

"If a man does not know the value of his own loneliness, how can he respect another's solitude?" says Merton. "It is at once our loneliness and our dignity to have an incommunicable personality that is ours, ours alone, and no one else's."[44] The more each individual develops and discovers the secret resources of his private world, the more he can understand others and contribute to society. The recluse who sits alone—spiritually naked and defenseless against the essential painfulness of temporal existence, digging deeply into the recesses of his soul—is living in the elemental reality of human existence that is shared by all. In that sense, Merton adds, "solitude is as necessary for society as silence is for language and air for the lungs and food for the body."[45]

Both Merton and Rilke begin, as I do, with the assumption that every human being is solitary by nature and that we delude ourselves by thinking otherwise. It is better, says Rilke, to have the courage to face and love our lonely condition. It is the general lack of such courage that makes it difficult or impossible to fathom the secret personality and the loneliness of others. We should have the audacity, says Rilke, to approach our existence as broadly as we can, encompassing the "the most strange, the most singular and the most inexplicable that we may encounter"—

> For it is not only indolence that causes human relationships to be repeated from case to case with such unspeakable monotony and boredom; it is timidity before any new inconceivable experience, which we don't think we can deal with. But only someone who is ready for everything, doesn't exclude any experience, even the most incomprehensible, will live the relationship with another person as something alive and will himself sound the depths of his own being.[46]

This acute sense of sympathy and understanding lies at the heart of what makes reclusive poets such as Rilke and religious hermits, from Saint Anthony to the Russian hermit Saint Seraphim, so attractive to troubled souls who read them or come to receive advice and blessings. Otherwise, how could one even think of asking a hermit—of all people!—for advice on how best to live in the world? It is virtually impossible to quantify the value of such advice from solitude; but, to my mind, it should certainly be included in the RNP.

It is a similar sense of deep empathy for another that Powys has in mind when he says that hermits make the best lovers, in both the spiritual the physical senses.

> True lovers are twin-hermits, carrying each other, in their separate imaginations, far away from the cares and amusement of the world, into those solitary places between land and sea, between earth and sky, alone with the clouds and the winds and the far-off constellations, where they can emphasize their division from the rest of our race.[47]

And, again, let us not overstate the value of action in the world. We should be skeptical, says Petrarch, about the motivations of those "virtuous" men who shun the cloister to take up their social duty—for example, as bishops who are guardians of the helpless sheep in their flocks. "Alas," he laments, "how much I fear that they are wolves eager to rend them alive."[48]

Montaigne made a similar observation, which can be applied to social life in every time and place. He did so in the year 1585, writing alone in his study on the third floor of his tower refuge, looking back on two decades of public service—and so, to my mind, he had the right to speak with authority on this issue:

> Let us leave aside the usual long comparisons between the solitary and the active life; and as for that fine statement under which greed and ambition take cover—that we are not born for our private selves, but for the public—let us boldly appeal to those who are in the midst of the dance. Let them cudgel their conscience and say whether, on the contrary, the titles, the offices, and the hustle and bustle of the world are not sought out to gain private profit from the public. The evil means men use in our day to push themselves show clearly that the end is not worth much.[49]

Robinson Jeffers came to about the same conclusion, writing several centuries later in the tower he built for solitary writing and contemplation at his Tor House retreat on the California coast. He asserted that nine-tenths of the energy of human civilization at its present level is devoted to self-frustration, self-incitement, self-tickling, and self-worship. "The waste is enormous," says Jeffers. Much of that time would be better spent going for a walk, admiring landscape, digging our gardens, or on "science and art; not to impress somebody, but for love of beauty that each discloses." We could even be quiet occasionally, he adds:

> Better than such discourse doth silence long,
> Long barren silence square with my desire.[50]

COMPROMISE

Another thing about the critiques of secular-minded hermit bashers is that they are directed mainly at the antiworldliness of soloists who chose a life of perpetual solitude. Again, there must be some misunderstanding. For secular Friends from Horace and Petrarch to Wang Wei do not argue against such things as friendship and simple enjoyment of life, but rather for greater balance between the life of solitude and that of society. Even the advocates of religious solitude find ways to balance the benefits of solitude with those of society over time. There is much room for compromise.

The simple fact, which I keep coming back to, is that all life necessarily involves such a compromise. Everyone is essentially alone in his or her consciousness and all humans are social to a degree. Even the longest, most physically isolated and curmudgeonly hermits ever known have all been on earth, not very far, in the scheme of things, from society. And none of the Friends I have researched was utterly solitary over time. They had mothers and lived in families of some sort in their early lives. Nearly all received friends or followers in their hermitages. Many took their wives or lovers along with them. Nearly all protracted solitudes, even the most famous of them, were punctuated by forays back into society.

Anthony left his mountain cave for a time and journeyed to Alexandria to help resolve a theological dispute. During his two-year stay at Walden Pond, Thoreau often returned home to sample his mother's apple pie and, on one occasion, to spend the night in jail in a show of civil disobedience against a poll tax he believed to be unjust. In these instances, neither Anthony nor Henry could be faulted for failing to answer the call of social responsibility. Some may think that Thoreau was uncomfortable in his one-room shack at Walden, but in his desert, at least, he didn't miss dessert.

Even where solitude has become an institution, there are many socially condoned trade-offs over time. Most monks take their vows after having lived normal worldly lives in childhood, adolescence, and parenthood. In Buddhist Thailand, young men are encouraged to spend a year or so living as mendicant monks before making their way in the world. I met some of them when I was working in the Peace Corps and they in a sort of "Nirvana Corps."

Such arrangements have their social advantages. The retreats of youthful Thais reinforce the element of equanimity in the national character, which came in handy recently as it enabled Thailand quickly to become a competitive member of the global economy of the late twentieth century. That same sense of composure helped Thais to respond promptly and confidently to a reverse of fortune when the nation's bubble economy burst beginning in 1997. The *New York Times* editorialist Thomas Friedman reports that few Thais he spoke with a year after the crash were embittered by the experience. One couple had profited handsomely during the boom times, then lost everything. Nevertheless, they cheerfully "set up a sandwich-making operation with many of their former employees and started delivering fresh ham-and-cheese around the streets of Bangkok."[51]

In Hindu civilization, the sanctioned postponement of solitude until later in life can also be viewed as a rather clever means for answering the complaints of Queen Janaka. For the proper Hindu following the Laws of Manu would have earned his right to the pleasures of solitude, having dedicated the physical prime of life to fulfillment of social duty. One might even say that this system neatly reduces the costs of old age retirement, while allowing the forest dweller the loving companionship of his wife, at least for a time, followed by the bliss of religious solitude.

There are also many forms of compromise with society among secular recluses. Horace, Wang Wei, Petrarch, and many others enjoyed the subtle pleasures and creative surges of solitude but they lived for long stretches of time in comfortable country retreats surrounded by friends, family, or servants. Still others balanced social life with periodic solitudes. Take for example, Seneca's recommendation in a letter to his young friend Lucilius that, to harden his moral strength against difficult times and for the good of his soul, he should "start cultivating a relationship with poverty" by appointing certain days on which he gives up everything and makes himself at home with next to nothing. "At the end of it, believe me," he says, "you will revel in being sated for a penny, and will come to see that security from care is not dependent on fortune—for even when she is angry she will always let us have what is enough."[52] In the same spirit, as we have heard, it was common for Roman gentlemen to build "poor rooms" in their houses to which they would retire occasionally to find tranquillity and to reconstitute their stoic resolve.

Some people I know engage in a daily regimen of meditation. Perhaps daily doses of surfing the Internet or old-fashioned reading or listening to music are heading in the same direction. If they do not train one's stoic will, at least they may relax the mind from the immediate aggravations of social life and may improve one's contribution to society in the process.

One might also find respite from the rigors of life amid the crowd by escaping for a week or two for a long walk in the woods; by going fishing, figuratively speaking, with a modern counterpart of Charles Cotton and his friend the Zen-like English angler Isaac Walton; by rowing on a lonely lake with Wordsworth or Rousseau; by enjoying time alone on weekends, as I do, at our dacha in New Paltz, New York, or as many others do in days of immobility with Sufi aspirants in Vermont.

Not all Friends, as we have heard, condone this secular compromise. Many religious soloists maintain that only through a complete flight from all worldly creatures can we expect to receive God's grace; only through complete isolation and dedication to the infinite do we have any hope of achieving enlightenment. All other solitudes, says Merton, are false. That is a strong perennial argument and for a long time I took it as debilitating to Friends of Solitude who are willing to bend to the pressures of worldly affairs. But then I realized that there are many equally serious responses to this call for "true" spiritual solitude.

In the first place, to be blunt, perhaps grace or enlightenment can wait. In the meantime we may enjoy a delightful, productive, and morally upright leisure here on earth. We may, as Petrarch argues, "enjoy the present and yet look forward to a better state, in place of a brief retirement from human society to partake of the perpetual companionship of the angels."[53]

In the second place, let's be realistic. No matter what we do, grace or enlightenment may never come; they may be illusory hopes that we have hastily created to meet a pressing psychic need. Even if they are real possibilities, what reason do we have to believe that they may be the product only of intense, obedient sequestration? Human life does not come with a roadmap for enlightenment, worldly or otherworldly. If God has somehow attempted to communicate such a map to us, there is no agreement between or within religions as to what that map should be. Enlightenment or grace may come in a way we cannot fathom in advance. So, again, in the meantime, let us try to enjoy, understand, and live life in the world as it is—and let us do so in periods of solitude which will quicken our sensibilities and possibly lead us to subtle answers to the unanswered questions.

MARKETING SOLITUDE

This mood, which is open to spirituality but thinks beyond any particular religion, is, I think, the usually unexpressed position of most Western Friends of Solitude since the Renaissance. It was also the position of Chinese recluse scholars and many ancient Greeks and Romans. And I see no reason why something similar could not catch on more widely around the world, particularly if solitude is balanced with social life. I like Richard Mahler's suggestion in *Stillness: Daily Gifts of Solitude* that "if silence and solitude could be bottled and sold, I'm sure they would." In no time, he adds, partly in jest, "a silence and solitude bottlers association would emerge. We would see TV commercials for silence and solitude bottled under fancy names, imported from the Swiss Alps, Hawaiian rainforests or Alaskan glaciers."[54]

Mahler, who spent a recent year alone in the mountains of northern New Mexico enjoying solitude and pondering its value, admits he is thankful such a scenario will never occur. The reason, he wisely concludes, is that there is no real money in it, adding that this may be just the reason why there is so little silence and solitude in the world at large.

Perhaps that is true. But money is a relative thing and many social causes are sponsored with very little of it. I can see nothing immoral in promoting occasional separation from society, which, I hope to have shown, can be a social good. It is an interesting idea. And in some sense it is already being done in the form of advertising that features "get-away" vacations and automobiles that can help one to escape the buzz and confusion of everyday life.

There is a demand for quiet time alone, as the sales pitches imply. And that demand appears to be growing as technology amplifies the pace and turbulence of social relations and removes old sources of privacy. The same technology further accentuates social mobility and contributes to the widespread sense of alienation for which positive-minded loneliness may be a helpful antidote.

The aging of the American population may add to that sense of loneliness; it may also fuel an untapped demand. For it is clear that an interest in solitude grows with time. Its "subtle feeling" is more likely to be appreciated and used by those over the important age of thirty-five. That certainly rings a bell with me, and it corresponds to the experience of many Friends. Anthony Storr puts it this way: in later life, the sexual energies which so dominate early life become less commanding, while other concerns naturally come to the fore, notably thoughts about the nature of life and its inevitable end. As I have found, age also stimulates a desire to get busy in the time left with directing one's energies to something significant as one enters the "darkening wood" of middle age. Later in life, the prospect or reality of retirement from the workplace may have a similar effect, as maturing workers leave the social world in which they resided for decades and enter intrepidly on a solitude of sorts, wondering what to do with the remaining time.

Ironically, the same marketing bombardments that so harass modern life have prepared the average consumer to expect change and to try something new. It's just a thought, but with an aggressive promotional campaign, including, say, a barrage of strategic ads featuring the benefits of tranquillity, extolling the creative power and promoting the potential for surging bliss and ecstasy in lonely contemplation; with a slogan such as "Solitude Works!" or "Fight loneliness with Loneliness"; with the right press releases, spokespersons, and talk show placements, maybe a hair-T-shirt, pole-sitting, or isolation-tank contest with associated photo-ops; with a "Hermits Only" or "Retirement Pays" Website and a secret chat room to bring optimistic loners together in cyberspace—with such a program, I see no reason why solitude could not sell as well as the latest brand of vitamins, say, or another self-help book.

It is true that most people these days prefer not to be alone and fear loneliness. But preferences derive largely from social norms and the recommendations of friends and other credible sources. I would argue that, with a positive, adventurous mind-set, most anyone can sufficiently calm his or her mind and passions to learn the art of being alone, and its associated gratifications. "Let the public consume the pleasures of solitude!" we could say, and I'm sure some environmentalists would endorse the idea. Libraries, book sellers, public parks, and travel agents might also be interested in the concept, since their offerings naturally involve the enjoyment of time spent away from the crowd. Some religious organizations and meditation groups might likewise come on board, because solitude and contemplation are integral to their efforts, and nothing that we will say in praise of solitude would run counter to any particular belief.

Possibilities aside, though, I agree with Mahler that the marketing of solitude could well be a bad thing. In addition to being somewhat self-contradictory, it would likely be counterproductive, given the tendency of consumerism to oversimplify and to debase what must be a subtle, personal, secret feeling if the gift of solitude is to work its magic.

Extreme Solitude

Finally, a word on behalf of those hairshirted "drunkards of God" whose ardent solitudes so incensed the likes of Gibbon and Nietzsche. The history of solitude, as we have heard, does contain an encyclopedic assortment of sensational ascetic practices, mystic swoons, and extremes of isolation. To a modern observer, most of these adventures in loneliness may seem pointless, the product of madness, hallucination, or the psychic inventions of blind faith.

But just what is it that we moderns dislike? Certainly, it is not the soloist's risk-taking. Hardly anyone questions the adventurous heroism of climbing parties that set out to scale treacherous peaks such as Mount Everest or K2, despite the fact that many climbers die in the process. Given that most such peaks have already been explored, the purpose of climbing them can only be the exhilaration of the experience or the glory of achievement in the eyes of the world. Perhaps a few more observers challenge the valor of race car drivers who risk their lives and often die in the name of sport. Nevertheless, the races go on.

Nor can it be the hermit's asceticism that appalls. For that, in a sense, is around us every day. We applaud the ascetic discipline of the champion bicyclist; the severity of military training; the quasi-military, "worldly ascetic" discipline of the corporate enterprise; and the rigors of nearly all ordinary life in Western civilization. Anticipating Max Weber by several decades, Henry Thoreau reminds us at the beginning of *Walden* that asceticism is just as much the lot of men tied to jobs and mortgage payments as it is the practice of religious hermits:

> What I have heard of Brahmins sitting exposed to four fires and looking in the face of the sun...or dwelling chained for life at the foot of a tree; or measuring with their bodies, like caterpillars, the

> breadth of vast empires,—even these forms of conscious penance are hardly more incredible and astonishing than the scenes which I daily witness.... How many poor immortal souls have I met well nigh crushed and smothered under its load, creeping down the road of life, pushing before it a barn seventy-five feet by forty, its Augean stables never cleansed, and one hundred acres of land, tillage, mowing, pasture, and wood-lot![1]

Even Nietzsche, it should be noted, does not question the value of asceticism. In fact, he welcomes its most extreme forms provided they are utilized as a kind of clarifying tool for philosophic excursions. "Let us not become gloomy as soon as we hear the word 'torture'," he says in his essay "What Is the Meaning of Ascetic Ideals?"—adding that "there may be plenty to offset and mitigate that word, even something to laugh at."

What Nietzsche finds laughable in the practices of religious hermits is not their asceticism but rather their inebriation and their suspicious aims. Saints, he says, employ solitude and self-deprivation as "a pretext for hibernation, their newest lust for glory, their repose in nothingness ('God'), their form of madness." For priests, says Nietzsche, the ascetic life is "their best instrument of power, also the 'supreme' license for power." But for philosophers, scholars, and sundry free spirits, self-deprivation and even lust for glory are justified because they constitute a "preparation of the intellect for its future 'objectivity.'" In that way, intense asceticism can be "something like a sense and instinct for the most favorable preconditions of higher spirituality."[2] For Wisdom, proclaims Nietzsche's Zarathustra, is a woman: "She always loves only a warrior."[3]

By contrast, I suspect that Gibbon, who converted to Catholicism at the age of sixteen, would not argue against the hermits' aims of being closer to God, but that their methods of doing so are unnecessarily manic and antiworldly. His critiques imply that the connection with God can be achieved just as well by other, less feverish means. This suggests that the aims and the methods of the hermits' extreme asceticism need to be considered separately.

THE CASE FOR MYSTICISM

Let us begin by assessing the methods of extreme solitude, which Gibbon derides as "quailing before the ghastly phantoms of a diseased brain." He employs his considerable rhetorical powers to portray the Christian hermits' mysticism as the product of delirium, and we can assume that Gibbon would take the same view of all such uses of solitude that involve spirit flights or altered states of consciousness.

But what are these mystic swoons? If we are willing to be a bit more charitable than Gibbon in our assessment, we can say that they are simply psychic states for which we have no immediate explanation. They may be hallucinations, supernatural experiences such as clairvoyance, mental telepathy, hearing voices from the beyond, or purported transports to union with the divine. But they may also include the more common mental phenomena of life: subconscious inklings and emotions, waking dreams, desires, the mental affairs that power artistic creativity, spiritual intuitions, or the subtle feeling of joy we now call "peak experience."

To another close observer of such mental phenomena, the American philosopher William James, they are secret psychic affairs outside the level of full sunlight consciousness, which reside in what he calls the "B-region," as opposed to the ordinary "A-region."[4] For example, says James, they may be "excitements like the emotions of love or ambition, gifts to our spirit by means of which facts already objectively before us fall into a new expressiveness and make a new connection without our active life."[5] James reasons that since such states are so frequently reported (certainly by religious hermits, but also by philosophers, poets, and other dreamers), it cannot be denied that they exist. We may challenge their validity or we may say that the person who has such experiences misinterprets them. But unless we assume that all those who report such mystic states are lying, we must accept them as real states of mind.

On that basis, James argues that "the existence of mystical states absolutely overthrows the pretension of non-mystical states to be the sole and ultimate dictators of what we may believe." He acknowledges that they "wield no authority due simply to their being mystical states."

Nevertheless, they may be "superior points of view, windows through which the mind looks out upon a more extensive and inclusive world." The higher ones among them, he adds, "point in directions to which the religious sentiments even of non-mystical men incline."

> They tell of the supremacy of the ideal, of vastness, of union, of safety, and of rest. They offer us *hypotheses*, hypotheses which we may voluntarily ignore, but which as thinkers we cannot possibly upset. The supernaturalism and optimism to which they would persuade us may, interpreted in one way or another, be after all the truest of insights into the meaning of this life.[6]

Nietzsche tells us that he frequently experienced such mystical inspirations, with the implication that they were an aid to his philosophy. I would venture to say that it is these "sparks and wonders" of his meditations which he has in mind when he speaks of the "subtle feeling called solitude." We can get an idea of what he is referring to in this passage from *Ecce Homo*:

> If one had the slightest residue of superstition left in one's system, one could hardly reject altogether the idea that one is merely incarnation, merely mouthpiece, merely a medium of overpowering forces. The concept of revelation—in the sense that suddenly, with indescribable certainty and subtlety, something becomes visible, audible, something that shakes one to the last depths and throws one down—that merely describes the facts. One hears, one does not seek; one accepts, one does not ask who gives; like lightning, a thought flashes up, with necessity, without hesitation regarding its form—I never had any choice.[7]

James reports that he, too, experienced a particularly unusual mystical encounter provoked by inhalation of laughing gas. He dictated sheet after sheet of phrases that occurred to him in that intoxicated state. To a sober reader, James conceded that they will seem to be meaningless drivel. But at the moment of transcribing, "they were fused in the fire of infinite rationality," and a reconciliation of opposites: "God and devil, good and evil, life and death, I and thou, sober and drunk, matter and form." It was partly from that altered-state experience that he derived the notion that such states could conceivably have great value. That would be the case, he ventures to say, if human beings began, for reasons of evolutionary advantage, to live in another world of consciousness and perception, just as many animals have developed means of perceiving the world using unusually high or low frequencies of light, sound waves alone, X rays, and so on.

One problem with any discussion of mystical states, of course, is that all are private affairs. To make matters more difficult, there is something like a Heisenberg Uncertainty Principle of consciousness at work here. In the micro-world of quantum mechanics, posited Heisenberg, the more precisely the position of a particle is known, the less precisely its momentum can be known. In the same way, it seems that the closer we try to get to an explanation of B-region experience, the less we can understand it using A-region thinking and terminology. One alternative in this situation is to reject B-region experience altogether, as many behavioral psychologists aim to do. But that is merely a convenient disavowal in the face of volumes of reports concerning B-region from ascetic hermits and other solitaries that we find in the literature of solitude. The only commonsensical alternative, it seems to me, is to listen to those reports and consider them in light of one's own private experience.

In my case, I do not purport to be a shaman, a religious ascetic, or someone who has experienced profound, life-changing mystical enlightenment. But I have been delicately overcome, always in time alone, with the oceanic feeling, which Freud said he could not reach. I would claim some sensitivity to spiritual, artistic, and thus mystical regions of thought. I often have experiences that I find difficult to describe and which seem to be beyond description. When I consider the mystic states recorded in the literature of solitude and then compare them with my own experience, there is something in me that senses an affinity with these further reaches of consciousness.

That leads me to a commonsense belief that mystic states may indeed be responsible for the rapturous joys that many Friends describe as a "bliss of angels" or a feeling "as high as heaven." But there, too, the reasons are difficult to describe. Then I think that there are so many things in my ordinary A-region that are similarly ineffable but commonplace that it is hard for me not to subscribe to a belief that the A-region and the B-region occur along a continuum in which both are always intertwined in mind and experience, like yin and yang in Chinese philosophy.

For example, I think, how is it that any human being can formulate a single sentence that can be comprehended by another mind in its isolation in another body and spirit? That everyday reality, like the nature of human consciousness itself, has not been fully explained by science, operating, as it necessarily does, in the A-region. I then ask myself further, how is it that a creative artist can magically breathe life into a work of art, which life can be comprehended by another thoughtful observer? That, too, is commonplace but not fully understood. And so I conclude that many of the other so-called mystical thoughts and experiences may be of the same order of things. Your own experience may lead you to the same conclusion.

Since B-region experiences are by nature private, ineffable, and poorly understood, it follows that many of the most valuable of them—such as profound creativity or spiritual enlightenment—might be evoked only through extreme practices of one sort or another, the workings of which are just as obscure to A-region sensibility. Such experiences may be wish-fulfilling fantasy and nothing more. But the possibility always remains that the very intensity of some "mystic swoons" in time alone may prompt delicate mental or spiritual explorations, of which we amid the ruction of ordinary life may know nothing, and will never know unless we are properly prepared.

Indeed, the fruits of such high-powered contemplation alone are widely attested. It was out in the Great Solitude that the first Iglulik shaman discovered shamanism and he later dove physically into the ground to discover the secrets of hunting. After days of fasting in solitude, the young Ojibwa initiate discovered the secrets of how to grow corn and thereby save his tribe. Buddha achieved enlightenment only after many years in ascetic solitude, when he looked like a skeleton with skin. And Saint John of the Cross made a point of saying that it was the "Dark Night" of his suffering in solitude that led to his unfathomable nearness with God.

JUDGMENT VERSUS FAITH

It is when mystic experiences are accepted uncritically rather than as hypotheses that the likes of Nietzsche become skeptical. What they vehemently oppose is the "drunken" assumption that because mystic raptures seem to derive from the ideal metaphysical world of the divine they are therefore true. He disliked the apparent blindness of faith with which Christian hermits in particular pursued that ideal, thinking that through humility and devotion some godly presence in the transcendent world—i.e., Jesus—would come from on high as in a fairy tale to bestow grace upon the loving hermit. Where that is the hope, the religious ascetic's vigils, his fasting, his failure to bathe, his perpetual seclusion, and especially his renunciation of self and the world for a "higher" netherworld are pointless, wrong-headed supplications to nothingness and a waste of precious time.

In this respect, Nietzsche is like the Christian Gnostics I mentioned earlier, many of whom believed that they could bring forth their own inner light by emulating Jesus to become enlightened spiritual beings like Him. The opposite camp, and the one that prevailed in Christianity, holds that no amount of self-interested striving can lead to salvation. Rather, one can only enter the Kingdom of Heaven or return to the pre-Adamic paradise in the Garden of Eden with help from outside: the grace of God. Individualistic efforts to rise to an enlightened spiritual state under one's own steam are viewed as vainglorious and hopeless. Without complete renunciation and devotion to the will of a loving and helpful God one can never reach the highest enlightenment.

Personally, I am not prepared to give supremacy to "blind faith," but neither is it wise to ignore such devotionalists, for the ultimate logic of their approach rests on very firm ground. "How is it," they may well ask us, "that you think the individual human mind with all its limitations of time and perspective can comprehend the essence of All—even in the depths of the evanescent and incommunicable meditations of your most profound cave? You cannot."

"Therefore," they would add, "the most you can hope for is a message or guidance from the All itself—from a muse, from a helping spirit, a revelation from God, thanks to his grace. If you think that you can manage on your own, not only are you deceiving yourself but your arrogant foolishness will be the greatest obstacle to a higher wisdom. You may call it blind faith. But that 'blindness' is often a necessity. It is in the nature of heaven and earth, which is so large—and you and I are so small."

"Yes," we may answer on Nietzsche's behalf, "we are small. Our perspective and capabilities are limited. But let us live and think with that truth in mind and not in quailing hope that some phantom from a nonexistent world beyond cares enough about us to offer guidance. That, sir, is the nature of heaven and earth. There is no Heaven! Your humble faith is blindness and nothing more! Living with eyes and ears open is the greatest spiritual heroism of all."

"If God exists and is so powerful," we might add, "why does he care a whit for what we may do to beg for His grace? Has He created the world as some sort of game in which the only winner is the one who acknowledges his power by supplication? If He is so all-knowing and intelligent, why does he not want us to exercise the intelligence and freedom of thought which He has bestowed to us?"

"But we know that grace exists. It is not a game," the religious man could answer, patiently. "We have witnessed it in the very existence of the world and ourselves. What is it keeps you going every day if not faith in something? Faith is worth the apparent absurdity. The greatest heroes are those who do the right things to cultivate that faith in humble supplication to the Almighty. And the result will be a thousandfold greater than anything you can dream of in your pitiful attempts to think your way to enlightenment through your own thought and judgment."

So the backtalk on this profound issue may continue forever until God himself comes down from his heavenly throne to settle the issue openly—for example, by appearing (as I once heard it prophesied on a cable TV program in New York City) simultaneously on all television sets in the world. Well, until something like that happens, one gets the strong impression that this issue will never be resolved. So it is wise not to be overly hasty with the gavel of judgment against the value of ardent faith in solitude.

At this point, the likes of Gibbon will agree that faith in God does indeed have great value, but they maintain that spiritual men and women can get faith without quailing before "ghastly phantoms." They need not be masochistic hermits. But, again, there is another view. Merton, for one, warns that true faith requires selfless, meditative prayer and stern discipline. "To keep ourselves spiritually alive," he says, "we must constantly renew our faith." That will require intense effort.

> It requires unending courage and perseverance, and those who are not willing to work at it patiently will finally end in compromise. Here, as elsewhere, compromise is only another name for failure.[8]

Ardent faith, then, may have its reasons; and so may highly disciplined asceticism that shuns the everyday world. If we are to be truly happy and fulfilled, to understand the rhyme and reason for All, or enter the tavern of ruin, then stronger medicine, more perseverance, and a jarring life experience may be required. These may be necessary if we are to renounce worldly desires and embrace sufferings—thereby to rise above both to another plane. And perhaps, if by our efforts we have become more sensitive to subtle B-region realities, we may open ourselves to insights into the nature of heaven and earth that are not available to A-region thinkers however profound their musings in solitude.

PSYCHOLOGY

Go sit in your cell and your cell will teach you everything.

—Abba Moses, fourth-century Egypt

PARADE OF HERMITS

SEVERAL YEARS AGO, when I began researching the literature of solitude, I had a fair idea that I would find much that is fertile, delightful, and otherwise beneficial to human life. But I had no idea that I would uncover this embarrassment of riches.

If true, the very abundance of the fruits of solitude would seem to place the hermit bashers in an awkward position. The problem, of course, is that many reports, particularly those of the ancient Friends before Petrarch, seem suspiciously to coincide with every wish-fulfilling fantasy imaginable. It is only reasonable to suspect, therefore, that the so-called powers of solitude are merely convenient flights of imagination or the work of sensationalizing storytellers. That lingering critique led me to begin formulating a psychology of solitude that would help to explain why time alone can produce such remarkable results and to show along the way whether they are merely the product of daydreams and hallucinations or whether they may be attributable to credible psychological mechanisms.

What I find is that fantasy and elements of James' B-region do indeed play a very important role, mainly as aids to thought and feeling rather than as fantasies in themselves. But there are other things at work, too, such as passion, suffering, and the time to think and work that separation from society naturally provides—each of which do not necessarily involve self-delusion or childhood fantasies. Together they show that simple—sometimes not so simple, sometimes very difficult, often soul-wrenching—time spent alone can produce some of the most extraordinary riches. They also suggest what facets of solitude might be emphasized to enhance its effects. Here is how I came to those conclusion based on an analysis of the history of solitude and with the help of a few psychologists, ancient as well as modern.

My first step was to define more precisely what the fruits of solitude entail. For assistance, I turned to Patanjali, the second-century B.C. grammarian and systematizer of Hindu mystic practices. In his *Yoga Sutras* Patanjali attempts to catalogue all the wondrous physical powers, or *siddhis*, that may be conjured in yogic meditation practiced in solitude. What came to be known as the "eight siddhis" are described by a later commentator, Shri Purohit Swami, as the power to take the smallest form, take the biggest form, take the lightest form, touch anything, control anything, create anything, penetrate anything, and bring about anything. The yogi's minor powers, says Shri Purohit, are innumerable. For example, his body may become "so sound that heat or cold cannot kill it, while the elements have no jurisdiction over it."[9]

That sweeping inventory would seem to cover the range of occult powers attributed to shamans, as well as such feats as Saint Anthony's power over animals, Chinese hsiens' ability to live for more than a thousand years, Bodhidharma's journey across the Yellow River on a bamboo stock, and Buddha's clairvoyance. The ability to "take the lightest form" would no doubt include feats of contemporary adepts of Tibetan *lung-gom* (which may be translated as "meditation on the dynamic vital principle"). Through a long program of secluded meditation—including up to nine years of solitary confinement in a Buddhist anchorage—such spiritual experts are said to become so light and powerful they may attain the ability of running as fast as a galloping horse over the rocky terrain of the Tibetan plateau.[10] And the "ability to create" anything would include the warrior Arjuna's ability through tapas of creating the all-powerful Pasupata Weapon, as well as the hermit-statesman Visvamitra's feat through equally ardent meditation of literally giving birth to a "new heaven."

Still, the eight siddhis don't even attempt to encompass the therapeutic sense of happiness and bliss associated with time alone, nor the more spiritual and intellectual powers of solitude. For that we may turn to the second-century B.C. Buddhist philosopher Nagasena. By his count, solitary meditation has more than two dozen mainly therapeutic or medicinal benefits:

> Secluded meditation guards him who meditates, lengthens his life, gives him strength, and shuts out faults; it removes ill-fame,

> and leads to good repute; it drives out discontent, and makes for contentment; it removes fear, and gives confidence; it removes sloth and generates vigor; it removes greed, hate, and delusion; it slays pride, breaks up preoccupations, makes thought one-pointed, softens the mind, generates gladness, makes one venerable, gives rise to much profit, makes one worthy of homage, brings exuberant joy, causes delight, shows the own-being of all conditioned things.[11]

Nagasena's listing would include the joy that Rousseau experienced in his retreat to Lake Bienne, when he says he was "so happy that it would have contented me for my whole existence without the desire for another state arising for a single instant in my soul."[12] And if solitude both softens the mind and makes thought one-pointed, as Nagasena says, then his catalogue probably would include such fruits of time alone as the prophesies of an Epimenides, the lawgiving of King Minos. It would also include more believable discoveries, such as Pythagoras' geometric theorems or the creative output in solitude of thinkers from Democritus to Chuang Tzu and writers from Petrarch to Proust.

The exuberant joy that Nagasena refers to might include the eremitic "bliss of angels" that Desert Fathers such as Abba Abraham estimated to be a hundred times greater than worldly life. But it fails to acknowledge what Patanjali emphasizes is the highest attainment of the yogi, who should finally renounce the siddhis and rise to the "infinite knowledge" and final liberation of the Self, which he calls the "Rain-Cloud of Divinity." Nor does it include the Buddha's achievement, after seven years of meditation, of "crossing over to the other shore" to the all-knowing, deathless state of nirvana or any of the other ineffable states of immortality, enlightenment, grace, or union with the divine that are so often associated with religious solitudes.

The catalogues of Patanjali and Nagasena provide an interesting perspective on the benefits of solitude, but they are still too complicated for our analysis. In their place, I suggest we think of the fruits of time alone in three broad, admittedly interrelated categories.

First, solitude may be *creative* by providing a mental environment that helps to produce something that wasn't there before. That may include ideas, discoveries, or physical effects. But to simplify things, we will leave the latter aside for the most part, taking the purported physical results of solitude to be metaphors for an underlying reality that emerges in the realm of thought. For example, we will assume that Visvamitra's "new heaven" was not an actual place in the heavens but a new concept of heaven. Admittedly, that will leave out quite a few miraculous effects associated with solitude; but the effects of thought—including mystical "thought"—are also remarkable, from the founding of religions to world-changing philosophies and scientific discoveries. In the end, these may be far more impressive than any occult powers.

Second, solitude may be *joyful.* Since joy is inevitably a matter of feeling that cannot be proven, when we hear Friends express joy, happiness, or contentment in solitude, we will take their word for it. Third, since so many Friends speak of a more intense form of happiness, something like bliss or *enlightenment* resulting in whole or in part from their time spent alone, we will take their word for that, too. The following discussion is divided, again, somewhat arbitrarily, into those three categories.

SEARCH FOR CONSISTENCIES

Determining what it is about being alone that might have caused or helped to bring about these results is just as problematic, and no one that I am aware of has suggested a typology of solitude to aid our analysis. What I have done is to comb through the history of solitude looking for consistencies that seem to be associated with the three major benefits of aloneness. I find that while the fruits of solitude are remarkably consistent across time and culture, there is little consistency in the outward circumstances of the Friends' eremitism. Friends in every culture spoke of the joys of solitude, often to the point of ecstasy, and there was some form of creative result associated with their time spent alone. But when we examine the places in which their retreats occurred, their personalities, and their activities, the first thing that strikes us is not the commonality of solitary experience, but rather its variety. What a rich spectrum of solitary life forms human beings on earth—we "social animals"—have produced. The lone state, in other words, is not a dull oneness. Seen in historical context, it is a long parade.

By definition, Friends retire to solitude in some way, to what virtually all Buddhist meditation guides refer to when they advise: "Find a lonely spot." Aside from its "loneliness," however, I can find no characteristic of any such refuge that makes it more creative or therapeutic than any other—not the place in which it occurs, the length of time spent alone, the degree of intensity, nor the Friends' personalities, their teachers, or their specific practices in time alone.

There is something about the open expanse of nature—whether in a desert, on mountaintops, or on a quiet lake—that may stimulate cosmic contemplation and a thoughtful, metaphysical mood, as is evident in the experiences of the Desert Fathers, Chinese hermits, and nature recluses such as Wordsworth. But many distinguished Friends ignored nature's grandeur altogether. In some of the Buddhist meditation manuals, for instance, monks are directed to find their lonely spot in a graveyard, preferably on top of a corpse, while many Christian hermits chose to live holed up in caves or in one-room anchorages attached to churches. Among secular-minded Friends, the Greek orator Demosthenes liked to retreat to the cellar under his Athenian home to focus undistracted on his speechwriting. But compare Socrates, who could enter his productive fits of philosophical concentration just about anywhere, on a field of battle or on a porch. And he, like many modern philosopher-hermits from Kierkegaard to Valéry, cultivated the advantages of solitude amid urban throngs.

In general, simplicity of life—and, at higher strength, poverty and asceticism—seem naturally to be associated with the life of solitude. But there are so many degrees of intensity along the simplicity-asceticism spectrum that it is impossible to judge which one represents the Lady at her best. Wang Wei's Wang River estate and Horace's Sabine farm were worlds apart from the ascetic heights of Saint Simeon's column. Yet they all loved and profited by solitude.

The Friends tend, by definition, to be introverts. But that is just another way of saying that they love solitude. It is true that many of the Friends have a curmudgeonly demeanor, if not an aggressively obnoxious disposition. It is impossible, for instance, to ignore the case of Myson of Chen, one of the Seven Sages of pre-Socratic Greece. According to

Diogenes Laertius, he was once spotted laughing to himself in a lonely spot. When asked why he took such pleasure when alone, he uttered this famous reply: "That is just the reason!" Heraclitus is said to have been "shrill, cuckoo-like, a mob-reviler." Such was often the case, too, with Thoreau. Henry James, Sr., remembered that he "was literally the most childlike, unconscious and unblushing egotist it has ever been my fortune to encounter in the ranks of manhood."[13]

Jean-Jacques Rousseau's reputation will always be sullied by the fact that, having written books on the importance of early education, he nevertheless consigned his own children to an orphanage. Petrarch was bitter as hell about the "busy men" of Avignon, not to mention weepy and melancholy about having been jilted by Laura. Rilke, it is reported, didn't attend his daughter's wedding because he was writing. And Robinson Jeffers seems perpetually serious as rock, as though wounded by life, a man with little sense of humor.

But compare Friends such as Yajnavalkya, Buddha, Jesus, Krishna, Chuang Tzu, T'ao Ch'ien, and many of the Desert Fathers. In them, we have an innate friendliness, love, and sympathy for the world. It is said that Democritus ripped his eyes out to avoid seeing the mob of mankind, but he also advised that bitterness of mind should be "avoided like a plague." Kierkegaard, like Nietzsche, fell in love with solitude at an early age and said that he lived thereafter as an "Isolated One." At the same time, his often light-hearted and ironic fictional style of philosophizing shows him to be something of a "laughing philosopher" on the order of Democritus. The same is true of Montaigne's tasty, meandering, warm-hearted essays, all penned in a productive retirement.

Another apparent consistency among the Friends of Solitude is that most had a strong early education, particularly in the relevant classical literature of their cultures, as did Petrarch and the recluse scholars of China. That education seems to have provided a discipline of thought that enabled them to get busy with creative output in time alone. But many Friends, such as Saint Anthony, were not so well educated and did not read books at all.

Similarly, there is a good deal of evidence that many Friends profited from the guidance of teachers as is typically the case with shamans, or from the traditions of earlier sages, as we see in the long list of predecessors to Yajnavalkya and the writings of Chinese Taoist philosophers. But there was virtually no transfer of such knowledge between modern Friends of Solitude. Each seems to have discovered the powers of solitude entirely through his or her own experience. As we have heard, the Iglulik Aua said that the greatest shamans cultivated their powers out in the tundra, without the help of a teacher.

There are many guides to the mystic raptures available in solitude, from Buddha's advice to his following as captured in the Pali Texts of his sermons to Climacus' *Ladder*. And as Evelyn Underhill shows in her enduring work, *Mysticism*, there is a remarkable consistency in the psychological processes along the "Mystic Way"—self-abandonment, self-purification, illumination, mystic pain, and, finally, union with the divine. Underhill admits, however, that her schema is a "discrete indulgence in the human passion for map-making."[14] There are many such charts, and actual practices vary considerably.

The only truly consistent commonality we are left with, then, brings us back where we started, to solitude itself: a purposeful—if sometimes unintended—detachment from the hubbub of society. That may sound tautological. But it explains why the fruits of solitude have accrued to religious and secular Friends alike across every culture and era, with little regard for the place or duration of their retreat or their specific methodologies or personalities.

Since at least the Paleolithic era humans have possessed large brains that have changed little over time and which are capable of consciousness—that is, awareness of the world, other people, self, death, pain, and consequences of actions. At the same time, we can assume that consciousness has never functioned in the manner of a conventional computer, which allows some processing to go on entirely separately from all other processing in the same machine. Instead, we are constantly distracted by the social noise of daily affairs, along with the internal residue of society in the form of memories, regrets, desires, and habits.

In that light, being alone may simply allow us to escape those disturbances in order to focus consciousness on aspects of our inner and outer worlds that might not otherwise have occurred to us. In that escape, whether it is a simple withdrawal from society or a more intense concentration facilitated by asceticism or suffering, being alone may provide time, freedom, and energy to think and work; and in such solitude, the soloist may be more alert to subtle, B-region perceptions and experiences. Let us examine more closely how it is we may get from there to the "subtle feeling called solitude" with its added potential for creativity, joy of living, and, on occasion, enlightenment.

Creativity

When asked why he chose to work in a remote research center far removed from the society that would eventually put his discoveries to practical use, the physicist Richard Feynman replied that it gave him time to think undisturbed. Feynman admitted that he missed the pleasures of a more active social life in the city; but he maintained that the nature of his work was so complex that, like building a house of cards, he required stillness and freedom from distraction in the surrounding atmosphere. Otherwise, the delicate structure of his reasoning would never make it past the first floor.

Similarly, time to think without interruption was probably the main driver of Democritus' creativity, as illustrated in the story that he never even noticed when his father sacrificed an ox in his garden study. That kind of dedication to thought, aside from any mystical forces acting there, makes solitude creatively potent. For it may be true, as the saying goes, that genius is nine-tenths perspiration and that solitude very simply offers the time for mental sweating.

Even for those Friends who bring with them a preprogrammed religious rule, isolation provides the freedom within which an active mind can surrender to its own reflections outside the strictures of habit, dogma, or observation by others. "The righteous man," says the Sufi al-Arusi, "is changed forty times a day, but the hypocrite remains in the same state for forty years."[15]

It is true that some people think or write best amid the excitement of a crowd—a general in the field, a journalist in the newsroom composing a story against the stimulus of a deadline, or a philosopher whose thinking may be inspired by repartee in a symposium. However, even they may agree that higher, more complex thoughts require a delicate chain of reflections and a quickened sensibility that can be shattered by the problems and passions inflamed by life in society.

REVERIE

Having the freedom to think and work undistracted is no doubt an important starting point for creativity. But we sense that some additional magic ingredient will be needed if we are to explain solitude's sparks and wonders. For it is possible to work very hard at something with no creative result. And if we are simply regrinding in solitude the thoughts we had in society we are only likely to end up with the same thoughts again.

Where do new thoughts come from? It must be that they are either there in nascent form or that they come from outside through some mysterious mystical channel. In either case, it is reasonable to posit that new thoughts are constructed from something in James' B-region—numinous, quasi-mystical inklings, inspirations, intuitions, intimations, hunches, daydreams, fantasies, or other mysterious building blocks of thought and feeling that are too subtle to be fully recognized amid the clamor of society. Solitude may simply help us to be more alert to them, to bring their significance into focus, then to use them to build new thoughts.

In his *Advantages and Disadvantages of Solitude*, Dr. Johann Zimmerman, put it well when he said, "Solitude leads the mind to those sources from whence the grandest conceptions are most likely to flow."[16] That is why Horace loved the country life, where he could "hearken to what the inner spirit sings." And it is why Philo counsels us to "be silent and hear."

Among the most common images used to explain this silent remedy is a quiet pool or, alternatively, a basin full of water. In an oft-quoted dialogue between a Christian hermit and two novices in the deserts of fourth century Egypt, for example, the hermit bids them to fill a vessel with water and look down into it. When he asked them, "What do you see?" they said they could see only cloudy water. But after the water became still he asked the same question again, to which they replied, "We see our own faces distinctly." "Thus is it with the man who dwelleth with men," said the hermit, "for by reason of the disturbance caused by this affair of the world he cannot see his sins; but if he lives in the peace and quietness of the desert he is able to see God clearly."[17]

Nearly a millennium earlier, secular-minded philosophers such as Pythagoras and Parmenides were employing quiet, reflective solitude in about the same way, if to different ends. Rather than yearning to see the God of All, per se, they listened in silence for *harmonia* or underlying principles that control all things. According to the third-century Roman philosopher Iamblichus, Pythagoras instructed his followers to take lonely walks each morning in temples, quiet groves, or sacred places to gain inner serenity and focus their reasoning powers for the day. And students hoping to be initiated into the Pythagorean circle were also required to complete a *quinquennial* silence, five years of "perfect silence" that was designed to "purify the dianoetic part of the soul" (the part that governs, or unleashes, intuitive understanding). The silent time was intended to prepare their psyches to comprehend the harmonies of mathematics and geometry and, at the highest level of attainment, to "hear the music of the spheres."[18]

Nor is this sort of quiet contemplation peculiar to the West. Confucius (as recorded in the *Chuang Tzu*) advised a similar inward examination—but with an important twist. "You must fast!" he says, for it is impossible to discover any truth through the common way of thinking and perceiving. By "fasting," he does not mean simply a restriction of diet, nor merely intense concentration alone. He advocates, rather, a complete emptying of the normal self, with its excess baggage of fears and habitual beliefs, so one can see and hear the truths inside. Says Confucius to Yen Hui:

> Look into that closed room, the empty chamber where brightness is born! Fortune and blessing gather where there is stillness. But if you do not keep still—this is what is called sitting but racing around. Let your ears and eyes communicate with what is inside, and put mind and knowledge on the outside. Then even gods and spirits will come to dwell, not to speak of men![19]

Several modern psychologists have theories to help us explain just what may be going on in the empty chamber of solitude—although I warn you in advance that their "scientific" terminology often seems only to cloud the picture.

Arthur J. Deikman argues that creative potential in solitude stems from a process akin to mysticism. In his paper "Deautomatization and the Mystic Experience," Deikman acknowledges that mysticism is generally assumed by modern psychologists to be a "regression to early infant-mother symbiotic relationship." He, on the other hand, views mysticism as something like that which happens in James' B-region: It is "the undoing of automatic perceptual and cognitive structures," which in turn "permits a gain in sensory intensity and richness at the expense of abstract categorization and differentiation." Stated another way, says Deikman, the undoing allows a return to a more "primitive" form of thinking typical of "uncivilized" cultures. To test his theory, Deikman conducted a series of experiments in which several individuals were isolated and asked to focus their attention for a prolonged period on a vase. As a result, he reports that the perceptual and cognitive changes in the subjects were "consistently in the direction of a more 'primitive' organization." Among a variety of responses, his subjects experienced increased vividness and richness of perception and an abundance of "syncretic thought."[20]

Another B-region psychologist, Silvano Arieti, argues that something similar—what he terms "paleologic thinking"—lies at the heart of creativity. Such thinking, he says in his book *Creativity: The Magic Synthesis*, employs all kinds of "amorphous cognition," including "past experiences, perceptions, memory traces, and images of things and movements," as well as primitive or repressed childhood images. These may not yet be organized into thoughts but are felt as an atmosphere or "global experience," about which "words spoil the feeling." In all cases, says Arieti, "Instead of rejecting the primitive (or whatever is archaic, absolute, or off the beaten path), the creative mind integrates it with normal logical process in what seems a 'magic' synthesis from which the new, the unexpected, and the desirable emerge."[21]

Not surprisingly, Arieti maintains that this synthesis is most likely to occur in time spent away from society. "A solitary individual," he explains, "is not constantly and directly exposed to the conventional stimulations and is less in danger of being overcome by the clichés of society."[22] As a result, it is more possible for him to listen to his inner self, to come in contact with his inner basic resources, as well as inspirations deriving from paleologic thinking.

Arieti acknowledges that living solely in a world of "global experiences" may be an unhealthy form of escape. But it can also provide a timely diversion from established ways of thinking. The creative person probably has good reason to seek release, because "he senses a defect, or incompleteness, in the usual order of concepts, or has some other motive for dissatisfaction with it." When that is the case, "he brings part of his mental activity back to the stage of amorphous cognition, to that great melting pot where suspense and indeterminacy reign, where simultaneity fuses with sequential time and unexpected transmutations recur."[23]

At the same time, as I have suggested above, Arieti emphasizes that solitude provides time for creative labor. He also cites the adage that creativity is ninety percent perspiration. By way of illustration, he refers to the classic example of Henri Poincaré's discovery of Fuchsian groups: after fifteen day's of intense study, the mathematician drank black coffee and spent a sleepless night during which he reports that "ideas rose in crowds; I felt them collide until pairs interlocked, so to speak, making a stable construction."[24] The following day, the Fuchsian discovery dawned on him as he stepped onto a bus. It is impossible to calculate just how much time Poincaré spent in the inspirational phase of his discovery, but it is clear that his undistracted study and his night of sleepless contemplation were necessary for his creativity. So was the time spent *after* his all-night labors, when, apparently, subconscious forces of "thought" came into play to lock the loose ends of his meditations into place.

Anthony Storr's account of the role of solitude in creativity is similar but adds a useful perspective. He begins with the observation that the world's greatest, most creative thinkers—he mentions recent ones, from Descartes to Wittgenstein—lived alone for most of their lives. Storr reasons that creation begins, in its first stage, with preparation, during which the creative person develops an interest in a particular subject, collects material, reads everything he can on the subject. Over time the accumulated material simmers in the mind. "We do not understand what goes on during this period of incubation," Storr admits, "but it is a necessary prelude to the next stage, that of illumination."[25] He hazards a guess about incubation, though, suggesting that it is like the resorting process that occurs in dreams.

Storr cites the psychologist Stanley Palombo's contention that dreams have an information-processing function, which is concerned with allotting new experiences to the right slot in permanent memory. He again concedes that what takes place in the brain remains a mystery, but adds that "the parallel with the scanning and sorting process, which occurs spontaneously in dreams or which is deliberately encouraged by prayer or meditation, is striking." That is why creative people tend to live alone and to be "greatly absorbed with their own thoughts." The absorption, says Storr, is partly the result of the creator's single-minded intensity of thought, but it is also accompanied by passive daydreaming reverie—"a state of mind in which ideas and images are allowed to appear and take their course spontaneously; but one in which the subject is sufficiently awake and conscious enough to observe and note their progress."[26]

In such a solitary, daydreaming state, the prepared mind, with its mysterious sorting process, may be better equipped for performing the essential and difficult creative task of "forming new links between formerly disparate entities." The sin qua non of such inspiration, says Storr (quoting Abraham Maslow), is the ability to become "lost in the present"—immersed, fascinated, absorbed. At the same time, the creator typically has "the ability to become timeless, selfless, outside of space, of society, of history." And the creative attitude depends, says Storr, "upon being free of other people; free, especially, from neurotic involvements, from 'historical hangovers from childhood,' but also free of obligations, duties, fears, and hopes."[27]

Most of the Friends did not take time to analyze the reasons for their creativity in time alone, but I think it is what Petrarch had in mind when he said solitude can foster a "divine fertility of intellect." Rousseau, a close observer of his own inner sentiments and humors, was a bit more specific. He represents the typical case of a Friend who found both creativity and joy when lost in the present. In *The Reveries,* he says that he never meditated more deliciously—nor were his intuitions more auspicious—than when he forgot himself. Thinking, he says, was always a painful process. But perhaps by way of compensation, his most intense meditations typically ended in a more pleasant and free-flowing reverie.

"In these wanderings," he said, "my soul rambles and glides through the universe on the wings of imagination, in ecstasies which surpass every other enjoyment." The best way to arrive at this state is through walking, forgetting, and a "cheerful imagination." "Movement which does not come from outside then occurs inside us," he explains. Then, somehow, the images of one's sensation and imagination "trace themselves upon the brain and there combine, as in sleep, without the help of the will; one lets all that go its own way, enjoying without acting."[28]

Rousseau says elsewhere that many of his most profound thoughts were inspired by the work of his emotions in states of meditative reverie that he learned in childhood. Early in life, he said, "I had thought about nothing; I had felt everything"—

> These confused emotions, which I had experienced one after the other, in no way affected the reason I had not yet acquired. But they did furnish me *reason of a different stamp* [my italics], and gave me strange and fanciful notions of human life of which experience and reflection have never quite cured me.[29]

PASSION

Like Rousseau, most of the Friends of Solitude were tremendously productive. Witness the Buddha's intricate philosophizing during his seven-year isolation, followed by years of sermonizing punctuated by solitude. We think of the abundant sayings of the Desert Fathers and the voluminous and imaginative sermons of a Yajnavalkya or Chuang Tzu, and the extensive writings of Petrarch and Nietzsche. How is it that one musters sufficient energy for creative work? Certainly not through reverie alone, or merely the added time for work. There is something in solitude that helps to *power* that work.

In part, solitude may preselect energetic creators, who are drawn to it to fill a fervent need to concentrate. But time away from the distractions of society may also fire passion for work by enabling a refocusing—or, to use the modern psychological term, a sublimation—of the main psychic urges that invigorate human life: aggression, sexuality, and self-preservation.

Among the most extreme forms of such sublimation, as we have seen, are those that occur in India. According to Hindu cosmology, the world itself was created by the god Brahma through the power of tapas; and it was through the same ascetic accumulation of powers in solitude that Arjuna created the all-powerful Brahma's Head Weapon.

Speaking from his own experience, Nietzsche states explicitly that by avoiding the distracting effects of both physical and social intercourse, inner resources of passion can be used to boost intellectual powers. "Those with the greatest power and the surest instincts do not need to learn this by experience," he says, "their 'maternal' instinct ruthlessly disposes of all other stores and accumulations of energy, of animal vigor, for the benefit of the evolving work: the greater then *uses up* the lesser."[30]

Many ancient Greeks likewise subscribed to the sublimation theory, recommending that warriors not engage in sexual activity well before a battle. As we have heard, this is precisely the point of Socrates' "eulogy to Love" in Plato's *Symposium*. To apprehend the highest truths, he argues, recounting the words of Diotima, the delicious charms of sexual passion must be led away from the senses toward spiritual beauty:

> For let me tell you, the right way to approach the things of love, or to be led there by another, is this: beginning from these beautiful things, to mount for that beauty's sake ever upwards, as by a flight of steps, from one to two, and from two to all beautiful bodies, and from beautiful bodies to beautiful pursuits and practices, and from practices to beautiful learnings, so that from learnings we may come at last to that perfect learning which is the learning solely of that beauty itself, and may know at last that which is the perfection of beauty.[31]

Petrarch said about the same thing when he attributed all his literary output to a sublimation of his unrequited love for Laura: "In her fair eyes I read there word by word all that I say of love and all I write."

While on this tantalizing subject, I cannot pass over a relevant theory put forth by the Jungian psychologist Erich Neumann. In his *Origins and History of Consciousness*, Neumann went so far as to label human consciousness (in blatant male chauvinist terms) "the 'higher phallus,' with the head as the seat of creative realization." Neumann explains that as consciousness develops in individuals it takes its impetus from innate animal instinct. That instinct, or libido, is required to make the ego strong enough to break away from the collective unconscious—that is, the collective transpersonal archetypes of the world, or what Neumann terms the "Earth Mother." As the conscious ego develops sufficient autonomy, it then has a desire to use the same libidinal energy to reenter the mysterious Earth Mother. The result is an enrichment of both consciousness and libido. The latter, he says, "makes itself felt, subjectively, as excitement, vivacity, and a joy that sometimes borders on intoxication; and, objectively, as a heightening of interest, a broadened and intensified capacity for work, mental alertness, etc."[32] Appropriately, Neumann calls it "Uroboric incest."

I'm not convinced that it is helpful to bring the concept of the collective unconscious into the analysis. We might as well call the Earth Mother the spirit world, since both are equally murky realms. But it is provocative terminology and it does underscore the importance of sublimation of instinctual energies in solitary creativity. Neumann adds that we can see the process of Uroboric incest in the desire for solitude and mortifications common to primitive initiation ceremonies and shamanism. You may recall that the Iglulik legend of the first shaman is a perfect example. During a time of famine and sickness in his tribe, the shaman took it upon himself to go behind a screen in his igloo and literally to dive headfirst into the earth to pay a visit to the Mother of the Sea Beasts. When asked how got the idea, he said that it came to him while he was out in the "great solitude" of the tundra.

Perhaps you thought solitude would be boring. Quite the contrary! In fact, we may conclude that when an otherwise passionate man or woman turns his or her life energies away from other people for a time and has the wherewithal to focus that energy on creative work, the results can be explosive.

INNER RESOURCES

The obvious problem with this source of creative energy is that human passions are very difficult to control, particularly in the resonant caverns of solitude. At Vaucluse, Petrarch still pined for Laura, and his desire for fame only grew stronger. In the deserts of the Middle East, the contemplations of Anthony and Jerome were bothered by visions of dancing girls and other worldly demons. And Montaigne's warning to recluses in his essay "On Solitude" is beyond doubt:

> Ambition, avarice, irresolution, fear and desires do not abandon us just because we have changed our landscape...They often follow us into the very cloister and the schools of philosophy. Neither deserts nor holds in cliffs nor hair-shirts nor fastings can disentangle us from them.[33]

How is it, then, that all Friends of Solitude were able to muster sufficient inner resources to mange these distractions? Many, particularly religious soloists with very intense aims of enlightenment and union with the divine, naturally look to equally intense ascetic practices. Nevertheless, even they tend to agree with Montaigne that asceticism is not the answer. In so many words, we have heard one of the Desert Fathers tell a novice that "your hairshirt won't do you a bit of good." And there is a common saying among monastics that monks must first and foremost be "called to solitude," meaning either that they will be called by God Himself or, in a more practical interpretation, that those best suited to monastic life will have something in their character and earlier experience or education that will enable them to endure solitude. In modern psychological terminology, they are more likely to be introverts who are most satisfied in life when they direct their attention upon themselves.

Storr cites research into similar psychological types that may shed some light here. Wilhelm Worringer, for one, studied the play behavior of children to find that some are what he calls "abstractionists" who prefer to detach themselves from the physical world, finding beauty "in the life-denying inorganic, in the crystalline or, in general terms, in all abstract law and necessity," where they find repose and personal integrity in a chaotic world.[34] In research on the artistic play of children, Howard Gardner found that some tend to be introverted "patterners," who "spurn the world of social relations, preferring instead to immerse (and perhaps lose) themselves in the world of (usually visual) patterns." When they get older, suggests Storr, "patterners will incline toward the sciences or philosophy."[35]

What such studies do not tell us is whether one is born to introversion or whether it is learned or nurtured by experience. The childhood psychologist Donald Winnicott seems to believe the latter. He suggests that what he calls "the capacity to be alone" is something developed early in life. In a paper by the same name, he maintains that this valuable ability originates "with the infant's experience of being alone in the presence of the mother."[36] In other words, the child's basic needs for food, warmth, and love are met, leaving him or her with time to discover personal life. There are many examples of this, but among the Friends whose early biographies are known in detail, Kierkegaard and Nietzsche stand out. Both, as Kierkegaard puts it, were "in love, fanatically in love...with thoughts" at an early age.[37] Both lived in relatively stable family situations in which they were protected but left to themselves. In other words, solitude was not discouraged as loneliness. Both, I believe, were first-born children, which meant automatically that their earliest childhood reveries would have been undisturbed by sibling rivalries. Moreover—and this is probably important—both had the example of contemplative fathers who liked to be alone and loved to philosophize.

In my own case, I grew up first-born in a Protestant family that was stable and supportive but left me alone. My father worked days in advertising and spent most of his nights away from home in social service activities ranging from the American Legion and the Cancer Society to United Way and the Boy Scouts. My mother was warm in her way but generally aloof, leaving me to myself, especially when I was sick with youthful asthma, which was often.

Father was no philosopher, per se, but he loved to read—the morning and evening newspapers mainly, mostly magazines beyond that (*Time* and *Saturday Review* were his favorites), along with such longer works as Churchill's autobiography, the story of Richard Burton's search for the source of the Nile, and, I shouldn't forget, Will Durant's *History of Philosophy*. I liked the way he fell asleep reading in his leather chair many nights when he was home. I liked the evenings we spent in our backyard at Inverness in Seattle and on our cruiser in Puget Sound, contemplating the stars and "solving the problems of life." I also liked the works of Montaigne and Emerson that appeared prominent in my father's library. I found out later that he bought them only to take to his army post in Alaska and never actually read them, but it fooled me, so only the perception mattered. More than anything, this fostered in me a love for wandering, adventurous, twinkling thought.

Such early exposure to philosophy seems to have been present in the biographies of a majority of the Friends of Solitude. In India, for example, Yajnavalkya was thoroughly versed in the knowledge and rites of the Vedas before he withdrew to the forest to ponder their inner meaning. As a young prince, the Buddha would likewise have been well trained in the Hindu classics of the time; and after he renounced princely life to become a wandering mendicant, we know that he spent years studying with all the important eremitic philosophers he could locate. In China, all of the recluse scholars were well trained in Chinese classical literature and philosophy. In Greece, Pythagoras and Democritus made journeys around the Mediterranean in search of the wisdom of philosophers. In Rome, Friends from Jerome and Evagrius to Horace and Seneca were highly educated classicists. Petrarch spent much of his time studying the Greco-Roman classics, while Nietzsche spent his early life as a professor of classical philology. In America, Emerson and Thoreau were well versed in the same European classical literature.

Works of literature and philosophy tend to become classics because they address essential problems of human life and death. Their language tends also to be challenging and complex, like a great and charming puzzle; so the job of learning the classics develops a manner of thought derived from study and discipline, which naturally promotes a love of abstract mental play, a sense of curiosity, and a nose for whimsy that can fill solitude to make it glow with the excitement of discovery. Other complex systems such as music, mathematics, or the sciences may also provide the mental schooling that can train thinking for subtle acrobatics and an ability to be engrossed in thought, in evanescent structures of insight that are seasoned with perennial wisdom.

Many pages back, we heard Petrarch tell us that solitude without literature and books is "exile, prison, and torture." But supply literature and solitude becomes "your country, freedom, and delight."[38] That, he says, is because the solid writings of the classic books afford their hosts "inestimable treasures of mind, spacious houses, brilliant attire, delightful entertainment, and most savory food."

And that, I think, is why Thoreau and even Gibbon could say they were never less alone than when they lived and busied themselves in solitude. To take another far-flung example, Alexandra David-Neel writes that the hermits she met on her journeys in Tibet in the early decades of the twentieth century were just as busy in their hermitages as Petrarch at Vaucluse or Nietzsche in his Genoan garret. The current idea in the West, she says, is that if a man lives in seclusion for a long time his brain will become disordered; he will become stupid and finally mad. But this, she maintains, does not apply to Tibetan hermits, who can live in isolation for ten or twenty years with only positive effects on their sanity:

> These men are prepared for loneliness...they have accumulated in their mind a store of ideas which keep them company. Moreover, they are not inactive during their retreat, long as it may be. Their days are occupied by methodical exercises in spiritual training, the search for occult knowledge or meditations on philosophic problems. And so, often passionately interested in these manifold investigations and introspections, they are actually very busy and hardly notice their solitude.[39]

To a degree, then, it seems that those who are best able to manage the wiles of solitude are, in one way or another, introverts. At the same time, personality is a multifaceted and secret thing with countless loopholes. There are many ways to turn an anxious, extroverted view of life into healthy introversion. It seems to help, in that regard, if one has built up the mental discipline and a storehouse of ideas through complex studies of some kind. It also helps if one has something to be passionate about—a problem to be solved, discovery to be made, or project to be completed—which will, in effect, distract one's attention from the distractions of society.

But the secret is in the doing, to get busy with something, and solitude is the best place both to ponder what that something ought to be and to get working on it. Either way, attitude and effort are key. That, I think, is why Samuel Johnson recommended a modification to Burton's direction—"Be not solitary; be not idle"—to his friend and biographer James Boswell. For "disordered men like you," he told Boswell, "if you are idle, be not solitary; if you are solitary, be not idle."[40]

Powys places still greater emphasis on self-motivation. In addition to using the inner resources of character and those developed through education, the endurance of solitude is a matter of remembering that time spent alone may lead to "avenues to planetary reverie." It is also a matter of having the courage, fortitude, and sense of adventure to follow those paths. The right outlook on life, he says in *A Philosophy of Solitude*, is to stand up not only against society but against everything outside one's inner self:

> It is our essential right as independent personalities to play the part of magicians, and to create and destroy this impinging Not-Self from the very start. By "creating" is meant the contemplative brooding which gives permanence and solidity; and by "destruction" is meant the annihilation by forgetting which is the ego's supreme weapon.[41]

ALTERED STATES

Not all creative output in solitude is a matter of intense effort, for the human mind also seems to like working in the secret domain of the subconscious. Sometimes the best thing is to set aside the burden of concentration and go for a walk. Petrarch tells us that he had his most profound inspirations when wandering in the woods and fields surrounding his Vauclusian retreat, just as Poincaré's insight struck him only after his night of contemplation as he stepped onto a bus. Moreover, as I have stressed, there are many ways to combine the virtues of solitude with those of society. An occasional return to society can ease the sense of loneliness and balance the mind, and nearly all of the Friends who we associate with extreme solitude made such forays.

Shamans likewise combine the two sides of life by playing important roles in their societies with focused bursts of solitude as needed to kindle their powers. When they do turn inward they aim to do all they can to take the creative potential in solitude to extremes through mental-spiritual journeys in what we term today altered states of consciousness. For others, too, a frightening, wrenching experience may push one into solitude and simultaneously alter one's perspective on things. The shock of isolation may serve to bring psychic powers to the fore that otherwise would have lain dormant—in other words, to provoke fantasies, hallucinations, and other mental activity that are similar to, but go well beyond, any of the deautomatization and primitive thinking mentioned so far.

Fear is a marvelous motivator. When accompanied by other strains on normal mental functioning (such as starvation, incessant drumming, or drug taking) the result may be a trance. More precisely, it may involve what Odd Nordland—in his paper "Shamanism as an 'Experiencing of the Unreal'"—describes as a "disconnection of the cerebrum" in which the entranced shaman may experience a deeper subconscious level of mental reality. That reality is dreamlike, but the shaman goes over the top to experience mental reality as worldly reality. Nordland suggests that this in-between state may be akin to hypnosis, in which "a monotonous influence, for example from a strong and dominating personality, can result in some of us again being able to cross the borderline between conscious and reflective experience, and the region where we journey, speak, and act without being masters over what takes place."[42]

Extreme solitude may have a similar effect, says Nordland, citing psychological experiments with sensory deprivation, which show that "each one of us is capable of having visual and auditory experiences which we would not count as 'real.'" In these experiments, subjects are kept for days at a time in isolation using darkened rooms, water tanks, and other paraphernalia that limit sensory input. The results are always surprising, frightening, and shocking to the one who is not prepared. For lack of another name, says Nordland, we must still call these cognitive experiences hallucinations. They occur, he believes, through the regulation of cerebral functions just at the time when the brain has a small variety of sensory impressions to react to.

In this altered state, the shaman may be in a useful position for problem solving on behalf of his tribe. He is free from taboo-conceptions and deprived of the usual critical powers that could inhibit creativity. "We can also imagine," writes Nordland, "that the problem may be of such a nature that it is not easy to think out logically and in full consciousness. Or it may demand abstractions, and make demands upon formulations and logical conclusions which make contemplation difficult."[43]

Shamanic states, in other words, may make possible in preliterate culture a form of thinking that employs intuitive abstraction without making use of the rational abstractions available to modern thinkers. "Where our society trains the scientist in the specialized use of symbols and language," Nordland concludes, "so the migratory cultures have their specialists who, in a crisis, can also employ the less conscious and less precise forms of problem-solving, on the level where man, in his thinking, parted company with his other fellow creatures."[44] We can surmise that anyone who enters an ecstatic state of altered consciousness in solitude—from Sufi "Perfect Ones" to Christian mystics—may avail themselves of similar powers of creativity.

VOICES

You may have noted that none of these considerations has brought us any closer to answering the basic question as to whether the creative inspirations in solitude come from inside the mind or from a divine source outside. Shamans must assume the latter, because they invariably say their powers are aided by "helping spirits" and that their occult work is not merely a matter of conjuring bright ideas but rather by exerting some influence on the spirit world to bring about a better state of affairs for their fellows. It may likewise be assumed that the collective unconscious of the Earth Mother resides somewhere outside in a metaphysical, albeit worldly, realm. Of course, most religions, with the apparent exception of Buddhism and Jainism, preach faith in a divinity outside the diminutive human realm. So, again, we are back to the question of faith and the validity of intimations of what may be true but are beyond concrete proof.

Where do the mystic intimations and hallucinations come from? Essentially, it is the same category of question as "What is the soul?" or "What is the mind?" and "Where do they go after death of the body?" I like the answer that the Sufi Dawud al-Ta'i gave to the question "Where were you?" when he inadvertently snapped back from being beside himself in ecstasy. "I have no idea," he said.

Even Nietzsche, as we heard, spoke of thoughts that flashed up of necessity, like lightning from an overwhelming force from outside him. But another modern philosopher, Henri Bergson, can be classified more squarely in the inspiration-from-outside camp. In *The Two Sources of Morality and Religion*, he speculates that the mystic "has felt the truth flow into him from its source like a force of action…His desire is with God's help to complete the creation of the human species. The mystic's direction is the very direction of the élan of life."

It is an effort to strike out beyond the limits of intelligence, says Bergson. The soul of the great-spirited mystic seeks a vision, a contact, a revelation of transcendent reality:

> Shaken to its depths by the current which is about to sweep it forward, the soul ceases to revolve round itself and escapes for a moment from the law which demands that the species and the individual should condition one another. It stops, as though to listen to a voice calling. Then it lets itself go, straight onward. It does not directly perceive the force that moves it, but it feels an indefinable presence, or divines it through a symbolic vision. Then comes a boundless joy, an all-absorbing ecstasy or an enthralling rapture: God is there, and the soul is in God. Mystery is no more. Problems vanish, darkness is dispelled; everything is flooded with light.[45]

Bergson declines to offer a precise explanation for how the light of inspiration is communicated to the enthralled mystic, except to say that it comes from the essential energy of things, the *élan*, which can only appear indirectly as a "presence." Perhaps he is right not to attempt explanation, for that would be to murder the mysterious wit, which is the soul of all creativity.

Likewise, it is unlikely that further researches into the workings of Arieti's paleologic thinking or the sorting-out process of daydreaming suggested by Storr or any other theories will reveal the true universal theory of creativity in solitude. Such researches may give us a better idea as to what the ingredients of creation might be and why these ingredients seem to be fostered best in solitude. But they will not explain the magic of how the ingredients are put together, deep in the hermit's inner cave.

Nor, ultimately, could they tell us how inspiration is fashioned into creative product. We will leave it at that, since the putting-together is itself prior to explanation. The "making" has already expired by the time the result is cast in words, or plastic art, or music.

Joy

We now switch gears for a moment, in a pleasant way. Some underpinnings of the creative fruits of solitude can sound, we must admit, rather stressful and unfriendly. Nevertheless, most of the Friends tell us otherwise. Horace wrote that he could "rise up as high as heaven" at his Sabine retreat. And Wang Wei's friend P'ei Ti could ask, "Oh Joy of solitude, will you ever come to an end?"[46] How can there be such joy in loneliness?

One obvious answer lies in the word "freedom." Just as subtraction from society leaves one free to think and work undistracted, so solitude leaves one free to enjoy life away from the annoyances of the crowd. Of course, the value of this aspect of time spent alone is widely acknowledged. Otherwise, vacations (from the Latin, *vacare*, to be free, empty) would not be so popular. One tourist package is even sold as an "antidote to civilization." It offers time on an island resort, where one's basic needs are satisfied, free of money and other unpleasant social realities. Those who take the trip are not exactly alone; nonetheless, the demand for such asylum suggests a strong yearning for escape from the troubles of work, family, and civilization at large.

Similarly, wealthy souls in many civilizations have paid dearly to build secluded country retreats. In the Roman Empire, most emperors such as Tiberius maintained rural estates called *latifundia*, as did Horace on a modest scale and with a helpful subsidy; in China, Wang Wei's elegant Wang River retreat is the best example; more recently in Europe we can point to the English country home and the Russian *dacha*.

Who would not like to have the financial wherewithal to afford such a retreat? And who at some turbulent, wrenching time in life does not dream of packing it all in and fleeing their current situation? At that point, they are likely to agree with the bitter line in Jean Paul Sartre's play *Nausea*:

"Hell is other people." Somewhere inside, they may even see some wisdom in the Buddha's harsh statement in Ashvagosha's *Saundarananda*: "To shun familiarity with others, as if they were a thorn in the flesh, shows a sound judgment."[47]

Still, the mere freedom from troubles is not enough to explain the greater joys to be found in time spent alone. If you have a rock in your shoe or a thorn in your side and you stop to remove it, then being free of that source of pain is an obvious, if temporary, pleasure. In that manner, withdrawal only brings you back to "normal" life, minus the buzz and clamor of society, a relief that doesn't necessarily add anything.

It is clear, however, that Lady Solitude can add value. For one thing, like childbirth, the creativity enhanced by time alone may be emotionally rewarding. It may afford the joy of solving a problem, say, or of making something beautiful or interesting. Storr reminds us that the resulting sense of satisfaction can be intense, because of what he calls a sudden "reconciliation of opposites"—the Eureka! effect. In the same way, one may also get a feeling of satisfaction if the creative powers of solitude are applied toward resolution of the problems in one's life.

Beyond that, the emptiness of being alone can have value in itself, aside from anything productive one *accomplishes* in solitude. That may happen particularly as the same creative energy and sensitivity is applied simply to the appreciation of life.

Being lazy myself, I am attracted to this sort of idleness, with its subtle, pixilated, tasty delights that are at once worldly and spiritual. It is perhaps because a solitude of appreciation is not directed at producing anything but happiness that it can be most productive in a subtler, aesthetic way by stirring the soul. Whereas thinking for productive purposes is hard work, in these moments less energy is required and thinking and feeling seem best when they are free-flowing and effortless. We take pleasure in reading alone, in quiet contemplation of the tracings the author has left behind in words. Fine music or plastic art is likewise best appreciated by mentally canceling out distractions to focus on the work. And if one can be profoundly elated by these, why not, with the right attitude, by anything in the great wide world?

The artist creates a work through skill and effort fired by passion, adding insight and spontaneity with the help of his greater sensitivity in solitude. The observer, in a sense, re-creates the work in solitude through a process of creative apperception, applying the same quiet sensitivity to the work in light of his or her own experience. As Lewis Mumford puts it,

> When we prolong the good moments, by holding the flavor of them on the tongue, we achieve a sense of completion and fulfillment that comes by no other method.[48]

What Mumford is pointing to is a kind of gourmet philosophy of life, which tells us existence must be savored if it is to be enjoyed. And there is no question that separation from society may put one in an appropriately savoring mood. Somewhere, Thoreau said that more than being a writer of books, he wanted to make his life a work of art. Often, he went a step further to advocate appreciating life as a transcendent work of art, in idleness. In his journal, Thoreau recounted one of his idle moments at Walden Pond where

> Drifting in a sultry day on the sluggish waters of the pond, I almost cease to live and begin to be.[49]

I think that captures the sensation. On another pond in a far distant place and time, Wang Wei's verse, "Drifting on the Lake," seems to evoke the same subtle feeling:

> Autumn air clear into the distance
> Far from the thresholds of men:
> Cranes alight on a sandy shore,
> Mountains rest beyond the clouds,
> Limpid waves disburse as evening comes.
> Tonight I trust my being to a single oar,
> As I drift alone, forgetting to return.[50]

To my mind, this love of lonely idleness is a wonderful and too much neglected feature of human consciousness, perhaps of existence itself. In animal life, one can sense this existential joy in the contentment of cows in a green pasture, or in a school of fish swimming effortlessly in a pond. In human life one can sense it in the language of musing poets, shepherds watching their flocks, fishermen at sea or by a river, my father who liked to stare vacantly at walls or the night sky at least once a day, and in the lives and writings of most Friends.

The American poet David Ignatov provides one of my favorite examples. "When I die," he wrote, "I want it to be said that I wasted hours in feeling absolutely useless and enjoyed it, sensing my life more strongly than when I worked at it."[51] Rousseau's delight in doing nothing is another. The precious *far niente* (Italian: "doing nothing"), he says, referring to his retreat to Lake Bienne, "was the first and the principal enjoyment I wanted to savor in all its sweetness, and all I did during my sojourn was in effect only the delicious and necessary pursuit of a man who has devoted himself to idleness."[52]

As witnessed by Wang Wei's poem quoted above, Chinese artistic and philosophical tradition takes a similar approach to the subtle virtues of doing nothing. But when Chuang Tzu writes of "free and easy wandering," it is hard to tell whether he's referring to the aesthetic pleasure of being alone or solitude's creative productivity. To Chuang, one senses, the two are inseparable:

> I have heard Confucius say that the sage does not work at anything, does not pursue profit, does not dodge harm, does not enjoy being sought after, does not follow the Way, says nothing yet says something, says something yet says nothing, and wanders beyond the dust and grime.[53]

Again, Chuang is pointing to the super-sensibility that solitude helps to engender with regard to one's most delicate and whimsical inward thoughts and outward perceptions. This, I think, is the most powerful source of the secular joys of solitude, because it may help to magnify the other related sources of pleasure we've been considering, enriching the joys of escape and seasoning the delights of living in the world as it presents itself before and behind our eyes.

MODERATION

Throughout the history of solitude we also hear, particularly from secular-minded Friends, a call to the proverbial "simple life." Detachment from society makes life simpler and outwardly less aggravating, almost by definition. But we also hear a general admonition that life alone will be better and happier to the degree that we are not enslaved by craving for wealth, status, fame, fancy food and clothing, or the other typical desires and trappings of social life.

In the West, this fundamental of the life of solitude finds its most famous expression in Epicurus' philosophy of the "good life." Despite the unfortunate connotation of the term epicure, his was not a philosophy of live-it-up-while-you-can hedonism, but rather one of strategic moderation. "The truest happiness," as the philosopher explains in his *Letter to Menoecus*, "does not come from enjoyment of physical pleasures, but from a simple life, free of anxiety, with the normal physical needs satisfied." One arrives at that pleasant state, he says, by means of a reasoned management of desire:

> Neither continual drinking and dancing, nor sexual love, nor the enjoyment of fish and whatever else the luxurious table offers brings about the pleasant life; rather, it is produced by reason which is sober, which examines the motive for every choice and rejection, and which drives away all those opinions through which the greatest tumult lays hold of the mind.[54]

This admonition to moderation lies at the heart of all Greek and Roman moral philosophy. As Seneca later put it in *On Tranquillity of Mind*, "We must not send our desires upon a distant quest, but we should permit them to have access to what is near, since they do not endure to be shut up altogether. Leaving those things that either cannot be done, or can be done only with difficulty, let us pursue what lies near at hand and allures our hope, but let us be aware that they are all equally trivial, diverse outwardly in appearance, inwardly alike vain."[55]

In eighth-century China, Han Shan said essentially the same thing in one of his more moralistic poems:

> a greedy man loves hoarding wealth,
> like an owl loves her chicks
> the chicks grow up and eat their mother
> wealth multiplies and swallows its owner
> spread it and blessings grow
> hoard it and disaster arises
> no wealth, no disaster
> flap your wings in the blue[56]

There's a simple, if sententious, logic to it. If your needs are uncomplicated and few in number, your chances of fulfilling them are far better than if you are hooked on immoderate desires for wealth or fame or social fun, all of which tend ultimately not to satisfy anyway, since they inevitably grow out of control, fueling a self-multiplying hunger for more wealth, more fame, more fun.

Abba Arsenius (the same desert hermit who God advised to "flee from men") taught his followers that a "cleaner conscience" is one of the greatest rewards of the secluded life. "In solitude," he said, "one is removed from the object of sin, from temptations as well as the influence of wrong-minded men." Arsenius, who had been a Roman courtier prior to his retreat, could have taken the idea directly from Seneca, perhaps from this excerpt from one of the philosopher's letters to Lucilius, probably written around the middle of the first century:

> When a mind is impressionable and has none too firm a hold on what is right, it must be rescued from the crowd: it is so easy for it to go over to the majority. A Socrates, a Cato or a Laelius might have been shaken in his principles by a multitude of people different from himself: such is the measure of the inability of each of us, even as we perfect our personality's adjustment, to withstand the onset of vices when they come with such a mighty following.[57]

Petrarch, we may recall, had a similar idea in mind when he wrote that Lady Solitude, "purest of all human possessions," preserves her wards not only from the irksomeness, but also the hateful contrivances of social life. More, says Petrarch, she assures that we are not "squeezed amid dancing throngs"; that we will not "unlearn humanity among men"; and that we will not, through satiety of feeling, grow, as our patriarch of solitude did before his retirement, "to hate things, hate people, hate business, hate whom you love, hate yourself!"

Religious soloists tend to take this conscience-cleansing principle to extremes in hopes of winning their way to heaven. The Desert Fathers made every attempt to avoid the Seven Deadly Sins: pride, envy, anger, lust, avarice, gluttony, and sloth. Mahavira believed that isolation from society and, indeed, from all evil influences and all possibility of doing wrong is the ultimate path to enlightenment and all the bliss that accrues from that achievement. A similar spirit of asceticism had probably been integral to Indian religious culture for millennia. If the solitary-ascetic practices of shamans from Australia to Greenland are any indication, it probably extends back to the earliest prehistoric human cultures.

Obviously, some nerve of essential human nature is being touched here. Religious solitaries must derive some satisfaction from appearing good in God's eyes—others, as we say these days, from "feeling good about themselves." Whether you are a Christian hermit in the desert, a Roman emperor in his fasting chamber, an Eskimo shaman out in the tundra, or a modern health club aficionado on a treadmill, there is the sense of well-being and physical and mental control that may be achieved by following a program of strenuous training—which, appropriately enough, is precisely the meaning of the Greek *askesis*, from which our word asceticism derives.

DEFENSE MECHANISMS

That is the bright side of the joys of solitude. Many psychologists, as I have said, mainly those with a Freudian bent, argue that these so-called pleasures are merely fantasies that are the product of defense mechanisms such as masochism and regression. In some perverse cases, that may be true. But if we examine these psychic "ailments," we find that they, too, may have value.

Masochism is generally defined as "the getting of pleasure from suffering physical or psychological pain, inflicted by others or oneself." This is where Lady Solitude may be said to be perverse, where she bids us to take pleasure in filth, hairshirts, and torturous nights in mosquito-infested swamps. Jeffrey Masson, as we have heard, maintains that ascetic masochism is simply a self-defensive response to trauma in early childhood, such as sexual molestation or loss of one's parents. Essentially, according to Masson, the ascetic tries to reenact the pains of childhood, which were his only source of love. It may also derive from a feeling of chaos and powerlessness, which is countered by an attempt to control the chaos by confronting it directly, reveling in it, and concocting delusions of grandeur along the way.

Saint Anthony, for instance, fled to a life of solitary asceticism in a tomb some time after both of his parents had died. Masson cites Flaubert's depiction of the hermit in *Temptation of Saint Anthony* as an example of how masochism may be employed as a desperate antidote for such despair. In this passage, Flaubert has a fellow hermit, Hilarion, tell Anthony:

> Hypocrite, sinking into solitude the better to license your outbreaks of greed! You abstain from meat, wine, baths, slaves and honors; but you let your imagination provide you with banquets, perfumes, naked women, and applauding crowds! Your chastity is only a more subtle corruption, and this scorn of the world nothing but your impotent hatred of it![58]

Perhaps the saint was in love with his self-inflicted tortures and got his jollies, as it were, from filling his mind with demons and fantasies. Indeed, that possibility should serve as a reminder of the hazards of living alone. But if masochism is merely the self-infliction—or, perhaps, self-testing—of pain, then there are certainly degrees of masochism. At the more moderate end of the spectrum, consider the arsenal of rhetorical techniques that recluse poets use to allay their feelings of sadness and melancholy. Or is it that melancholy itself—like singin' the blues—is a form of defense against life's sorrows? Many recluse poets found some consolation in well-turned verse, which, if not expunging, at least mollified the sadness by expressing it beautifully.

Most of Petrarch's reflections in the *Canzoniere* are intended to manage the pain, magnified in solitude, of his unrequited love for Laura. And finding solace in regret and melancholy has been a central feature of Chinese poetry for millennia, as when Juan Chi says:

> I only fear that, in a moment,
> My life will disintegrate in the wind.
> I've always walked on thin ice.
> But no one knows it![59]

Likewise, the Indian hermit-poet Bhartrihari seems to have been more than half in love with easeful death but found solace in poetic expression of life's woes. "All desire for pleasure has waned," he laments in one poem. Friends and colleagues have passed on, he can't walk without a cane, and his eyes are veiled in darkness: "How bold this body is to fear the final blow of death."[60] There is a difference between being in love with death and confronting its reality. But the two are so commonly combined and, as in the case of Petrarch, Juan Chi, and Bhartrihari, so poetically poignant that I, for one, am willing to admit the artistic value of these melancholy ruminations.

As for the stronger asceticism of religious hermits such as Anthony or Mahavira, it is difficult *not* to agree with Masson that some ascetics in the eremitism of India and early Christianity must have employed their vast and imaginative menu of ascetic practices—spending the night in mosquito-infested swamps, living like a cow, hanging perpetually upside down from a tree-limb, and so on—as psychotic defense mechanisms pure and simple, where the pain inflicted is the objective rather than a means to a higher end. But perversion enters the picture when we lose our sense of perspective and dive mindlessly into fanaticism, when we find ourselves content with such strange and tortuous psychological tricks.

For the most part, it seems to me that spiritually adventurous hermits, including most of the Desert Fathers, did not lose their balance. As we have heard, they were not at all preoccupied with intense asceticism, and they emphasized strongly that fasting and all-night vigils are not ends in themselves, but only means to achieving God's grace. As the Sufis rejected harsh ascetic practices as hindrances to union with the Infinite, so the Buddha is said to have achieved enlightenment just at the time when he turned away from his self-starvation under the Bodhi Tree and ate a bowl of porridge. In one of his later sermons, the Buddha says that Mara, Hindu god of pestilence and mortal disease, then appeared, to tell him that by giving up his self-mortification he had gone astray and was not yet enlightened. But the Buddha replied:

> I understand how these austere ascetic practices are entirely destructive to my purpose like oar and rudder in a ship on land. I develop the path of morality, concentration and insight for the realization of the truth and I have attained supreme purity. O Mara, you are vanquished.[61]

At the same time, the Buddha continued to recommend a balanced asceticism in the form of mendicancy and self control. And as I have already argued on behalf of extreme ascetic and solitary practices, it may be that such intensity, commitment, and suffering are necessary to finally free the self from selfish distractions so as to provide a sense of joy, not to mention union with the divine. If this is merely psychotic play-acting, how can we explain the volumes of homespun philosophy of the Desert Fathers or Mahavira's intricate anti-theology? Surely these are not ruses or self-delusions designed to conceal a psychological perversion "discovered" only a century ago by modern scientists.

Much the same can be said about the theory that would attribute the religious hermit's happiness or bliss to the psychiatric concept of regression. In his 1931 paper primly titled "Buddhistic Training as an Artificial Catatonia," F. Alexander posits that the solitude and meditation techniques of Buddhist training work by means of "a withdrawal of libido from the world to be reinvested in the ego until an intra-uterine narcissism is achieved—'the pure narcissism of the sperm.'"[62] And according to Freud, the "oceanic feeling" which the mystic aims to achieve is merely "memory of a relatively undifferentiated infantile ego state."[63] In this scenario, the hermit or recluse uses ascetic training to tear away the normal faculties of reason and perception developed through adulthood in order to regress to a dumb but blissful child-like state—in other words, a "return to the womb" that can supply the regressor with a godlike feeling of omnipotence or ecstatic delusions of grandeur. It is possible, for example, to apply that interpretation to Julian of Norwich's vision of herself, along with Christ, as larger than the entire universe.

But again, as there are degrees of masochism, so there may are different forms and degrees of regression. Dr. Freud may have thought he was being boldly objective by asserting that regression is merely a desperate and pointless defense mechanism. But his contemporary Rilke, recommends it highly. In fact, one gets the impression that Rilke spent his entire poetic life advocating a return to the marvelous solitude of early youth, as he says in one of his letters to the young poet he refers to as Mr. Kappus:

> What is necessary, after all, is only this: solitude, great inner solitude. To walk inside yourself and meet no one for hours—that is what you must be able to attain. To be solitary as you were when you were a child, when the grownups walked around involved with matters that seemed large and important because *they* looked so busy and because you didn't understand a thing about what they were doing...
>
> Think, dear Sir, of the world you carry inside you, and call this thinking whatever you want to: a remembering of your own childhood or a yearning toward future of your own—only be attentive to what is arising within you, and place that above everything you perceive around you.[64]

There is no doubt that this sort of "regression" fueled Rilke's creativity. It is obvious that his poetry is not a concatenation of self-intoxicating appeals to return to an infantile ego-state, but rather an invitation to a deeper mental adventure and an authentic cause for joy.

Likewise, we might do well to listen more closely to the French philosopher Gaston Bachelard on these matters. "In his happy solitudes," writes Bachelard, "the dreaming child knows the cosmic reveries which unite us to the world." There are moments in which every child "is the astonishment of being." Even as we grow older, says Bachelard, "childhood remains within us a principle of deep life, of life always in harmony with the possibilities of new beginnings."[65]

SELF-AGGRANDIZEMENT

While on the subject of negative-minded solitudes, this is as good a place as any to consider that the antics of some Friends—the showy rejection of society or the extraordinary physical feats such as pole-sitting and even the self-immolation—may simply be attention-getting devices. Ironically, they may be used to increase the soloist's stature in the eyes of the very society they have supposedly rejected. But, again, there is a bright side in the effects that even apparently self-interested solitudes may bring about for the individual and for society.

Seclusion, in itself, regales the hermit with a convenient aura of mystery and sagacity. There is a natural human tendency to assume that anyone capable of living away from the comforts and attractions of society must be an extraordinary person, a curmudgeonly misogynist perhaps, but possibly a saint or a wizard with unusual spiritual or intellectual powers.

In every culture, the literature of solitude is replete with stories of nobles who pay visits to saints or sages in their hermitages. The main purpose of these tales is to show that the spiritual life of the hermit is greater than that of the most powerful king, as when King Visvamitra confronted the hermit Vasistha in the forest and declared that his occult powers—and we may assume, his spiritual wisdom—were far greater than that of any worldly noble. Visvamitra went on to become a great hermit himself, and the stories of Emperor Huang Ti and King William of Orange convey the same moral.

Ironically, in those eras when the solitude became a widely acknowledged feature of society it was also a source of income for hermits. Shamans are typically paid in kind for their mystic services in the form of food, clothing, or other valuables. Indian monks and recluses have from ancient times earned their way in society by begging, through which food and lodging are received implicitly in return for blessings bestowed.

According to the Hindu *Artha Sastra,* some ascetic recluses were routinely paid to serve as spies by using their spiritual status as a means for infiltrating opposing kingdoms.[66] And in the West, there were many eremitic descendants of the Desert Fathers who were contracted at annual salaries to be the resident holy men, or "ornamental hermits," in the gardens of English estates.

There is, for instance, an elegant hermitage on the grounds of Warkworth Castle in Northumberland, England, with its fine gothic arches, alter, piscina, quatrefoil window, and hagioscope all hewn out of solid rock. In the early sixteenth century, hermits who resided there were patronized by the earl of Northumberland. In return for saying prayers for a number of nobles listed by the earl, each successive hermit received pasture for twelve cows, a garden, twenty loads of firewood, fish every Sunday, and £20 a year.

That a hermit's prime motivation may be power over others is still a more damning critique. It is all too easy to imagine, for instance, that the Anatolian pole-sitting hermits such as Saint Simeon must have felt a sense of accomplishment from the fact that so many followers gathered around them to ask their blessings and advice, to care for their needs, and to worship them—which is why the column on which Simeon resided for thirty years was several times built higher the better to protect him from his throngs of followers.

As Nietzsche puts it, when the religious hermit shows us that he is striving for a higher world, "he wants to fly longer and farther and higher than men of affirmation." As such a hermit "stands before us, enveloped in his cowl, and as the soul of a hairshirt," says Nietzsche, he derives satisfaction from the effect he makes upon us:

> He wants to keep concealed from us his desire, his pride, his intention of flying above us.—Yes. He is wiser than we thought, and so courteous towards us—this affirmer! For that is what he is, like us, even in his self-renunciation.[67]

Nietzsche maintains that this striving for power can be put to good use so long as it is truthful and grounded in real earthly life. But Masson asserts that the hermit's asceticism is only a show. "The image of the monk who lives alone," he argues, "strikes the reader as so much bravado—like the child who packs his bags and leaves for the open country, all the while desperately awaiting the sign from his parents that will allow him to abandon his spite and rush to the waiting arms of the loving parent."[68] Applying that theory to the Indian adolescent—"who has been forced by his culture to make what can only be termed pathologically excessive restrictions on his libidinal life"—Masson reasons that the ascetics of the subcontinent (and all others) take vengeance "through a mocking compliance by later turning into a genuine ascetic who massively and permanently denies all physical enjoyment. It is as if he is telling his parents: 'You wanted me to renounce. I will do more than you ever expected; I will renounce everything—you included.'"[69] Thus, in addition to any self-aggrandizing pleasure that the hermit-ascetic may thereby enjoy, he or she may also savor the satisfactions of revenge.

No doubt, these are real aspects of time alone that must be accounted for in any serious psychology of solitude. Nevertheless, we must acknowledge again that all human life is underpinned by complex motivations that may seem pitiful or perverse to some observers but which can nevertheless bear constructive results. The show-off strategies of some Friends were mingled with elements of public protest of value to society. Diogenes the Cynic may have had reason to harbor a grudge against society, as his family was disgraced and exiled from his native home in Sinope when his father was convicted, rightly or wrongly, of debasing the coinage. But his words and deeds later served to demonstrate the value of a simple life and to take some of the wind out of Plato's idealist philosophy. He also proclaimed that freedom of speech is the most beautiful thing in the world; and he helped to turn the focus of Greek thought onto the value of the individual, a development which contributed to the later spread of Christianity. There is no doubt his protests were well accepted and highly influential. Alexander himself said, "Had I not been Alexander, I should have liked to be Diogenes."[70]

Mahatma Gandhi found political value in the showiness of radical simplicity, which led to a philosophy of peaceful resistance that influenced

Martin Luther King's campaign for social equality in the United States. In effect, that is precisely what the reclusive lives of the Desert Fathers did to promote Christianity during the last centuries of the Roman Empire, and it is the same leverage that Chinese recluse scholars exerted against unjust regimes.

We may critique the use of that power if we disagree with the ends to which it is put. As a public relations man myself, I can say that such "grandstanding" seclusion and an associated projection of honesty and simplicity of life will work, just as any positive publicity can provide political or economic leverage to achieve goals in the world. But it does not mean that such a public hermit may not have experienced the creative and joyful fruits of solitude in other ways.

One possible sign of sincerity is that religious Friends such as the Desert Father Saint Hilarion moved repeatedly to even more remote retreats to escape well-meaning cave-followers—which, of course, only served to increase his fame. Moreover, with a few exceptions such as Diogenes and Peregrinus, few Friends intentionally advertised their solitude or the asceticism. While I have seen many manuals dedicated to helping otherwise reclusive authors achieve fame and fortune through publishing, I have never seen such a manual for hermits. In the end, though, we can never be completely sure, for the sincerity or falseness of the hermit's solitude lies only within his or her own head.

Enlightenment

If you are at all like me, the thoughts in the last two sections gave you a rather warm feeling, a reassuring sense that solitude can be something other than a vainglorious pose or a psychotic desire for a return to the womb. But we have yet to understand why Lady Solitude can bestow the protracted "bliss of angels" that the Desert Fathers of Egypt talked about or the *quamaneq* enlightenment described by Iglulik shamans.

Seen from that perspective, her creative benefits, the escape to simplicity that she encourages, and her enjoyable idleness are still rather weak attempts to make the best of a bad situation. They may afford much, but in the end they change little. They do not answer the unanswered questions of human existence. "We see that this whole world is decaying," says King Brihadratha, so "what is the good of enjoyment of desires?" As Petrarch put it in his *Letter to Posterity*, "But alas! nothing mortal is enduring and there is nothing sweet which sooner or later does not become bitter."[71] Death, to paraphrase Horace, is still the finish line for all.[72]

We can see why Horace might be temporarily "charmed" in his quiet Sabine retreat and, metaphorically at least, how he might "rise up as high as heaven." But it is still difficult to fathom why some Friends seem literally to have transported their souls to heaven, nirvana, or some such realm, apparently to abide there permanently. Not only did the Buddha achieve such raptures in his solitude, it is said that his enlightenment was so comprehensive that he literally conquered death and all suffering throughout the universe, past, present, and future. Even if we take this achievement metaphorically, we have to admit that the friendly (and not-so-friendly) features of lonely joy that we have been discussing cannot yet account for the bliss of enlightenment.

No doubt, the word "enlightenment" covers a lot of very tricky ground—from attaining a state of what the Hindus call "liberation," the

Buddhists "nirvana," and the Chinese Taoists "the Tao" to what Christians are more likely to call "the grace of God." For purposes of this psychoanalysis, I will take the term enlightenment in its ordinary-language sense to be synonymous with these and other similar religious terms.

I will also include a form of enlightenment that is, for want of a better term, more secular. It could, for example, be a state or realization akin to what some modern psychologists call "the process of individuation." As Storr puts it, individuation is a condition of wholeness and integration in which "the different elements of the psyche, both conscious and unconscious, become welded together in a new unity."[73] Jung wrote that this new integration is an internal matter, "an attitude that is beyond the reach of emotional entanglements and violent shocks—a consciousness detached from the world."[74]

The "enlightenment" that Storr and Jung are referring to is probably about the same thing that Abraham Maslow calls peak experience, which experiences are typically associated with a feeling that the universe is "perceived as an integrated and unified whole." They may or may not lead to a "solution" to the problem of human suffering and death, but they can, says Maslow, produce a clear perception that "the universe is all of a piece and one has one's place in it." In his research, Maslow found that peak experiences may be egoless, self-validating, timeless, beautiful, humbling, frightening, and perplexing. They typically involve "a sense of the sacred glimpsed *in* and *through* the particular instance of the momentary, the secular, and the worldly." Like Bergson, Maslow suggests that such experiences are in fact the original mystic raptures from which the great religions derive and which they ultimately hold in common. "Usually, perhaps always," he explains, "the prophets of high religions have had these experiences when they were alone." Organized religion, he adds, can be seen as the "punch card or IBM version" of that original revelation designed to make it "suitable for group use or administrative convenience."[75]

These words pointing to enlightenment or something like it are, of course, just that—words. As I am writing this, I get the feeling that I am attempting to swim with Maslow, et al, but we all have our winter clothes on. We may take comfort, however, albeit cold comfort, in the reality that most of those who would speak of enlightenment will agree that it is real and powerful, but ultimately indefinable. So we will leave it at that.

How is it then that some clever Friends of Solitude have been able to achieve enlightenment or quasi-enlightenment so un-defined? In short, my "answer"—more an intrepid hypothesis—is that the same solo-mechanisms underpinning creative and joyful solitude are at work in blissful, enlightening solitude. But now they are taken to the nth degree, as it were, such that the delights of being alone may combine with solitude's inspirational powers to accommodate a profound understanding of and adjustment to the realities of life.

DETACHMENT

It is no surprise that those Friends whose lives and writings are most associated with enlightenment tend to take solitude to extremes. And many, as we have heard, advocate a complete isolation from all created, illusory things. The hope, simply stated, is that one might thereby migrate from this world of pain and illusion to a divine region of bliss and purity of thought, where all things work in harmony, and all the unanswered questions are answered. That strategy is reasonable, of course. For, as Emerson puts it, "thought makes free." It "dissolves the material universe by carrying the mind up into a sphere where all is plastic."[76]

Indeed, such an abstract realm might be a fine place to live forever like an angel, an idea in the mind of God, or an ineffable something in the Parmenidean "heart of well-rounded Truth." By climbing out of Plato's cave we might achieve true happiness and immortality in a realm of Truth beyond all reflected images. As Diotima told Socrates, by living "apart and alone" and "having brought forth and nurtured true goodness" such a man or woman "will have the privilege of being beloved of God, and become, if ever a man can, immortal himself."[77]

Plotinus likewise plotted the course to that immortal realm through a flight to the Primal Beauty of the Alone. "To attain it," he says, "is for those that will take the upward path," and enter the celebrations of the Mysteries laying aside garments, "in nakedness, until passing on the upward way all that is other than God, each in the solitude of himself shall behold that solitary-dwelling Existence, the Apart, the Unmingled, the Pure."[78] Dionysius the Areopagite, as we have heard, counsels a similar flight from "all things in this world of nothingness" to a true perception of God: "where the simple, absolute, and unchangeable mysteries of heavenly Truth lie hidden in the dazzling obscurity of the secret Silence."[79] Rabi'a echoes the same hope when she says, speaking of the unnamable God of All: "Ever since I knew him, I turned my back on all creatures." So it was with Julian of Norwich: "No soul can rest," she said, "until it is detached from all creation."

Among Indian philosophies of isolation, the Jains represent the most extreme form, if not the most interesting case of such antiworldliness. For the Jains are also anti-idealist. They believe, instead, that the universe runs on an entirely material process of karma; there is no brahman, just things themselves that interact over time according to the moral laws of reward and retribution. It follows, therefore, that it is only through complete isolation from all the sin and ugliness of the world, over countless rebirths, that one can successfully rise above any further incarnation, finally to achieve a state that the Jains in fact call "Isolation."

Mahavira is said to have risen to that state after having renounced worldly life, when he lived in a state of wandering homelessness. He was "single and alone like the horn of a rhinoceros…free like a bird, steady and firm like Mount Mandara, deep like the ocean, mild like the moon, refulgent like the sun, pure like excellent gold; like the earth he patiently bore everything; like a well-kindled fire he shone in his splendor."[80] Then, in the summer of the thirteenth year of his homeless wandering, having fasted for days and while in deep meditation, Mahavira is said to have "reached the highest knowledge and intuition, called *Kevala* [Isolation], which is infinite, supreme, unobstructed, unimpeded, complete, and full."[81]

From a commonsense point of view, there is an obvious problem with these strategies for enlightenment in that they posit a separate world of truth, which may simply be a matter of wishful thinking. For what if there is no reincarnation; or even if there is, what if we continue our series of rebirths to discover that there is no highest tip of the universe, that it was just a metaphor for something more profound? What if, as the result of an ardent escape from illusion, we confront the Parmenidean goddess or the Uncreated face-to-face and they do not cooperate or they simply inform us that, like Wrong-Way Corrigan, we have only succeeded in making a useless touchdown at our own goal? Worldly life, with all its messiness and temporality, was already the greatest gift we could have received, they might say. And what if we can't find them at all, because they do not exist?

Fortunately, there is another way of thinking about detachment that does not require—and does not contradict—recourse to either a transcendent divine essence or laws of karma. It is what Dionysius calls "the unceasing and absolute renunciation of thyself" and what others specify, not as a renunciation of the world, but a relinquishing of all selfish desire for worldly things. If you do not renounce desire a hundred times, says Fakhruddin 'Iraqi, you will never embrace your Desire. As a Sufi, 'Iraqi's Desire (with a capital "D") is union with the infinite God. But if we hold back on specifying that indefinable goal for a moment, we can substitute the all-encompassing word enlightenment: "If you do not renounce desire, you will never attain enlightenment."

The logic of detachment is as simple as it is hard hitting, which probably explains its pervasiveness in every culture of solitude, secular as well as religious. Essentially, it takes Epicurus' management of desire to extremes—in fact, down to "zero." Stated another way, if you have nothing, you have nothing to lose; if you desire nothing you have everything to win. One divided by zero is infinity.

This spiritual strategy has been known by many names: surrender, disinterest, equanimity, apatheia, humility, emptiness, "breaking the will." As a first step, the world renouncer says, in essence, that there is no hope of achieving a true and lasting happiness in the world as it appears to us viewed through the lens of desire. The only true course, therefore, is to disassociate one's self from the whole world, fruit and seed alike. The natural conclusion from that line of reasoning is suicide, as Hamlet contemplated and the Greek and Roman Stoics offered as a commonsensical escape when the sea of troubles became overwhelming. But logically, continues the renunciate, suicide is just another form of self-caring and desire. So truly to give up desire, one must give up desire for death, perhaps even desire for enlightenment, along with one's incessant pessimism.

As a second step, then, one may think: "Instead of isolating myself from the world, why not just give up the idea that I deserve or might win any further rewards from the world than the mysterious majesty of existence that already presents itself before me? What more do I want?" At that point, something miraculous seems to happen. For aside from all the philosophy and religious dogma that later come into play to quicken the process, optimism begins to grow, seemingly from nothing.

Here is how Yajnavalkya explained it toward the end of one of his famous dialogues with King Janaka around the ninth or tenth century before Christ:

> He who is without desire, who is freed from desire, whose desire is satisfied, whose desire is the Soul—his breaths do not depart. Being very Brahma, he goes to Brahma.[82]

For Yajnavalkya, as for so many others, the object of detachment is to get closer to the divine. But if one believes that one's essential soul and the essence of the universe—atman and brahman—are the same thing, there is no valid reason why its realization may not also be corporeal. As Chuang Tzu knew, the strategy of zero desire must work in both realms. In characteristically direct prose, he advises:

> If you abandon the affairs of the world, your body will be without toil. If you forget life, your vitality will be unimpaired.[83]

William James is saying about the same thing in this description of release that leads, if not to full-blown enlightenment or heavenly bliss in the traditional sense, at least to a sense of well-being beyond joy:

> The transition from tenseness, self-responsibility, and worry, to equanimity, receptivity, and peace, is the most wonderful of all those shiftings of inner equilibrium, those changes of the personal center of energy, which I have analyzed so often; and the chief wonder of it is that it so often comes about, not by doing, but by simply relaxing and throwing the burden down.[84]

As James implies, there is something magical about this flight from desire and worry. That in itself might be the eternal secret of human happiness and bliss. But several obvious and very serious questions remain: How is it that we can possibly muster enough energy and wisdom to give up all desires without giving up life itself? And what is it that we should give up? Are we to renounce all desires, including the desire for truth and blissful union with the uncreated essence of things?

The history of solitude as we have reviewed it does not contain simple answers to these questions, but the Friends do point the way to answers of a sort in an often wayward and mystically-charged language which is appropriate to the subject. Invariably, a relative level of detachment is as a starting point from which there are three broad strategies for enhancing the intensity of that detachment.

Two of these parallel the main paths to spiritual enlightenment in Indian mystic philosophy, as laid out by the god Krishna in the Bhagavadgita. One has to do with love and the redirection of human passions; it is what the Gita calls *bhaktimarg*, the path of devotion to the divine. The other pertains more to the mind; it is what the Gita calls *jnanamarg*, the path of "knowing." But, as we will see, the *Cloud* author was closer to the mark when he called it *unknowing*. To these two we may add what I will term the path of experience, under which rubric I will include the psychological shocks or dark night experiences that can bring about salutary changes in perspective.

SELFLESS LOVE

We've seen that sublimation can provide a sensational boost to creativity in solitude, and there is little doubt that the same energy can be enjoyed in its own right. Together, the two effects may be sufficiently strong to elevate detached contemplation to the warmth of a higher plane of joy, if not the bliss of illumination.

Among the most palpable demonstrations of this comes from those soloists who report that they can, through intense solitary meditation, generate sufficient inner heat to warm themselves in the coldest weather.

We've heard that by remaining completely still, the Hudson's Bay shaman Igjugarjuk was able to stay alive while sitting naked in an igloo for an entire month and, in the course of that trial, to achieve enlightenment. Perhaps that is why the Desert Father Abba Joseph told his followers that "You cannot be a monk unless you become like a consuming fire." The delightful "fire of love" that Richard Rolle felt when meditating alone for years in his hermitage seems to involve a similar process.

Rolle says that the feeling came entirely from within and had no material cause, "but was the gift of my Maker." Nevertheless, based in her experiences in Tibet, Alexandra David-Neel suggests that the ability to generate inner heat may come about through a somewhat more mundane process. The technique, known as *tumo*, is what enabled the Tibetan hermit-saint Milarepa to reside for nine years scantily clothed in cold mountain caves. But David-Neel adds that she too learned that art by following a venerable lama's instructions to "go to a lonely spot, bathe in an icy mountain stream, and then, without drying my body or putting on my clothes, to spend the night motionless in meditation."[85] She describes an alternative visualization which can enable any serious-minded adept to generate tumo within a few hours by concentrating on a thin band of fire down the length of the body then gradually widening the band through the power of meditation until it fills one's entire frame. David-Neel adds that this esoteric method once came in handy when she used it to warm herself after she fell into a mountain river and her clothing literally froze on her body.

There is another form of tumo that is used more precisely for purposes of enlightenment and appears to be more in line with Rolle's fire of love. It arises spontaneously, says David-Neel, "in the course of peculiar raptures and, gradually, folds the mystic in the 'soft, warm mantle of the gods.'"[86] Perhaps there is some physical explanation for this psychic phenomenon. The heat may be unleashed as a byproduct of intense meditation by a widening of the arteries or some chemical reaction or other yet unknown to medicine. It may work something like adrenaline or the narcotic effect of endorphins or other peptides, which are generated internally by long-distance runners and women in childbirth. According to Tibetan mystic lore, however, the warmth seems to derive from a process of sublimation with an explicitly sexual origin.

Some lamas, says David-Neel, describe tumo as "the subtle fire which warms the generative fluid and drives the energy in it, 'till it runs all over the body along the tiny channels of the *tsas* [veins, arteries, and nerves]." In support of that theory, she cites the story of Lama Reschungpa, whose young wife, unhappy with his selfish austerities, stabbed him one day to find that sperm instead of blood ran out of the wound. Perhaps she thought that this was the only way she could receive the seed of her celibate husband. The more sagacious lamas that David-Neel spoke with on this subject, however, emphasized that tumo is not sperm in the gross material sense, but rather an "invisible energy (*shugs*)" which fills the body, not with generative fluid, but with generative force.[87]

A similar linkage between love energy and enlightenment is common across the history of solitude. The prophetess Diotima, according to Socrates, said that the power of Eros can drive a thoughtful soul not only to understanding of Truth and Beauty, but to the bliss of immortality. Ruysbroek, we recall, advised that one can only become a bride of Christ through a "fierce tumult of love." And the author of the *Ancren Wisse*, the twelfth-century guide for Christian anchoresses, likewise advised female hermits to "forget the world," then to redirect their natural sexual yearnings to a higher plane:

> Stretch out your love to Jesus Christ. You have won Him! Touch him with as much love as you sometimes feel for a man. He is yours to do with all that you will.[88]

John Climacus was still more explicit about the spiritual power of love in *The Ladder of Divine Ascent*. It is literally eroticism, he writes, which gives chaste souls the energy or motivation to climb the spiritual ladder to God: "I have watched impure souls mad for physical love, but turning what they know of such love into a reason for penance and transferring that same capacity for love to the Lord."[89] The object is to drive out bodily love by means of spiritual love. "My love," God whispers to John's soul at the top rung of his ladder to heaven, "you will never be able to know how beautiful I am unless you get away from the grossness of the flesh." The reward of that vigorous sublimation, God adds, is great: "…faith, hope, and love, these three. But love is the greatest of them all." "Love," Climacus explains, "grants prophesy, miracles. It is an abyss of illumination, a fountain of fire, bubbling up to inflame a thirsty soul. It is the condition of angels, and the progress of eternity."[90]

Suppose, then, that sublimation in solitude may provide the energy one needs to climb metaphorically out of Plato's cave to an ideal and blissful world of Form or to God's Heavenly Kingdom. And suppose that accumulation of the inner force of love might serve to multiply the already blissful effect of renunciation. That is a potent combination, but the strategy of love or devotion to the divine may have other advantages. Depending on one's belief, it may prepare the way through surrender and humility for an enlightening action from God Himself who descends to minister the devoted soul; or, in nonreligious terms, love may simply fuel faith in the ultimate order of things, whatever that turns out to be.

Strange as it may seem, this is where Friends as diverse as Jesus, Krishna, Rumi, and even Nietzsche meet. For Christians it is a matter of taking Christ into one's heart through love, whereby one has the hope of receiving greater divine love in return. For many Hindus it may be loving devotion to Krishna, allowing him to drive the chariot of one's life. "Renounce all actions to me and worship me, meditating with singular discipline," says Krishna in the Bhagavadgita. When men are "intent on me" and "entrust reason to me," he adds, "I soon arise to rescue them from the ocean of death and rebirth."[91]

For Rumi, love is the only worthwhile thing in the world:

> That spirit which does not wear
> the inner garment of Love
> should never have been.
> Its being is just shame.[92]

Tellingly, Rumi emphasizes that love and renunciation are the same. "If they ask what Love is," he says, "tell them it is the sacrifice of will. For if you have not left your will behind, you have no will at all."[93]

For Nietzsche, the way to his brand of "enlightenment" is likewise through the energy of love. But in his case, it is not specifically love of God, but something called love of one's fate. In *Ecce Homo*, he proclaims that

> My formula for greatness in a human being is *amor fati*, that one wants nothing to be different, not forward, not backward, not in all eternity. Not merely bear what is necessary, still less conceal it—all idealism is mendaciousness in the face of what is necessary—but love it.[94]

The likes of Nietzsche, of course, make a point of rejecting all abstract notions of deity or any ideal realm of Truth. But what is the difference between loving God and loving the fate that God has given us? Not all Friends, even the devotionalists among them, actually met God face-to-face. In fact they tend to be suspicious of those who say they did so. We have heard the Desert Fathers warn that "If you see a young monk by his own will climbing up into heaven, take him by the foot at the throw him to the ground." "If you see the Buddha on the road, kill him!" is a famous Zen statement. And in the last century Thomas Merton made a point of saying that the hermit sitting in his cell will have his stomach aches like any other man and will spend most of his time dwelling in the raw reality of existence without any word from on high. Such contemplation, says Merton, is essentially "a listening in silence, an expectancy." The contemplative in solitude does not anticipate a special kind of transformation; nor does he demand light instead of darkness—rather:

> He waits on the Word of God in silence, and when he is 'answered,' it is not so much by a word that bursts into his silence. It is by his silence itself suddenly, inexplicably, revealing itself to him as a word of great power.[95]

In the hermit's cave, the question of whether one will meet God may therefore be moot. Like Moses, one may see only His hind parts. It is certain that the hermit will meet the essence of human existence head on; and, probably, he will find a way to love that fate and reality. Sitting in his cell it may occur to him, as it has to so many others, that love is the essence of all, what Dylan Thomas called "the force that through the green fuse drives the flower." He may sense that the fire which lights the universe is the same as that which lights the soul, as does Sakayanya in the *Maitri Upanishad*: "For as it has been said, 'He who is in the fire, and he who is here in the heart, and he who is in yonder sun—he is one.'"

One could also quote Rabi'a and dozens of other enlightened Friends on the value of selfless love. But I will be satisfied here to quote a thought by Carlo Carretto, which expresses the power of the eremitic equation—*detachment X love = bliss*—about as clearly as can be. I found it many years ago in his book *In Search of the Beyond*. But, to my mind, there is nothing "beyond" or idealist about it:

> Yes, to become lowly, lowlier still—as lowly as possible. This is the great secret of the mystical life. And then, having reduced oneself to a single point and become nothing more than a soul which watches attentively and a heart which loves, to get used to a complete reversal of the usual position—the eternal position of pride, and the uneasy position of the ego which always sees itself as the center of the universe.[96]

The bliss-seeking heart, then, is humble to the point of complete renunciation of desire and loves either god or the world, or both. Note that Senior Carretto includes another aspect of eremitic bliss in his spiritual counsel: a soul that watches attentively. That points to a second widespread means for magnifying the effects of detachment: philosophy.

THOUGHTLESS PHILOSOPHY

The notion that one may achieve enlightenment through philosophy or any form of reasoning sounds fishy. But what we hear across the history of solitude is not that enlightenment may be obtained by thinking in the ordinary twenty-first-century sense of the term, but rather through a kind of thinking that is more akin to the alert reverie characteristic of creative and joyful solitude. I call it "thoughtless philosophy" because it is philosophy in the original sense of the term, which means "love of wisdom." It is "thoughtless" because one of the most consistent admonitions among the

Friends of Solitude is that one can only achieve the bliss of enlightenment by unloading one's baggage of habits and self-imposed illusions though *not* thinking.

In India, as we have heard, Yajnavalkya insisted that true understanding is "not this, not that." In ancient China, Master Kuang advised the Yellow Emperor that the only way to understand and live in the essence of things is to be perfectly still and quiescent and to destroy all concepts. Philo's advice to "be silent and hear" seems to say the same thing. In Christianity, that strategy is typified by the *via negativa* of Dionysius and *Cloud* author's advice that true understanding of the divine can only come in a "cloud of unknowing." And al-Ghazali maintained that mystic experience in such a cloud, or whatever one wishes to call it, is the most profound form of knowing—"the light of the lamp of prophetic revelation."

Again, words are getting in our way. Perhaps we can begin to understand if we recognize that thinking, to say the least, occurs in a complex, mysterious realm, which we do not fully comprehend and, perhaps, never will. It is clear, however, that there is thinking…and then there is thinking. There is logical thinking, left-brain thinking, right-brain thinking, primitive thinking, intuitive thinking, daydreaming, ecstatic thinking, "out-of-the-box" thinking, and so on. Each of these may be prone to a wishy-washy mysticism and wish-fulfilling fantasy. But we have already seen that even the most apparently illogical of these processes may hold insights and inspirations for which thinking is a misleading label. They may be akin, for example, to the mysterious goings-on in the mind of a creative artist who gives life and spontaneity to a work of art or the blissful sense of union with the oneness of things that Thoreau and Wang Wei felt deeply as they drifted lonely on their separate lakes, when they ceased to "live" and "began to be."

In this light, the call for thoughtless philosophy is simply a call for a more thoroughgoing mental-spiritual solitude that is alert to being. In essence, the mystic Friends are telling us that we may never get the "subtle feeling called solitude" until we forget rigid logic, unexamined supposition, cultural baggage, and all the ingrained habits of dogma and tradition, including preprogrammed techniques of meditation. In the same way, we must forget the myriad distractions that the mind creates each instant—the fears, regrets, pains, and sorrows that come from society—and get down to real thinking about "what the inner spirit brings."

As we wipe all ordinary thoughts from our minds, we may begin to "think" in a different way, not with our minds, perhaps, but with our souls. Listening to Zen Master Dogen, we may learn the art of "nonthinking." To explain, Dogen cites the story of Great Master Hongdao who was asked by a monk: "What is thinking in steadfast composure like?" When the master answered, "Think not thinking," the monk asked what that is, and the master offered this subtle clarification: "Nonthinking." That does not seem to bring us much closer to understanding, at least in translation. Nevertheless, knowing something of Dogen's Soto Zen, we may interpret "not thinking" as referring to a complete emptiness of mind, which may be either impossible or unproductive, since it may just be empty-headedness or a frozen death-like mental state. Nonthinking, by contrast, would be an unrestricted state of mind in which one may stand back from thoughts, allowing them to flow as they will, trying neither to develop nor suppress them. That separation from thoughts may allow us to experience our souls, something inexpressible between our souls and or thoughts, or just the essential emptiness underlying thoughts and things.[97]

If all this seems unnecessarily esoteric, think of it this way: nonthinking may be something like that which financial journalists try to evoke when economists refuse to give an intuitive opinion, by saying—"Tell me what you feel, in your gut." In this regard, the best practical advice may be to forget about confusing matters such as thinking and nonthinking altogether. In the same spirit, the anonymous author of the *Cloud of Unknowing* recommends that we put *everything* material and spiritual beneath a cloud of forgetting. Without forgetting everything inside and outside consciousness, he says, there is no chance of getting nearer to God.

Chuang Tzu likewise emphasizes again and again that to "understand" the Way one must forget things, as well as thinking—

> Only when there is no pondering and no cognition will you get to know the Way. Only when you have no surroundings and follow no practices will you find rest in the Way. Only when there is no path and no procedure can you get to the Way.[98]

Buddha, who challenged anyone to dissect the logic of his path to enlightenment, preached a similar mindlessness to achieve what he called "living in the fullness of the void." What one needs, he explains to his disciple Ananda in a dialogue generally translated as "Lesser Discourse on Emptiness," is the right mind-set. It can be accomplished in successive stages. He tells Ananda to shift his mind from the creaturely, day-to-day perception of villages or human beings to a "perception of the forest." Going several metaphysical steps further, Ananda should direct his mind away from all earthly thoughts to thoughts of "the sphere of infinite space"—then away from that to "the perception that consciousness itself is nothing." Going still further, he directs Ananda to reside in "the sphere of neither-perception-nor-nonperception," and finally away from that, too, to "the concentration of mind wherein awareness and feeling cease." That, says the Buddha, is the "true, not mistaken and utterly purified and incomparably highest realization of the void"—in a word, enlightenment.[99]

In the modern West, Paul Valéry came to about the same conclusion that thought is best when it comes from a place other than (ordinary) thought. Speaking through his experimental character Monsieur Teste, he speculates that "There are individuals who feel that their senses separate them from the real, from being." Such thinkers say, simply—"Away with everything that I might see!" "What I see blinds me," says Teste "What I hear deafens me. That by which I know makes me ignorant. I am ignorant inasmuch, and insofar, as I know."[100]

Unknowing, forgetting, holding aloof even from joy—it all sounds rather cool, not to say hard-hearted. But many of the Friends emphasized that the energy of love and philosophical reverie may work together. The *Cloud* author, we recall, emphasized that the objective of unknowning is always divine love and that the cloud may be pierced by a "dart of love." Sufis such as al-Ghazali spent a great deal of time philosophizing about the world and enlightenment, but they always maintained that one can only light the lamp of revelation through love in a tavern of ruin. And Socrates seems to have taken Diotima's admonition to heart that true philosophy is powered by Eros. Nietzsche speculates, longingly it seems, that many ancient Greek philosophers did the same. Referring, I think, to Friends from Epimenides to Heraclitus, he says that such thinkers prided themselves in, and were appreciated for, the passionate, inspired power of their philosophical sportings. "To abstract oneself from sensory perception, to exalt oneself to contemplation of abstractions—that was at one time actually felt as exaltation," he says, adding:

> To revel in pallid images of words and things, to sport with such invisible, inaudible, impalpable beings, was, out of contempt for the sensorily tangible, seductive, and evil world, felt as a life in another higher world. "These abstracta are certainly not seductive, but they can offer us guidance!"—with that one lifted oneself upwards. It is not the content of these sportings of spirituality, it is they themselves which constituted "the higher life" in the prehistoric ages of science.[101]

Nietzsche laments that we can no longer quite enter into this feeling. But I'm not convinced that such exultant moods are entirely lost in modern times. Ludwig Wittgenstein, for one, is said to have abstracted himself with remarkable intensity when solving a philosophical problem in his head—like a teakettle at the boil, or a snorting athlete pressing weights just beyond his maximum, or, indeed, a mother giving birth. There is also a lingering notion among Wittgenstein aficionados that his kind of superphilosophizing is the "higher life."

Wittgenstein spent much of his time thinking about thinking, particularly logical thinking. In his early life, while working on his first groundbreaking philosophical work, *Tractatus Logico Philosophicus*, he spent a year in a remote hut in Norway thinking and writing. Many of the readers of that work took him to be a coldly mathematical analytical philosopher, as he seemed to imply in statements such as "The facts in logical space are the world" and "Whereof one cannot speak, thereof one must remain silent." But he stressed in the same work that to see the world rightly, the reader must "surmount these propositions"—

> He who understands me finally recognizes them as senseless, when he has climbed out of them, on them, over them. (He must so to speak throw away the ladder, after he has climbed up on it.)[102]

Later in life, Wittgenstein said that he had made some "serious mistakes" in his earlier way of thinking, and he shifted to a more open, questioning approach in such penetrating statements as

> Ask yourself: How does a man learn to get a 'nose' for something? And how can this nose be used?[103]

This is my interpretation, but when I ask myself that question, my answer is that the best place to get a nose for thought—that is, intuition—is in silence. As to how it should be used, I would say the answer appears in another of Wittgenstein's later aphorisms:

> God grant the philosopher insight into what lies in front of everyone's eyes.[104]

When I think about what lies before my eyes I am in a quandary. If I try to think "logically," I feel as though I am facing a wall of rock. I can't tell whether my spiritual vision is murky or whether I am being blinded by the brilliance of things considered in time alone. But when I try to think with my "nose," as it were, and put energy into it, the no-thinking seems to make sense. I think of the Paleolithic shamans scratching on cave walls to conjure visions of the essence of things that lie within and am reminded of the "auspicious enigmatizing" of the Vedic munis. I can almost hear those renegade priests of silence thinking with their "noses" as they sit in the brahmanic contest ground:

> A firm light placed for vision—a mind
> most fleet of all that fly!
>
> Far beyond soar my ears, far beyond
> my eyes, far away to this light which is
> set in my heart!
>
> Far beyond wanders my mind, its
> spirit goes to remote distances.
> What really shall I say? What indeed
> shall I even think?[105]

That questioning and wandering beyond rote ritual and mandated conceptions is part of the game. I think, too, of Lao Tzu, when he sat utterly motionless in "Solitude itself," then explained to Confucius that he was letting his mind "wander in the Beginning of things." And I think of Ruysbroek's statement that to become a true bride of Christ one must not only become lost in a fierce tumult of love; the lonely contemplator must also have "lost himself in a Waylessness and in a Darkness, in which all contemplative men wander in fruition and wherein they never again can find themselves in a creaturely way." Only then will the loving contemplative behold God in a mysterious brightness so great that he "sees and feels nothing but incomprehensible Light."

In the end, there is no way to confirm whether the nonthought adventures of any of these Friends led to enlightenment, because not one of them defined it. But they certainly had good things to say about the experience—or perhaps they mean non-experience. And in one way or another, they all say that you can't have enlightenment or the self-sufficing power of solitude without finally throwing ordinary thinking aside, while using the power of Eros to climb Wittgenstein's ladder, then toss it away. Combining the three facets outlined so far, the perennial path to enlightenment in solitude might then be stated in this equation: *detachment X love X nonthought = bliss.*

EXPERIENCE

One can try ardently to love God and the world using energies stored up in solitude and to understand the universe via twinkling mystic nonthought; or one can try a combination of both. It may work. But for some, there is still not enough energy or inclination to turn the battleship of ordinary life in the right direction. To truly make it to enlightenment, to cross over to the "other shore," we may need a jolt, a kick in the head, so to speak, to adopt a more universal perspective on things and to concentrate the mind and heart on the real work.

For most of the Friends, life itself kindly supplied the wake-up call—loss of parents or a friend, a love affair gone sour, imprisonment, severe disappointment with the state of current society or, possibly, an early experience such as childhood molestation. For some, the experience came as a specific soul-quaking shock. Such experiences are generally associated with religious conversion or enlightenment, such as the godly "showings" that Julian of Norwich received during her sickness unto death or the Dark Night of the Soul experience that guided Saint John of the Cross "more surely than the light of noon" to union with God.

But Emily Dickinson writes that she came upon a similar dark night experience when she says "I felt a Funeral, in my Brain" in a poem written sometime during the 1880s in her bedroom-study in her father's house at Amherst, Massachusetts. She does not say what precipitated that funereal jolt. It may have been depression over unrequited love, her bachelor isolation, her failure to publish, or her innate sensitivity. Whatever it was, I suggest it was not her first and that such inner experiences must have clarified her outlook on life and deepened her poetry. As she put it, the experience helped her to break through reason:

> As all the Heavens were a bell,
> And Being, but an Ear,
> And I, and Silence, some strange Race
> Wrecked, solitary, here—
>
> And then a plank in Reason, broke,
> And I dropped down, and down—
> And hit a World, at every plunge,
> And finished knowing—then—[106]

What would such a dark night experience be like? We all know the pain of utter hopelessness following the death of a loved one or some other loss or adversity when we become despondent, wonder about the point of it all, even to the point of hating life and God Himself. In this psychologically precarious position, Lady Solitude can provoke an intense confrontation with emptiness, a thundering nothingness that grabs you by the throat, threatens a showdown with death. But amid your melancholy, if you are not destroyed in the process, the experience may then serve as a psychological purgative that forces a reconsideration of our precarious yet wondrous position in phenomenal reality.

Perhaps this scare-tactic process is similar to what happens in Russian roulette, the famous end-game in which a distressed soul, troubled with existence to the point of suicide, places a bullet in one chamber of a six-cylinder pistol, spins the casing, points barrel at his head, and pulls the trigger. If the gun fires, then the player has been granted his wish: death. If not, he suddenly sees the world from the perspective of not-being, but he is alive…which must have a way of generating a new gratitude for the majesty of existence.

From the perspective of mortality demonstrated physically, anything looks good, worth our joyous loving attention. And from the perspective of nothingness, the psyche, now returned unexpectedly to life, tends to expand to fill the universe and to ponder ultimate questions—perhaps, suddenly, to sense answers. I don't think one has actually to hold a loaded gun to one's head to get the idea of what it might be like; it can be done as a mental experiment which illustrates—or provokes—the wisdom of "letting go."

As we have seen, the use of isolation as such a scare tactic is common in primitive initiation rites throughout the world. According to Mircea Eliade, such rites are methods for causing a psychological rebirth—or death and resurrection—into a new life that is more spiritually and culturally alert. Youth are initiated into adulthood by "killing" their youthful ways, by being taken away from the protection of their mothers and families, and by being introduced forcefully to the great but also fearsome world outside the tribe where ancestors and good and evil spirits lurk. As Eliade puts it, the initiate "dies" to the temporal, profane world and is reborn into the world of the sacred, which is beyond time and the font of the group's culture, spiritual values, and protections. The initiatory death, he says, "provides the clean slate on which will be written the successive revelations whose end is the formation of a new man. This life is conceived as the true human existence, for it is open to the values of spirit."

We have seen further that neophyte shamans in many of the same primitive cultures undergo periods of transformative solitude designed not merely to introduce him or her to the broader spiritual culture of the tribe, but to make them as spiritual adventurers capable of traveling to remote sacred realms for the good of their tribes, often for their own benefit. We think particularly of the Arunta of Australia, who can only achieve shamanhood if they undergo the needed trials to receive, out alone in the outback, a new set of intestines.

Likewise, the Iglulik Aua, who reports that to gain his powers a neophyte shaman must spend time in the great solitude until he "sees himself as a skeleton." Buddha did essentially the same through self-emaciating starvation prior to his enlightenment, after which he, too, looked like a skeleton. And in the Tibetan chöd rite, the neophyte must find a "solitary, awe-inspiring place," visualize himself as a gigantic corpse and his intellect as a "Wrathful Goddess" who cuts off the initiate's head then serves up his body and all his thoughts as a grizzly offering to demons. As a result, the neophyte should now be emancipated from all concepts, pious and impious.

What I find even more interesting is that these sorts of exhortations to a soul-transforming shock are common among secular as well as religious Friends of Solitude. Petrarch, as we have seen, advocated that to achieve clarification of thought on profound matters one must dive into "the hidden recesses of solitude" by means of a meditation on death to the point that one should "tremble and turn pale."

Epicurus advised a similar tactic. Happiness, he said, is relatively easy to attain, providing one contemplates the existential realities of life and death, "by day and by night, alone or with a like-minded friend." Those realities, or "vexations," include "our dread of the phenomena above us, our fear lest death concern us, and our inability to discern the limits of pains and desires."

According to Epicurus, each of these can be exorcised by philosophy, or what he calls "natural science." It begins with what might be termed an active, alert acceptance of what is, the most central fact being the inevitability of death and the impossibility of finding happiness in ordinary pleasures. Following his program of meditation on these and related matters, Epicurus wrote to Menoecus, "you will never experience anxiety, waking or sleeping, but you will live like a god among men. For a human being who lives in the midst of immortal blessings is no way like mortal man!"[107]

Powys recommends a meditation, not on death, per se, but rather on solid, elemental being, what he calls "not-self." First, says Powys, we should make a salubrious "image-gesture" in order to think of the soul as independent of the body and "our consciousness as an indwelling power holding the body in its control."

> To enhance this image-gesture and make it more effective, nothing could be better than to think of our body—thus dominated by our mind—in the form, which in all probability it will eventually take, of a skeleton.
>
> In this thinking of our body as a skeleton, made to gesticulate and move about and patiently endure many evils, there will be attained a wonderfully close relationship with the elements.[108]

Powys may have come across this skeleton image while reading Rasmussen's account of Iglulik shamanism, a translation of which was published just a few years before he wrote his philosophy of solitude. In any case, this ability to see oneself in the context of the elements is the essence of what Powys has to say. "We do not need philosophy to drive us to work. Necessity will do that," he says. Rather, we need philosophy to "kill boredom, to destroy inertia, to dispel lethargy, to drive away weariness, to overcome a sense of futility." The only philosophy that can do this, he adds, "is one that is based upon the actual life-quiver, life-pulsation, life-thrust of the self, as it wrestles with the not-self."[109]

Seeing oneself as a skeleton is also a process of forgetting, which, says Powys, requires something stronger than an admiring contemplation of reality; rather, it needs "a habit of thought that is a habit of war." Our happiness, he adds, is not something that is easily drifted into, in a relaxed and passive acceptance of the Universe. Rather, it requires a struggle:

> We must philosophize with our malice. We must be as gods, selecting and rejecting. To accept the Cosmos in its entirety is the gesture of a slave not of a man. Thus when our loneliness is invaded and the magical silence in which every spirit has a right to live is impinged upon by the crowd there is a wonderful comfort to be derived by stripping ourselves, not only of our clothes but of our flesh and blood, until there is nothing for them to torment but the forked, straddling skeleton and a skull that may be held in human hands a thousand years hence![110]

BRIHADRATHA'S LESSON

There is clearly something very potent in these dark night experiences. Nevertheless, one of the great lessons in the history of solitude, as most of the Friends warn, is that in the end such psychodramatic techniques and mystic methodologies are merely aids to enlightenment.

One of the most apt demonstrations of this is the story of King Brihadratha. In a mood of depression, the king renounced worldly life and spent 1,000 days sitting naked in the desert, his hands perpetually raised in penance, starring at the sun in hopes that his ardent asceticism will grant him release. Fortunately for the former king, the seer Sakayanya appeared, "glowing like a smokeless fire," to set him straight. "I am like a frog in a waterless well," he pleads. "Sir, you are our only way of escape!"

The seer makes it clear to the king that his penance, no matter how fervent, will do him little good until he cultivates an understanding of his own Soul, which is also the Soul of the universe. Mankind was created, he explains, when the seer Prajpati, a mind-born son of Brahma, saw that he was alone without enjoyment and decided to create numerous offspring by meditating on himself. But his creations were lifeless, so he "made himself like wind" and entered into their bodies to animate them. The way to release is thus to know the Soul, the "wind" of Brahma. "The Soul," he says, "is all gods and all things. Obviously, it is He you should desire to know."

So Sakayanya tells the king that, having gone out into the desert and put all objects of sense outside his body, he should aim to unite not with mere sunlight but with the essence of the "thousand-rayed, hundredfold-revolving sun"—Brahma:

> Incomprehensible is the supreme Soul, unlimited, unborn, unthinkable—His soul is space itself! In the dissolution of the world, He alone remains awake. From space He awakens this world, which is a mass of thought. It is thought by Him and in Him it disappears...He who is in the fire, and he who is here in the heart, and he who is yonder in the sun—he is one.[111]

Brihadratha's naked asceticism didn't seem to aid him in that regard, but it did prepare him through renunciation for Sakayanya's message. In a spirit of inclusiveness, the seer describes several alternative methods he might have used to the same effect. For instance, he could have employed the "Six-Fold Yoga"—restraint of breath, withdrawal of the senses, meditation, concentration, contemplation, and absorption. Or, he could have emulated sages of the past who prepared for achieving the light of Brahma by closing their ears with their thumbs so that they could "hear the sound of space within the heart." That inner space, says Sakayanya, may sound like a flowing river, a bell, a brazen vessel, a wheel, croaking frogs, rain, or like speaking in a sheltered place. The idea, though, is to pass beyond these various Brahma sounds, in which case "men disappear in the supreme, the non-sound, the unmanifest Brahma. There they are unqualified, indistinguishable, like the various juices which have reached the condition of honey."[112]

But beyond all these methods, and having restrained one's mind and senses, the sage makes it clear that the king will not reach the condition of honey until he, in a sense, gets back to the basics—first, through a complete renunciation of desire:

> Om! One should be pure, in a pure place, abiding in purity, studying divine Reality, speaking of Reality, meditating on Reality. Then, in the real Brahma which longs for the Real, the adept becomes completely other. His fetters are cut. He is void of expectation, free of fear of others, void of desire. He attains imperishable, immeasurable happiness…
>
> Verily, freedom from desire is like the choicest extract from the choicest treasure. For a person who is made up of all desires, who has the marks of determination, conception, and self conceit, is bound. By being the opposite of that one is liberated.[113]

In addition, then, the king must emulate earlier sages by taking the "highest course," which brings us back to the perennial mystic wisdom of no-thought thought:

> That which is non-thought, but stands in the midst of thought,
> The unthinkable, supreme mystery!
> Thereon let one concentrate one's thought.[114]

Enlightenment will only come, says Sakayanya, when "the intellect stirs not." Looking more broadly across the history of solitude, his spiritual advice coincides with that of most if not all of the Friends of Solitude. Not one of them proposed a recipe for enlightenment by any definition, nor for the secret of creativity or joy in solitude. Instead, they begin, by definition, with the perennial advice to "find a lonely spot." From there, advice differs widely according to the thoroughgoing intensity of one's objectives.

Among what we may broadly term secular soloists such as Petrarch, the advice is generally that a more moderate solitude coupled with a management of desires can suffice to promote creativity and joy. This occurs through the freedom to think and enjoy life, the added sensitivity to what we have called B-region intuitions, and the refocusing of human passions that separation from society naturally provides. Along the way, having the character for solitude, preparation that provides a storehouse of ideas and mental discipline are helpful, while patience, personal effort, and a sense of adventure in solitude are key.

For religious-or spiritually-oriented Friends who speak of union with the divine and "answers" to the unanswered questions, all of these features of solitude may come into play. In addition, the general admonition is that some form of asceticism, associated methodology, guidance of a spiritual master, or the "shock therapy" of a Dark Night of the Soul may be required to renounce desires and to become, insofar as possible, selfless. But the clear message from all such Friends is that these are only starting points. Enlightenment, as Sakayanya says, will only come in the mystical world of no-thinking meditation, while others such as most Sufis and medieval Christians emphasize the value of passionate love of the unfathomable divine. Among those who fall somewhere in between, perhaps Metchtild of Magdeburg offers the most epigrammatic summation when she says:

> Love the nothing,
> Flee the self.
> Stand alone.

Overall, we may conclude that detachment from society and its cloying residue in the self can help to foster the "embarrassment of riches" that we have found across the history of solitude. The ability to realize those treasures seems to reside, at the highest level, with selfless love and non-thinking, a kind of thinking that is beyond conception. But their true source resides in the secret, indefinable workings of the mind and the spirit. And there is no recipe for success in nurturing the fruits of time spent alone. That is why the wisest advice that I have heard—which is applicable both to secular and religious retreats—is that which I quoted at the beginning of this section from the Desert Father Abba Moses: "Go sit in your cell and your cell will teach you everything."[115]

SOLITUDE IN SOCIETY

Those who do well, do well wherever they are.

—Meister Eckhart, Fourteenth Century

Alienation

THERE IS ONE VEHEMENT GROUP OF HERMIT BASHERS—more precisely, solitude bashers—that I have intentionally saved until now. In the last century, particularly before the fall of the Soviet Union and the ensuing demise of Marxist ideology, not only was solitude "detested as a curse," as Kierkegaard lamented, it was fashionable for social scientists to theorize that all inhabitants of modern civilization are painfully and irrevocably alone. Robert Sayer aptly labeled this condition "solitude in society." In a book by the same name published in 1978, a he defines it as "a generalized and radical social fragmentation that causes the isolation of each individual within the social framework," along with "his inability to communicate adequately with others." It is, Sayer maintains, "one aspect of the fundamental crisis of capitalism: alienation."[1]

Sayer's position, following Marx and many others, is that the feeling of alienation is getting worse over time as mass society and capitalism extend their vulgar net around the globe. Societies based on this economic footing have given the individual an ever expanding range of choices in geographic location, lifestyle, and belief.

But the choices are bewildering. The freedom of movement and the impersonal pressure of competition combine to transform people into commodities. As such, we no longer belong in the fullest traditional sense to the community—particularly, to the corporate community, to which we sell our labor and from which we may be fired at any time in the name of profit. Family life is thereby weakened and each person no longer has a definite link to a social world of manageable size, which was the once and rightful source of human love, a sense of belonging, and beliefs and mores that could be accepted as given without the need for anxious choice.

Marx's analysis of this modern malady begins with his reading of Aristotle's perennial definition of man: "Man is in the most literal sense of the word a *zoon politikon*, not only a social animal, but an animal which can develop into an individual only in society."[2]

This, of course, is a misinterpretation of Aristotle, since it leaves out the philosopher's point that contemplation, which is essentially asocial, is a primary end of the zoon politikon. Nevertheless, Marx goes on to posit that over time, as the world's socio-economic superstructure develops into capitalism, social life becomes so remote and impersonal that neither men nor women can any longer develop into contented individuals. Instead, we are cogs in a machine over which we have no control; community is illusory; money replaces the heart at the center of life. The result, says Marx, is a multifaceted separation: alienation of man from nature, from his labor, from his "species being," from other men.

I like Frederick Engles' description of this historical dilemma—especially for its Petrarchan rhetoric. Engles wrote it in London in 1844, when capitalism, according to Sayer, had achieved its full realization and the isolated individual attained his most absolute form, in the city.

> The hundreds of thousands of all classes and ranks crowding past each other, are they not all human beings with the same qualities and powers, and with the same interest in being happy?...And still they crowd one another as though they had nothing in common, nothing to do with one another...The brutal indifference, the unfeeling isolation of each in his private interest becomes the more repellent and offensive, the more these individuals are crowded together within a limited space. And however much one may be aware that isolation of the individual, this narrow self-seeking is the fundamental principle of our society everywhere, it is nowhere so shamelessly barefaced, so self-conscious as just here in the crowding of the great city. The dissolution of mankind into monads, of which each one has a separate principle, the world of atoms, is here carried out to its utmost extreme.[3]

This hellfire preaching packs an emotional punch. We feel pity for all those orphaned monads, especially when we consider that we and ours are merely atoms, too, in this vast disintegrating social universe. And in the meantime, history has further developed, adding additional instruments of subtle torture—in the form of constant media bombardments on our delicate souls, global telecommunications that don't provide "true" human communication, proliferation of computers that digitize our minds, nine-to-five jobs that so sap our spirit we never have time to come back to ourselves.

Since Engles, many others have appeared on the alienation podium to rant about the fearful, depressing woes of our social-psychological state of affairs. Among the more measured of these, the French sociologist Emile Durkheim demonstrated a link between rising suicide rates in France and the dislocation of community—what he called *anomie*—that came with industrialization in Europe. More recently, Christopher Lasch went a step further to make the point (in *Culture of Narcissism*) that not only are we alienated from our fellow men and our true human potential, we have fallen in love with our own images. Taking narcissistic pleasure in what is in reality a defense mechanism, we cannot see beyond our own self-gratification and thus live desperate lives of lonely isolation.

Lasch blames these developments on "the culture of competitive individualism, which in its decadence has carried the logic of individualism to the extreme of a war of all against all, the pursuit of happiness to the dead end of a narcissistic preoccupation with the self."[4] The modern narcissist, according to Lasch, is "facile at managing the impressions he gives to others, ravenous for admiration but contemptuous of those he manipulates into providing it; unappeasably hungry for emotional experiences with which to fill an inner void; terrified of aging and death."[5]

Lasch acknowledges that this development in personality is a logical response to the social-economic structure in which we find ourselves. Narcissism, he explains, "appears realistically to represent the best way of coping with the tensions and anxieties of modern life, and the prevailing social conditions therefore tend to bring out narcissistic traits that are present, in varying degrees, in everyone."[6]

A warlike society tends, in other words, to produce men and women who are at heart antisocial. It should therefore not surprise us to find that although the narcissist conforms to social norms for fear of external retribution, he often thinks of himself as an outlaw and sees others in the same way "as basically dishonest and unreliable, or only reliable because of external pressures."

But it is not only the conditions of economic warfare, crime, and social chaos that shape the narcissist of our times, says Lasch. His condition is rooted in "the subjective experience of emptiness and isolation." The narcissist's ethic of self-preservation, he concludes, "reflects the conviction—as much a projection of inner anxieties as a perception of the way things are—that envy and exploitation dominate even the most intimate relations." In response, the narcissist may turn to the literature of self-help and what Lasch terms "the ideology of personal growth." But this, he argues, is only superficially optimistic. It "radiates a profound despair and resignation. It is the faith of those without faith."[7]

WHAT IS TO BE DONE?

We must admit that these social analysts have a point. Modern society is categorically different from, say, an agricultural or a hunting and gathering society. And solitude can indeed be a painful experience, even for a Friend, but especially for those who see no value in it and are not prepared for it. My position, nevertheless, is that man is *by nature* a solitary animal, as well as a social one. We have ties to society, whether we like it or not; and we are essentially solitary, also whether we like it or not. It is very possible to ignore our essential condition of loneliness through the warmth and distraction of continuous socializing, which many traditional, precapitalist cultures seem to have afforded, at least in retrospect. When the certainties, the warm connections, and the sure guidance of the group are replaced by mass society, competitive economic systems, and freedom of choice, then it is not surprising that man's essential solitude would come to the fore.

But what shall we do about it? When it comes to solutions, Marx issued the boldest call to action when he cried out for a revolutionary reconstruction of society through a "positive supercession of private property"—in other words, communism—a recommendation that spawned many of the great calamities of the twentieth century. As for more contemporary theorists, one must read the footnotes or carefully examine concluding paragraphs to find a cogent proposal.

Sayer confines himself to an analysis of the disease, saying nothing about a cure. Durkheim suggests that occupational groups, or what he calls "corporations," including "all workers of the same sort, in association," should be formed to provide a greater sense of community.[8] Lasch ventures an offhanded solution only on the last two pages of *The Culture of Narcissism*, where he calls for a "struggle against capitalism itself," in which "citizens will have to take the solution of their problems into their own hands." They will have to create their own "communities of competence" and reinvigorate the surviving traditions of localism, self-help, and community action with a "moral discipline formerly associated with the work ethic."[9]

With some exceptions, then, these academics are notoriously poor at providing practical solutions to the ills that they analyze so meticulously. I would suggest that the problem with their recommendations lies not only in the inability to lay out a credible plan. Their failure, it seems to me, goes deeper than that. It is an inability to think past the abstractions that are the tools of the social scientist's trade in order to address concrete, living reality. The real world can be analyzed as a "structure." But it cannot ultimately be treated, lived, or profoundly changed as a structure without unintended consequences that are likely to be horrendous.

It is true that society and historical circumstance, in some sense, create the man. In society, we learn language, culture, and how to live. No one can live entirely outside society or history. Moreover, given the individual's infinitesimally small representation in the demographics of mass society, the chances that he or she will actually redirect the course of world history are proportionately small. Lacking a "name," the genius and rhetorical skills of a Marx or a Petrarch, and more than a bit of luck, the individual is unlikely to make the slightest splash in the river of history.

But if the individual is "made" by society, it is also through the individual that all history must be processed and through which social change must flow. It may take time, perhaps a century or a millennium, but ultimately, it is we individuals who make the world by perceiving and acting from our particular viewpoints and the willed structure of our consciousness. Short of wider influence on society, however, it is clearly the case that we have the ability right now to make our own inner, spiritual worlds for ourselves, regardless of the state of society.

Had these academics of alienation been less caught up in grandiose dreams of social change they might also have noticed that more alienation—more intentional solitude in society and, yes, more loneliness—might not only be inevitable in the modern world, it may be a good thing. More detachment on their parts might have improved the quality of their social analysis. They might have paid closer attention to Hegel's basic point that alienation—in other words, solitude in society—is essential to individual human maturity and dignity.

It was a desirable event, to paraphrase Hegel, when men and women cultivated the ability and the inclination to "alienate" themselves from the substance of society and thus, by stepping back, obtain perspective on their societies, on themselves, and on the wide world in which they resided. Otherwise, how is consciousness possible in the truest sense of the term? The emergence of distinct individuality and independent existence is necessary, says Hegel, if man's essential nature is to be realized completely. Prior to that, man accepts the world of sense passively and is completely identified with it—"Just because he himself is simply world, there is no world yet for him. Not until he sets it outside himself or contemplates it, in his aesthetic status, does his personality become distinct from it, and a world appears to him because he has ceased to identify himself with it."[10]

Richard Schacht follows the same line of thinking in his useful book *Alienation*, which traces the multitude of conflicting and confusing uses of the term in modern sociological, theological, and philosophical literature. In the preface to his book, Walter Kaufmann, sums up Schacht's position, insisting that alienation is in fact an inevitable and important part of human life:

> Whoever would try to protect the young from alienation has despaired of man. It would be more in keeping with the spirit of the Hebrew prophets, Confucius, and Socrates to say instead: Life without estrangement is scarcely worth living; what matters is to increase men's capacity to cope with alienation.[11]

In the Hegelian-Schachtian view, it is only when we intentionally cultivate alienation and actively set the world outside ourselves once in a while that we will have a chance of seeing the world as it is. It may be that this thoughtful form of alienation will help us to cope with the egregious social alienation that we fear. If Marx thought he turned Hegel on his head, we may thereby turn him on his feet again, and we will be the richer, I am sure.

Consider, further, that alienation from society is not only needed for a sense of perspective. According to many religious leaders, it is essential to authentic spirituality. Without alienation from the world, they say, one cannot know God. The worst form of estrangement in society is not one's separation from a warm, well-tempered community—which, in any case, is generally viewed as impossible—but one's isolation from the transcendent, all-powerful One, which is the only true reality. Speaking of this form of spiritual alienation, the Christian theologian Paul Tillich states the matter succinctly: "The state of existence is the state of estrangement... Man as he exists is not what he essentially is and ought to be. He is estranged from this true being."[12]

In Tillich's view, we should fight alienation from our true being, God, with occasional alienation from society. "In moments of solitude," he writes in his essay *Loneliness and Society*, "something is done to us. The center of our being, the innermost self that is the ground of our aloneness, is elevated to the divine center and taken into it. Therein can we rest without losing ourselves."[13] "In the poverty of solitude," he adds, "all riches are present. Let us dare to have solitude—to face the eternal, to find others, to see ourselves."[14]

In various ways, we hear essentially the same spiritual advice from religious hermits throughout the history of solitude, from Taoists to Sufis. Richard Rolle put it this way:

> Those who criticize my solitude and say "Woe to him who is alone!" do not define "alone" as being "without God," but understand it to mean "without company." A man is alone indeed if God is not with him.[15]

In a sense, therefore, loneliness may be the best medicine for loneliness, whether it is directed to God, to a return to our true selves, to our souls—or all three. We have heard Emily Dickinson say that there is "another

Loneliness." In the remainder of the poem she points to the means for achieving that state:

Not want of friend occasions it
Or circumstance of Lot

But nature, sometimes, sometimes thought
And whoso it befall
Is richer than could be revealed
By mortal numeral—[16]

The contemporary American poet David Ignatov put it another way in his memoirs, where he says that his philosophy, developed over some time, is to strive for a kind of balance between solitary life and social life, between self and others. During his middle years, Ignatov began to realize that people around him were experiencing the same sadness and sense of inner deprivation. But, as he puts it, they were simply using "laughter and arm-in-arm walking with others" to hold their sadness at bay. "It was then," the poet writes, that "I began to grow more cheerful in myself."

> From dread of this loneliness as the mark of myself, I came to treasure it as my security and place of being, while the commonality I first hailed as a relief from my loneliness came to have an ambivalent meaning for me. While I needed it to feel myself not utterly alone and meaningless for that reason, it also held a threat to my being as I understand it now, that sense of apartness which always would be me. And so now I negotiate carefully between this self and the other to try to keep both in balance, without losing the value of either, if I can.[17]

The Japanese poet Buson put it still another way in one of his haikus:

Loneliness!
It, too, is joy.
An autumn eve.[18]

Perhaps the ways of expressing and the ways of finding happiness in loneliness are infinite, because the experience is necessarily a private one and the ways will vary according to the makeup of the person. But the simple admonition to rest in aloneness and stillness is the same for all Friends.

DELETING LONELINESS

Since I began researching this book, attitudes toward solitude in society have changed. One of the key people behind that change, somewhat surprisingly, was President Ronald Reagan, as symbolized by his famous phrase: "Mr. Gorbachev, tear down this wall!" Reagan played a conspicuous role in precipitating the fall of the Soviet Union and the just as dramatic decline in the notion that capitalism is ruining our spiritual lives. Rapid improvements in technology further helped to promote the globalization of trade and ideas, along with the success of free-market capitalism, which is now embraced by most countries around the world.

As a result, it is now virtually impossible to locate any social commentator who would find the cause of modern loneliness in socioeconomic structure or a cure for alienation through a change in that structure. Still, the feeling of alienation and social abandonment has not abated. That reality of contemporary life is obvious. But it was made abundantly clear to me when I searched the Internet recently to find thousands of items containing the word "loneliness." In addition to complaints of the lovelorn, I found many warnings that the sense of loneliness will continue to increase with changes in demographics, along with advances in technology and instant global communications.

At one site, offered by a Christian group called Probe Ministries, for example, Kirby Anderson cautions that "the baby boom generation is headed for a crisis of loneliness."[19] In previous generations, he says, where extended families dominated the social landscape, a sizable proportion of adults living alone was unthinkable. In the 1950s, about one in every ten thousand US households had only one person in them, but by the mid-1990s census statistics showed that one in four households was a single-person household, and sociologists project that the ratio will rise to one in three very soon. Kirby cites a sharp rise in late marriages, increasing cohabitation without marriage, a rise in divorce rates, and a suspected increase in cohabitations that break up. He also points to a pernicious rise in what he calls "LTL" (living-together-loneliness) and an increase in our urban and suburban communities of people who are physically very close to each other but emotionally distant. "Close proximity," he wisely notes, "does not translate into close community." People are uprooted again and again by job changes and as communities undergo upheaval. And we can expect increased isolation, as hectic work schedules cause people to be away from home at different times or unavailable to friends.

This certainly warrants Anderson's characterization that we baby boomers are in a "chilling" situation. Anderson concludes that this presents Christians with an opportunity to minister to people cut off from normal, healthy relationships. Churches can provide opportunities for outreach and fellowship in their communities. Meanwhile, he says, "individual Christians must reach out to lonely people and become their friends. And ultimately we must help a lost, lonely world realize that their best friend of all is Jesus Christ."

Another site, sponsored by the University of Florida Counseling Center, suggests a more secular approach, stating that we only contribute to our sense of loneliness by being passive and doing nothing about it.[20] Instead, we should accept those feelings. We should see where they are coming from and what they are connected to in our lives so that we can begin to make changes. We should also become more active about sharing our feelings with an understanding friend, pastor, teacher, or counselor. And we should get involved with activities or clubs to "take our minds off of feeling lonely." Other sites tell us to get a hobby, realize that other people are also lonely, don't look to sex for the answer, don't drink too much, and don't wait for someone to call: Call them!

This is all good advice, I suppose, especially since it addresses individuals rather than social structures. But I am most attracted to the take-charge recommendation offered by Dr. Luann Linquist on her Web page titled "Delete Loneliness."[21] To do so, she says, "lonely people must rid themselves of negative feelings and thoughts of loneliness." "If you are lonely," she explains, "but you really want to attract and maintain satisfying relationships, you must rid yourself of your loneliness."

I think Dr. Linquist may be on to something precisely because her advice is tautological. I have often heard it said that the best way to be happy is to be happy. The same may apply if we are to fight loneliness. I do not know exactly what Dr. Linquist's telephone therapy would consist of, having not engaged it myself, but the implication is clear that loneliness should be treated essentially as a psychic "mirage" and a matter of attitude.

If we turn back to the advice and examples of the Friends of Solitude, we find a similar spirit of optimistic fortitude. The first step is to choose solitude, to find a lonely spot, a place that you can love and where you might escape your toils, troubles, and distractions. There, you might listen to your timeless self; sort things out; moderate desires; or ponder how best to redirect your life to something important and true, something that will fire your passion. You might think or, better yet, stop thinking and forget everything, then see what comes of it. You might simply enjoy idleness, here and now, with a deeper sense of being. You might aim for a complete selflessness that resides solely in the love of God or the ineffable emptiness that underlies all things.

To follow the likes of the Buddha, Lao Tzu, or Christ to the higher levels of enlightenment you may, of course, need the guidance of teacher and methods of contemplation. But the clear lesson from the history of solitude is that there are no sure-fire steps to enlightenment, because the very hope that there is a recipe to follow will only get in the way. Another lesson that I take away, and advocate here, is that time spent alone can be of great personal value, even when one does not hope to attain mystic union with the infinite. The joys and powers of a more down-to-earth detachment are open to everyone; and there is certainly no reason to be ashamed of reveling in such a solitude, provided it is honest, open, and balanced with society.

In all cases, there are no guarantees that time alone will not be treacherous, that your worldly thoughts and fears will not follow you and be magnified there. Your worst fear, in addition to thoughts of death, is likely to be your fear of separation from the safety and nurturing warmth of society. But that is part of the adventure. Perhaps the most important thing to remember is that separation is also freedom. You may have reason to fear it, but the same freedom can also open one to the fertility of intellect, the penetrating intuitions, the sense of liberation, and all the other riches so evident in the history of solitude.

The logical admonition would be to press on and have the courage, as Rilke says, to dig deeper into the dark hours of your loneliness. You may get lost as you descend, or ascend, as the case may be; but if you lose yourself in a waylessness, you may discover something wonderful there. You may not find the happiness you expect, but you may discover something larger that is beyond your expectations and for which, like all art, music, solo journeys of shamans, philosophy, and religion, words can spoil the meaning.

INNER SOLITUDE

THERE IS STILL ANOTHER VIEW of solitude in society that may sound paradoxical at first but may in fact be the best answer to those hermit bashers who maintain that seeking intentionally to be alone is immoral. For many Friends in the long history of solitude have advocated not only that one may embrace solitude as something of a cure for loneliness but that it is possible and preferable to be solitary in a positive sense *in* society—simultaneously and continuously.

That perennial thought is found across the eremitic literature and, as far as I can tell, in every major religion. In India, it seems to have found its first expression in the karma yoga of the Bhagavadgita, and in Mahayana Buddhism. In Christianity, we find it in Meister Eckhart's admonition to disinterest and in Kierkegaard's concept of the Knight of Faith. In Islam, we find it in Sufism. It is essential to Taoism. Moreover, it has been championed by a surprisingly diverse range of secular writers.

It is, it seems to me, the most ingenious compromise imaginable between solitude and society, a profound conundrum. After all, the spiritual value of quiet meditation should not depend on where the Friend happens to be, but on whether or not his or her mind, heart, and spirit are inwardly attuned. Just as one may be lonely in a crowd, one can be humble, inward, and enlightened there.

I find it remarkable that Daniel Defoe's Robinson Crusoe finally came to the same conclusion. After returning from his own long and lonely sojourn on a deserted island, he criticized the solitudes of both the religious hermit and the philosopher. The solitary life, says Crusoe, is a "mere cheat." In his "Serious Reflections," ostensibly written in London, Defoe has him say that "those religious, hermit-like solitudes, which men value themselves so much upon, are but acknowledgments of the defect or imperfection of our resolutions."[22]

As for the ascetic solitude of the religious hermit, Crusoe, presaging the complaints of Nietzsche and Gibbon by a century, calls it a "rape upon human nature." I can imagine he would agree with Merton that true Christian solitude is selfless and always cleaving to God through Christ. But Defoe's Crusoe maintains that such solitude is best carried out in the midst of society. Be they Christian hermits or philosophers, if they desire spiritual transport, says Crusoe, "let them learn to retreat in the world, and they shall enjoy a perfect solitude. If a mind be truly master of itself, there is no need for wildernesses or desolate islands in the sea to quicken one's meditations." In all circumstances, he adds, "it is not want of an opportunity for solitude, but the want of a capacity for being solitary" that inhibits men from enjoying the fruits of aloneness.[23]

I haven't mentioned it yet, but Petrarch came up with essentially the same psychological technique several hundred years earlier. Of course, he always preferred to "seek solitude in her own retreat," particularly amid woods and fields; but under pressure of circumstance he could evoke a solitude of mind no matter where he was. Even in the city, the poet says he could create "a haven of refuge in the midst of a tempest, using a device, not generally known, of so controlling the senses that they do not perceive what they perceive."[24]

Powys says something similar when he advises modern men oppressed by the toils and trammels of twentieth-century society to turn inward wherever we may be—on the factory floor, in our offices, or on the city streets—to forget the outside world, and, with malice if need be, to dive down to the elemental essence of life by thinking that we are, for example, skeletons lying on a seashore or mental beings at one with the raw majesty of the Atlantic Ocean.

The problem, of course, is that through such mental gymnastics we may get lost in the dream-like ocean of our consciousness. We may find ourselves adrift in a sea of existential immobility, an antilife of "preferring not to." If we are truly able to abstract ourselves to such a degree that we can enjoy a perfect solitude, we may not have sufficient strength to reside in the elemental ocean of being, while also remaining active in the world. Like Melville's Bartleby the Scrivener, we may end up despairing of both solitude and society. If we do so, we are only recapitulating the isolationist hermit's presumptuous error of antiworldliness.

But it is possible to maintain inner solitude in a subtle way. It can be done in the same spirit as one can savor the inner thoughts and experiences evoked by a poem, a musical sonata, a painting, or one's own daydreaming digressions, while at the same time maintaining effective connection with the world in a way that is not overly taxing. One way, which I often employ, is to meditate not on the ocean or the starry heavens but on that which happens to be before me here and now. In that way, through a neat legerdemain of the soul, I can be in my office, but not of my office; engaged, but not tied.

KARMA YOGA

This condition of detached engagement is possible under ordinary circumstances of life. But I can imagine a situation, of war, say, or some other horrendous human atrocity or turn of fate, in which focusing upon the here and now would be too painful to contemplate and I would prefer to retire to the forest or my study. Interestingly, that is precisely the topic of the Bhagavadgita, a dialogue between the hermit-warrior Arjuna and the god Krishna that occurred just before the great battle recounted in Mahabharata.

As forces gather on both sides, Arjuna suddenly thinks twice about his impending actions. Rather than killing his brothers and their soldiers in battle, he considers that the moral course would be to take the traditional Hindu option of retreat to a life of religious eremitism. There he could avoid the buildup of bad karma and work toward his spiritual enlightenment. It is then that Krishna, who is serving as Arjuna's charioteer, issues his famous speech on karma yoga, the way of enlightened action in the world.

"Why has a mood of cowardice come over you at this bad time?" asks Krishna. "Do not behave as a eunuch," he says. "It is time to act."[25] After all, he explains, "no one exists for even an instant without performing action; however unwilling, every being is forced to act by the qualities of nature."[26] Whether Arjuna fights or retreats to the forest, he will be acting either way—therefore subject to the laws of karma; that is, the laws of "action." (In Sanskrit, karma refers both to action in the world and to the just rewards of those actions.)

But Krishna says that there is another way of viewing action that has been forgotten by contemporary men. It is not to relinquish worldly action, but all attachment to the *fruits* of that action. "This is my decisive idea," says the god.

As the ignorant act with attachment
to actions, Arjuna,
so wise men should act with detachment
to preserve the world.[27]

Krishna does not tell Arjuna that his action in fighting this particular enemy is morally the right thing in a worldly sense. His message is of a higher order and one that would presumably apply to both sides. It is more along the lines of the lesson that Siva taught the Pine Forest Sages—that action in itself is necessary to preserve the balance and order of the world, even under the most adverse circumstances and, sometimes, even when it seems impossible to judge the moral correctness of those actions. In that light, action in the world to live out one's fate is something of a spiritual duty. Just as important, by acting with detachment, as Krishna does, one can avoid karmic retribution. "Gathering in my own nature," he explains, "I freely create the myriad forms of life, helpless in the force of my nature." Nevertheless, says the god:

These actions do not bind me,
since I remain detached
in all my actions, Arjuna,
as if I stood apart from them.[28]

The reason for this, he continues, is simple (at least in concept). For if one truly follows the yoga of detachment, that inner solitude can lead to the "heaven" of enlightenment regardless of where one happens to be. The result, in contemporary terms, is a win-win situation. Says Krishna:

If you are killed, you win heaven;
if you triumph, you enjoy the earth;
therefore, Arjuna, stand up
and resolve to fight the battle![29]

One obvious question, then, is this: How can one act without yearning? The answer seems to be that one should shift desire from selfish worldly interests to selfless love of the Infinite, as represented by Krishna. The world, too, is part of the Infinite. It is therefore divine if perceived and lived with the right spiritual attitude. And Krishna by his divine presence shows that it is possible for a man or woman to be profoundly spiritual—and joyful—in the world.

> Detached from external contacts,
> he discovers joy in himself;
> joined by discipline to the infinite spirit,
> the self attains inexhaustible joy.[30]

In fact, the warrior who possesses such decisive inner tranquillity and fortitude and who, figuratively speaking, fights with Krishna by his side, is likely to be a more courageous and powerful warrior than those who lack this spiritual anchor. "The man who knows my power," he says, "is armed with unwavering discipline."

Krishna's message must have been clearly received, because Arjuna went on to fight the battle with the god of karma yoga at his side. As it turned out, his forces triumphed in a worldly sense. The next day, when the dust had settled, Arjuna delivered a similar message of worldly spirituality to his brother Yudhisthira, as the great king sat dumbstruck on the battlefield, his body pierced by spears, contemplating the horrific carnage in which untold numbers of men had perished and he had killed his brothers. "Now," says Yudhisthira, "my grief is stupefying me." So he resolves to escape from the ties of this world to wander as a hermit in the forest. Without affection for anything, he plans to perform the most austere of penances to atone for his terrible deeds. But Arjuna admonishes him not to escape his responsibilities and his fate in the world:

> Oh, how painful, how distressing! I grieve to see this great agitation of thy heart, since having achieved such a superhuman feat, thou acquired the sovereignty of the earth which has been won through observance of duties of thy own class, why shouldst thou abandon everything through fickleness of heart?…If thou

> retirest into the woods, in thy absence dishonest men will destroy sacrifices. That sin will certainly pollute thee.[31]

The message is all the more poignant for those who listened carefully to the whole Mahabharata and recall that Arjuna himself was once an ascetic hermit in the Himalayas whose tapas was sufficiently ardent to conjure the powerful Pasupata Weapon. What we are hearing from both Krishna and Arjuna is obviously a response by Hindu culture to India's epidemic of eremitism. The Bhagavadgita advocates not so much saving the joys of time alone for the latter half of life, but rather solitude in society, acceptance of fate, and responsibility in the world accompanied by spiritual innerness…also in the world.

A later Hindu text, the Ashtavakragita, makes precisely the same case for a higher spirituality in the world, but in more direct language and with greater emphasis on the stratagem of renunciation of self in a way that does not necessarily involve the assistance of a god. In this gita, the Master of Life (a *karma yogin*) advises us to love our true selves, which are "naturally happy," and to awaken to our own natures, with the result that "delusion melts like a dream." The sorrows of social duty may have scorched our hearts like the heat of the sun, says the Master—

> But let stillness fall on you
> With its sweet and cooling showers,
> And you will find happiness.[32]

He makes it clear, further, that inner stillness can be achieved irrespective of one's situation or location. Such is the way of every karma yogin:

> His nature is free of conditions.
>
> Win or lose,
> It makes no difference to him.
>
> Alone in the forest or out in the world,
> A god in heaven or a simple beggar,
> It makes no difference![33]

Essentially, the Master's profound power of serenity stems from a strategic and conscious will to desirelessness, which is, in a sense, payment toward a much greater happiness. The liberated master of karma yoga is awake, selfless, busy but doing nothing, and free from distraction, even without the support of meditation. "The master is always at peace," he says, "because he understands how things are"—

> The fool tries to control his mind
> How can he ever succeed?
>
> Mastery always comes naturally
> To the man who is wise
> And who loves himself...
>
> His mind is calm.
>
> Never seeking the solitude of the forest,
> Nor running from the crowd.
>
> Always and everywhere,
> He is one and the same.[34]

THE KNIGHT OF FAITH

In Buddhism, another spiritual-material compromise known as the *Mahayana* (the path of the Greater Vehicle) takes a similar tack. Among many things, it allows that one need not be an ascetic or antisocial to achieve enlightenment. A Buddhist who is on the cusp of attaining enlightenment may choose, out of compassion for worldly beings, to become a *bodhisattva.* Such an "enlightenment being" maintains an inner oneness borne of solitude and metaphysical wisdom but remains in the world, typically to show others the way to spiritual enlightenment.

Such was the case with one of the Buddha's greatest followers, the householder saint Vimalakirti. Vimalakirti is also noted in Buddhist history as the follower who exhibited his enlightenment to the Buddha when he answered the question "What is the Bodhisattva's initiation into the non-dual Dharma" (the path of oneness) simply by raising his hand and remaining silent. That silence, thereafter known as Vimalakirti's "thundering silence," is taken as a pointed recognition that the world of sense and the world of spirit are one and the same, that the way of the world and the way of the spirit should also be regarded as the same, but that the reason for it is not expressible in words.

Many Chinese recluse poets were influenced by this profundity. Wang Wei was proud to note that a form of his name (*Wei Mojie*) is the transliteration of Vimalakirti in Chinese and that his life, too, combined action in the world of affairs with the tranquillity of inner retirement. The poems of T'ao Ch'ien, as we have heard, suggest understanding of a similar underling principle, as when he says, "With the mind detached, one's place becomes remote."

The poet probably learned that trick from Taoist rather than the Buddhist sources. That is not surprising, because from the very beginning, as we have seen, the Chinese view of the power of solitude combined the worldly with the spiritual. The sage, in common Taoist parlance, lives in the world of change and practical activity; but he holds himself to the realm of non-activity. In one sense, he is confined in the "walls of the nameable," yet his empty spirit resides in the "open country of what transcends speech."[35] That thought is expressed still more concisely in this Chinese saying: "The small hermit lives in the mountains. The great hermit lives in a town."[36]

Among the Sufis, the mingling of the worldly with the spiritual is seen in the use of mundane imagery such as drunkenness and sexual ecstasy to evoke mystic transports. Despite the early interest in ascetic solitude by some Sufis, it was not long before most rejected ascetic withdrawal as a veiled form of worldliness. "The world is like a bride," says al-Ghazali, "He who loves her combs and decorates her hair. The ascetic blackens her face, tears her hair out, and rends her clothes. But he who possesses the knowledge of God is completely absorbed in God and does not worry about her at all."[37] The Sufi Yahya ibn Mu'adh went further in this spirit of worldly apatheia when he asked, "How can I refrain from loving the world, wherein God has given me love and nourishment, whereby I am able to preserve my earthly life, the life in which I can achieve that obedience to God which guides me to the next world?"[38]

The notion of worldly religiousness has, of course, found a place in the Christian West, particularly in the Protestant spirit of what Max Weber called "worldly asceticism." But that of worldly spirituality has not generally been accepted in Christian thought, even though Christ can, in a sense, be seen as the supreme bodhisattva—not only an enlightened one, but God Himself, who chose to be born into this mortal coil to live a normal early life as a carpenter's son. Westerners who do see the value and possibility of spiritual solitude in the world tend to be novelists, philosophers, or heretics.

We've already heard from Petrarch, Defoe, and Powys in that regard. In thirteenth-century Germany, Meister Eckhart likewise made it clear to his followers that one may achieve enlightenment or "god-consciousness" in the street as well as the in church or a desert place. "I was asked this question," he writes in "On Solitude and the Attainment of God," "'Some people withdraw from society and prefer to be alone; their peace of mind depends on it; wouldn't it be better for them to be in the church?' I replied, No! And you shall see why." Following on from the brief quote at the beginning of this section, Eckhart explains in words that need no further elaboration:

> Those who do well, do well wherever they are, and in whatever company, and those who do badly, do badly wherever they are and in whatever company. But if a man does well, God is really in him, and with him everywhere, on the streets and among people, just as much in church, or desert place, or a cell. If he really has God and only God, then nothing disturbs him…
>
> To be sure, this requires effort and love, a careful cultivation of the spiritual life, and a watchful, honest, active oversight of all one's mental attitudes toward things and people. It is not to be learned by world-flight, running away from things, turning solitary and going apart from the world. Rather, one must learn an inner solitude, wherever or with whomsoever he may be. He must learn to penetrate things and find God there, to get a strong impression of God firmly fixed in his mind.[39]

The noise of cultural idiosyncrasy aside, I can't see much difference between Eckhart's basic position and that of the Bhagavadgita. True nearness to the divine essence of the universe or enlightenment by whatever definition cannot depend upon outward things but rather on spiritual reality, which is evanescent and inward.

Finally, Søren Kierkegaard took essentially the same position when he maintained that the highest form of spiritual being—his Knight of Faith—would live concealed in ordinary life. He, too, reasons that faith and spiritual enlightenment are wholly inward affairs, adding that the completely isolated, antiworldly life of religious solitude is immoral, a presumptuous flight from the God-given reality in front of our noses.

Kierkegaard admitted that he could find no example of such a being, even though every second man might be one. If he ever heard of the existence of a Knight of Faith, he said that he would be prepared to make a pilgrimage on foot to watch the man's every movement. And if they were introduced, he expected that the occasion would be surprising:

> Here he is. Acquaintance made, I am introduced to him. The moment I set eyes on him I instantly push him from me, I myself leap backwards, I clasp my hands and say half aloud, "Good Lord, is this the man? Is it really he? Why, he looks like a tax-collector!"[40]

Perhaps you are such a Knight, or potentially so, without knowing it.

Sources, Further Reading

Note: This bibliography is organized for convenient reference to works by and about Friends of Solitude following the groupings in which they are presented in the brief history of solitude above—*Primitives*, including shamans; hermits and other lovers of solitude in *India*, *Greece/Rome*, *China/Japan*; *Christians*; and *Sufis*. *Modern European* and *Modern American* Friends from Petrarch to date are listed separately. All other source materials are listed in the last section: *Historians, Philosophers, Psychologists.*

Primitives

Clottes, Jean, and David Lewis-Williams. *The Shamans of Prehistory: Trance and Magic in the Painted Caves.* Sophie Hawkes, trans. Harry N. Abrams, 1996.

David-Neel, Alexandra. *Magic and Mystery in Tibet.* Dover, 1971.

Eliade, Mircea. *Rites and Symbols of Initiation: The Mysteries of Birth and Rebirth.* Harper Torchbooks, 1958.

——. *Shamanism: Archaic Techniques of Ecstasy.* Willard R. Trask, trans. Princeton University Press, 1972.

——. *Zalmoxis: The Vanishing God.* University of Chicago Press, 1970.

Evans-Wentz, W.Y. *Tibetan Yoga and Secret Doctrines.* Oxford University Press, 1958.

——. *Tibet's Great Yogi Milarepa: A Biography from the Tibetan.* Oxford University Press, 1928.

Govinda, Lama Anagarika. *The Way of the White Clouds: A Buddhist Pilgrim in Tibet.* Shambala, 1970.

Halifax, Joan. *Shamanic Voices: A Survey of Visionary Narratives.* E.P. Dutton, 1979.

Harner, Michael. *The Way of the Shaman.* HarperSanFrancisco, 1990.

Nordland, Odd. "Shamanism as an Experiencing of 'the Unreal.'" In Carl-Martin Edsman, ed.; *Studies in Shamanism*; Almquist & Wiksell, Stockholm; 1963.

Rasmussen, Knud. *Across Arctic America: Narrative of the Fifth Thule Expedition.* Greenwood Press, 1969.

——. *Intellectual Culture of the Iglulik Eskimos: Report of the Fifth Thule Expedition, 1921-24.* William Worster, trans. Copenhagen: Glydendalske Boghandel, Nordisk Forlag, 1929.

Schoolcraft, Henry Rowe. See Mentor L. Williams, ed.; *Schoolcraft's Indian Legends*; Michigan State University Press, 1956.

Spencer, W.B., and F.J. Gillen. *The Native Tribes of Central Australia.* Macmillan, 1899.

India

Ashtavakragita. *The Heart of Awareness: A Translation of the Ashtavakra Gita.* Thomas Byrom, trans. Shambala, 1990.

Ashvagosha. *The Saundarananda of Aśvaghosa.* E.H. Johnston, trans. Motilal Banarsidass, Delhi, 1975.

Batchelor, Stephen. *Alone With Others: An Existential Approach to Buddhism.* Grove Press, 1983.

Bhagat, M.G. *Ancient Indian Asceticism.* Munshiram Manoharlal, New Delhi, 1976.

Bhagavadgita. *The Bhagavadgita in the Mahabharata.* J.A.B. van Buitenen, trans. University of Chicago Press, 1981.

——. *The Bhagavad-Gita: Krishna's Counsel in Time of War.* Barbara Stoller Miller, trans. Bantam Books, 1986.

Bhartrihari. *The Hermit and the Love Thief: Sanskrit Poems of Bhartrihari and Bilhana.* Barbara Stoller Miller, trans. Columbia University Press, 1967.

Buddha. *The Lion's Roar: An Anthology of the Buddha's Teaching Selected from the Pali Canon.* David Maurice, trans. Rider & Company, 1962.

——. *Dialogues of the Buddha: Digha-Nikaya.* T.W. Rhys Davids, trans. Oxford University Press, 1899.

Conze, Edward, ed. *Buddhist Scriptures.* Penguin Books, 1959.

Deussen, Paul. *The Philosophy of the Upanishads.* Dover, 1966.

Dimmit, Cornelia, and J.A.B. van Buitenen. *Classical Hindu Mythology: A Reader in the Classical Sanskrit Puranas.* Temple University Press, 1978.

Eliade, Mircea. *Yoga: Immortality and Freedom.* Willard R. Trask, trans. Princeton University Press, 1969.

Jacobi, Herman. *Jaina Sutras.* Dover, 1968.

Johnson, Willard. *Poetry and Speculation of the Rg Veda.* University of California Press, Berkeley, 1980.

Mahabharata. *The Mahābhārata.* Books 1–5 in three volumes. J.A.B. van Buitenen, trans. University of Chicago Press, 1973-78.

——. *The Mahabharata.* Kisari Mohan Ganguli, trans. Munshiram Manoharlal, New Delhi, 1981.

Malalaskera, ed. *Encyclopedia of Buddhism.* Government of Ceylon, 1996.

O'Flaherty, Wendy D. *Hindu Myths.* Penguin Books, 1975.

Patanjali. *Aphorisms of Yoga by Bhagwan Shri Patanjali.* Shri Purohit Swami, trans. Faber and Faber, 1973.

Radhakrishnan, Sarvepalli, and Charles A. Moore, eds. *A Sourcebook in Indian Philosophy.* Princeton University Press, 1957.

Rig Veda. *The Rig Veda: An Anthology.* Wendy Doniger O'Flaherty, trans. Penguin Books, 1981.

Shantideva, Acharya. *Guide to the Bodhisattva's Way of Life.* Stephen Batchelor, trans. Library of Tibetan Works & Archives, Dharamsala, 1981.

Thapar, Romila. *A History of India: Volume One.* Penguin Books, 1966.

Thomas, Edward J. *The Life of Buddha as Legend and History.* Routledge & Kegan Paul, 1927.

Thurman, Robert A.F. *The Holy Teaching of Vimalakirti: A Mahayana Scripture.* Pennsylvania State University Press, 1983.

Upanishads. *The Thirteen Principal Upanishads.* Robert Ernest Hume, trans. Oxford University Press, 1931.

Zimmer, Heinrich. *Philosophies of India.* Joseph Campbell, ed. Princeton University Press, 1951.

Greece, Rome

Aristotle. *Aristotle: The Politics*. T.A. Sinclair, trans.; revised by Trevor J. Saunders. Penguin Books, 1981.

——. *The Complete Works of Aristotle: The Revised Oxford Translation*. Jonathan Barnes, ed. Princeton University Press, 1984.

——. *The Ethics of Aristotle: The Nichomachian Ethics*. J.A.K. Thomson, trans.; revised by Hugh Tredennick. Penguin Books, 1976.

Arrian. *The Campaigns of Alexander*. Aubrey de Sélincourt, trans., revised by J.R. Hamilton. Penguin Books, 1971.

Aurelius, Marcus. *Meditations*. Maxwell Staniforth, trans. Penguin Books, 1964.

Austin, Scott. *Parmenides: Being, Bounds, and Logic*. Yale University Press, 1986.

Bolton, James David Pennington. *Aristeas of Proconnesus*. Clarendon Press, 1962.

Dillon, John M. *The Middle Platonists: A Study of Platonism, 80 B.C. to A.D. 220*. Duckworth, 1977.

Diogenes Laertius. *Lives of the Eminent Philosophers*. R.D. Hicks, trans. Harvard University Press, 1925.

Dodds, E.R. *The Greeks and the Irrational*. University of California Press, 1951.

Epicurus. *Letters, Principal Doctrines, and Vatican Sayings: Epicurus*. Russel M. Geer, trans. Bobbs-Merrill, 1964.

——. *The Philosophy of Epicurus*. George K. Strodach, trans. Northwestern University Press, 1963.

Freeman, Kathleen, trans. *Ancilla to the Pre-Socratic Philosophers*. Harvard University Press, 1948.

Gorman, Peter. *Pythagoras: A Life*. Routledge & Kegan Paul, 1979.

Graves, Robert. *The Greek Myths*. Penguin Books 1955.

Guthrie, Kenneth Sylvan, ed. *The Pythagorean Sourcebook and Library*. Phanes Press, 1987.

Guthrie, W.K.C. *A History of Greek Philosophy*. Cambridge University Press, 1962.

Heraclitus. *The Art and Thought of Heraclitus.* Charles H. Khan, trans. Cambridge University Press, 1990.

Horace. *The Essential Horace: Odes, Epodes, Satires, and Epistles.* Burton Raffel, trans. North Point Press, 1983.

——. *Horace's Satires and Epistles.* Jacob Fuchs, trans. W.W. Norton and Company, 1977.

——. *The Odes and Epodes of Horace.* Joseph P. Clancy, trans. University of Chicago Press, 1960.

——. *Satires and Epistles of Horace.* Smith Palmer Bovie, trans. University of Chicago Press, 1959

Lucian. "The Passing of Peregrinus." In *The Works of Lucian*; A.M. Harmon, trans.; Harvard University Press, 1936.

Lucretius. *Lucretius: The Way Things Are.* Rolphe Humphries, trans. Indiana University Press, 1968.

Ovid. *The Metamorphoses.* Horace Gregory, trans. New American Library, 1958.

Philo. *Philo of Alexandria: The Complete Life, The Giants, and Selections.* David Winston, trans. Paulist Press, 1981.

Plato. *The Complete Texts of Great Dialogues of Plato.* W.H.D. Rouse, trans. New American Library, 1956.

Plotinus. *The Essence of Plotinus.* Stephen MacKenna, trans.; complied by Grace H. Turnbull. Oxford University Press, 1948.

Rist, J.M. *Plotinus: The Road to Reality.* Cambridge University Press, 1960.

Sandmel, Samuel. *Philo of Alexandria: An Introduction.* Oxford University Press, 1979.

Sedgwick, Henry Dwight. *Horace: A Biography.* Russell & Russell, 1947.

Seneca. *Letters from a Stoic: Epistulae Morales ad Lucilium.* Robin Campbell, trans. Penguin Books, 1969.

——. "On Tranquillity of Mind." In *Seneca II, Moral Essays II*; J.W. Basore, trans.; Harvard University Press, 1970.

Vernant, Jean-Pierre. *The Origins of Greek Thought.* Cornell University Press, 1982.

China, Japan

Basho. *Basho: Narrow Road to the Deep North and Other Travel Sketches.* Nobuyuki Yuasa, trans. Penguin Books, 1966.

Birch, Cyril, ed. *Anthology of Chinese Literature*. Penguin Books, 1967.

Bodhidharma. *The Zen Teachings of Bodhidharma*. Red Pine, trans. North Point Press, 1989.

Buson. In, Steward W. Holmes and Chimyo Horioka; *Zen Art for Meditation*; Charles E. Tuttle Company, Inc. of Boston, Massachusetts, and Tokyo, Japan, 1973.

Chuang Tzu. *The Complete Works of Chuang Tzu.* Burton Watson, trans. Columbia University Press, 1968.

Cleary, Thomas. *The Essential Tao.* HarperSanFrancisco, 1991.

Confucius. *The Analects of Confucius.* Arthur Waley, trans. Vintage Books, 1938.

Davis, A.R. *The Narrow Lane: Some Observations on the Recluse in Traditional Chinese Society.* The Australian University, 1959.

Dogen, Eihei. *Moon in a Dewdrop: Writings of Zen Master Dogen*. Kazuaki Tanahashi, et al., trans. North Point Press, 1985.

Han Fei Tzu. *Han Fei Tzu: Basic Writings.* Burton Watson, trans. Columbia University Press, 1964.

Han Shan. *Cold Mountain: 100 Poems by the T'ang Poet Han-shan*. Burton Watson, trans. Columbia University Press, 1970.

——. *The Collected Songs of Cold Mountain*. Red Pine, trans. Copper Canyon Press, 1983.

——. *Riprap & Cold Mountain Poems*. Gary Snyder, trans. Four Seasons Foundation, 1977.

Hawkes, David. *The Songs of the South: An Anthology of Ancient Chinese Poems by Qu Yuan and Other Poets*. Penguin Books, 1985.

Hoover, Thomas. *The Zen Experience*. New American Library, 1980.

Kuan Tzu. *Kuan-tzu: A Repository of Early Chinese Thought.* W. Allyn Rickett, trans. Hong Kong University Press, 1965.

Matthiessen, Peter. *Nine-Headed Dragon River: Zen Journals 1969-82.* Shambala, 1985.

Schuhmacher, Stephen, and Gert Woerner, eds. *The Encyclopedia of Eastern Philosophy and Religion*. Shambala, 1989.

Stonehouse. *The Zen Works of Stonehouse: Poems and Talks of a Fourteenth-Century Chinese Hermit.* Red Pine, trans. Mercury House, 1999.

Suzuki, D.T. *Manual of Zen Buddhism*. Grove Press, 1960.

T'ao Ch'ien (Tao Yuan-ming). *Gleanings from Tao Yuan-ming (Prose and Poetry).* Roland C. Fang, trans. The Commercial Press, Hong Kong, 1980.

——. *The Poetry of T'ao Ch'ien*. James Robert Hightower, trans. Clarendon Press, 1970.

Waley, Arthur. *The Way and It's Power: A Study of the Tao Te Ching and Its Place in Chinese Thought.* Grove Press, 1958.

Wang Wei. *Poems of Wang Wei*. G. W. Robinson, trans. Penguin Books, 1973.

——. *The Poetry of Wang Wei: New Translations and Commentary*. Indiana University Press, 1980.

Wagner, Marsha L. *Wang Wei*. Twayne Publishers, 1981.

Christians

Anonymous. *The Cloud of Unknowing and Other Works.* Clifton Wolters, trans. Penguin Books, 1961.

Athanasius. *Athanasius: The Life of Anthony and the Letter to Marcellinus.* Robert C. Gregg, trans. Paulist Press, 1980.

Bede, The Venerable. "Life of Cuthbert." In *Lives of the Saints*; J.F. Webb, trans.; Penguin Books, 1981.

Brown, Peter. *The Making of Late Antiquity.* Harvard University Press, 1978.

Budge, Ernest A. Wallis. *'Anan Isho: The Paradise, or the Garden of the Holy Fathers.* Burton Franklin, 1972.

Capps, Walter Holden, and Wendy M. Wright, eds. *Silent Fire: An Invitation to Western Mysticism.* Harper & Row, Publishers, 1978.

Carretto, Carlo. Sarah Fawcett, trans. *In Search of the Beyond.* Doubleday & Company, 1975.

Cassian, John. *Conferences.* Colm Luibheid, trans. Paulist Press, 1985.

Chadwick, Owen. *Western Asceticism* (including *The Sayings of the Fathers* and *The Conferences of Cassian).* Owen Chadwick, trans. Westminster Press, MCMLVIII.

Clay, Rotha Mary. *The Hermits and Anchorites of England.* Methuen & Co., 1914; reissued by Singing Tree Press, 1968.

Dionysius the Areopagite. *The Divine Names & The Mystical Theology.* C.E. Rolt, trans. SPCK, 1920.

——. *Pseudo-Dionysius: The Complete Works.* Colm Luibheid, trans. Paulist Press, 1987.

Eckhart, Meister. *Meister Eckhart: A Modern Translation.* Raymond B. Blakney, trans. Harper Torchbooks, 1941.

Eusebius. *The Ecclesiastical History.* J.E.L. Oulton, trans. Harvard University Press, 1932.

Evagrius of Pontus. *Evagrius Ponticus: The Praktikos and Chapters on Prayer.* John Eudes Bamberger, OCO, trans. Cistercian Publications, 1980.

Georgianna, Linda. *The Solitary Self: Individuality in the Ancren Wisse.* Harvard University Press, 1981.

Jackson, Kenneth Hurlstone, trans. *A Celtic Miscellany: Translations from the Celtic Literatures.* Penguin Books, 1971.

Jerome, Saint. *Select Letters of Saint Jerome.* F.A. Wright, trans. G.P. Putnam and Sons, 1933.

John Climacus, Saint. *The Ladder of Divine Ascent.* Colm Luibheid and Norman Russell, trans. Paulist Press, 1982.

John of the Cross, Saint. *The Collected Works of Saint John of the Cross.* Kieran Kavanaugh and Otilio Rodriguez, trans. ICS Publications, 1979.

Julian of Norwich. *Revelations of Divine Love.* Translated into modern English by Clifton Wolters. Penguin Books, 1966.

Mechthild of Magdeburg. *Mechthild of Magdeburg: The Flowing Light of the Godhead.* Frank Tobin, trans. Paulist Press, 1998.

——. *Meditations With Mechtild of Magdeburg.* Sue Woodruff, trans. Bear & Company, 1982.

Merton, Thomas. Listed in "Modern Americans" below.

Palmer, G.E.H., Philip Sherrard, and Kallistos Ware. *The Philokalia: The Complete Text.* Faber and Faber, 1979.

Robinson, James M., ed. *The Nag Hammadi Library.* Translated by members of the Coptic Gnostic Library Project of the Institute for Antiquity and Christianity. Harper & Row, 1977.

Rolle, Richard, Hermit of Hampole. *The Fire of Love.* Clifton Wolters, trans. Penguin Books, 1972.

Ruysbroek, John. *The Spiritual Espousals and Other Works.* James A. Wiseman, trans. Paulist Press, 1985.

Theodoret of Cyrus. *History of the Monks of Syria.* R.M. Price, trans. Cistercian Publications, 1985.

Waddell, Helen. *The Desert Fathers: Translations from the Latin With an Introduction.* Constable, 1936. Reprinted in Vintage Spiritual Classics, Random House, 1998.

Ward, Benedicta, trans. *The Sayings of the Desert Fathers.* Cistercian Publications, 1975.

Workman, Herbert B. *The Evolution of the Monastic Ideal.* Epworth Press, London, 1917.

Sufis

Al-Ghazali, Abu Hamid Muhammad. *Al-Ghazali's Path to Sufism: His Deliverance from Error.* R.J. McCarthy, trans. Fons Vitae, 2000.

Andre, Tor. *In the Garden of the Myrtles: Studies in Early Islamic Mysticism.* Birgitta Sharpe, trans. State University of New York Press, 1987.

Attar, Farid al-Din. *Muslim Saints and Mystics: Episodes from the Tadhkirat al-Auliya (Memorial of the Saints).* A.J. Arberry, trans. Routledge & Kegan Paul, 1966.

Glubb, Sir John. *The Life and Times of Muhammad.* Madison Books, 1998.

Hafiz of Shiraz. *The Teachings of Hafiz.* Gertrude Lowthian Bell, trans. The Octagon Press, 1979.

'Iraqi, Fakruddin. *Fakruddin 'Iraqi: Divine Flashes.* William C. Chittick and Peter Wilson, trans. Paulist Press, 1982

Kritzeck, James, ed. *Anthology of Islamic Literature From the Rise of Islam to Modern Times.* New American Library, 1964.

Nurbakhash, Dr. Javad. *In the Tavern of Ruin: Seven Essays on Sufism.* Khaniqahi-Nimatullahi Publications, 1978.

Rabi'a al-Adawiyya. *Doorkeeper of the Heart: Versions of Rabi'a.* Charles Upton, trans. Threshold Books, 1988.

Rumi, Jelaluddin. *The Essential Rumi.* Coleman Barks, with John Moyne, trans. Castle Books, 1995.

——. *The Ruins of the Heart: Selected Lyric Poetry of Jelaluddin Rumi.* Edmund Helminski, trans. Threshold Books, 1981.

Schimmel, Annemarie. *Mystical Dimensions of Islam.* University of North Carolina Press, 1975.

Tufail, Abu Bakr Muhammad bin. *The Journey of the Soul: The Story of Hai bin Yaqzan.* Raid Kocache, trans. The Octagon Press, 1982.

Modern Europeans

Bishop, Morris. *Petrarch and His World.* Indiana University Press, 1963.

Burton, Robert. *The Anatomy of Melancholy.* Vintage Books, 1977.

Cowley, Abraham. *Abraham Cowley: Poetry & Prose.* Oxford at the Clarendon Press, 1949.

Defoe, Daniel. "The Serious Reflections of Robinson Crusoe," in *Robinson Crusoe*, Vol. III. Logographic Press, London, 1790.

Descartes, René. *Discourse on Method and the Meditations.* F.E. Sutcliffe, trans. Penguin Books, 1968.

Donne, John. *John Donne: Poetry and Prose.* Frank J. Warnke, ed. Modern Library, 1967.

Flaubert, Gustave. *The Temptation of Saint Anthony.* Kitty Mrosovsky, trans. Penguin Books, 1990.

Forster, Kenelm. *Petrarch: Poet and Humanist.* Edinburgh University Press, 1984.

Hayman, Ronald. *Nietzsche: A Critical Life.* Penguin Books, 1982.

Kierkegaard, Søren. *The Diary of Søren Kierkegaard.* Peter Rohde, ed. Philosophical Library, 1960.

——. *Either/Or: A Fragment of Life Edited by Victor Eremita.* Howard V. Hong and Edna H. Hong, trans. Princeton University Press, 1987.

——. *Fear and Trembling: Dialectical Lyric by Johannes de Silentio*. Alastair Hannay, trans. Penguin Books, 1985.

Lowrie, Walter. *A Short Life of Kierkegaard*. Princeton University Press, 1970.

Montaigne, Michel de. *The Complete Essays of Montaigne*. Donald M. Frame, trans. Stanford University Press, 1958.

Nietzsche, Friedrich. *Beyond Good and Evil*. R. J. Hollingdale, trans. Penguin Books, 1972.

——. *Daybreak: Thoughts on the Prejudices of Morality*. R.J. Hollingdale, trans. Cambridge University Press, 1982.

——. *The Genealogy of Morals and Ecce Homo*. Walter Kaufmann, trans. Random House, 1968.

——. *Human, All Too Human: A Book for Free Spirits*. Marion Faber, with Stephen Lehman, trans. University of Nebraska Press, 1984.

——. *Joyful Wisdom*. Kurt F. Reinhardt, trans. Frederick Ungar, 1981.

——. *Thus Spake Zarathustra*. Thomas Common, trans. Modern Library.

Petrarch, Francesco. *The Life of Solitude by Francis Petrarch*. Jacob Zeitlin, trans. University of Illinois Press, 1924.

——. *Petrarch: The Canzoniere; or Rerum Vulgarium Fragmentum*. Mark Musa, trans. Indiana University Press, 1996.

——. *Petrarch: Selections from the Canzoniere and Other Works*. Mark Musa, trans. Oxford University Press, 1985.

——. *Petrarch at Vaucluse: Letters in Verse and Prose*. Ernest Hatch Wilkins, trans. University of Chicago Press, 1958.

Pound, Ezra. *The Spirit of Romance*. New Directions, 1968.

Powys, John Cowper. *A Philosophy of Solitude*. Simon and Schuster, 1933.

Rilke, Rainer Maria. *Letters to a Young Poet*. Stephen Mitchell, trans. Random House, 1984.

——. *Selected Poems of Rainer Maria Rilke*. Robert Bly, trans. Harper and Row, 1981.

Rousseau, Jean-Jacques. *Reveries of the Solitary Walker*. Charles E. Butterworth, trans. Harper Colophon, 1982.

——. "The Social Contract" in *The Essential Rousseau*. Lowell Bair, trans. New American Library, 1974.

Shattuck, Roger. *Marcel Proust*. Viking Press, 1974.

Trinkaus, Charles. *The Poet as Philosopher: Petrarch and the Formation of the Renaissance Consciousness.* Yale University Press, 1979.

Valéry, Paul. *Collected Works of Paul Valéry, Volume 6: Monsieur Teste.* Jackson Matthews, trans. Princeton University Press, 1973.

Wordsworth, William. *The Prelude, With A Selection from the Shorter Poems, the Sonnets, The Recluse, and The Excursion.* Holt, Rinehart and Winston, 1965.

Wittgenstein, Ludwig. *Culture and Value.* G.H. von Wright, ed.; Peter Winch, trans. University of Chicago Press, 1980.

——. *Philosophical Investigations.* G.E.M. Anscombe, trans. B. Blackwell, 1967.

——. *Tractatus Logico-Philosophicus.* C.K. Ogden, trans. Routledge & Keegan Paul, 1933.

Zimmerman, Johann George. *The Pleasures of Solitude.* Philip Allan & Co., 1924.

Modern Americans

Bly, Robert. *Jumping Out of Bed.* White Pine Press, 1987.

Dickinson, Emily. *The Complete Poems of Emily Dickinson.* Thomas H. Johnson, ed. Little Brown and Company, 1980.

Emerson, Ralph Waldo. *Essays and Lectures.* The Library of America, 1983.

Harding, Walter, ed. *Henry David Thoreau: A Profile.* Hill and Wang, 1971.

Ignatov, David. *The One in the Many: A Poet's Memoirs.* Wesleyan University Press, 1988.

——. *Whisper to the Earth.* Little, Brown and Company, 1981.

Jeffers, Robinson. *The Double Axe and Other Poems.* Liveright, 1977.

Mahler, Richard. *Stillness: Daily Gifts of Solitude.* Red Wheel/Weiser, 2003.

Merton, Thomas. *Confessions of a Guilty Bystander.* Image Books, 1968.

——. *Contemplative Prayer.* Doubleday, 1972.

——. *No Man is an Island.* Harcourt Brace Jovanovich, 1955.

——. "Philosophy of Solitude." In *Disputed Questions*; Farrar, Straus and Giroux, 1953.

——. *Thoughts in Solitude.* Farrar, Straus and Giroux, 1956.

——. *The Wisdom of the Desert.* New Directions, 1970.

Snyder, Gary. *The Real Work: Interviews & Talks*. New Directions Publishing, 1980.

Stevens, Wallace. *The Collected Poems.* Vintage Books, 1982.

Thoreau, Henry D. *The Illustrated Walden.* Princeton University Press, 1973

——. *The Heart of Thoreau's Journals.* Odell Shepard, ed. Dover Publications, 1971.

Whitman, Walt. *Specimen Days*, in *The Portable Walt Whitman.* Mark Van Doren, ed. Penguin Books, 1945.

Historians, Philosophers, Psychologists

Arieti, Silvano. *Creativity: The Magic Synthesis.* Basic Books, 1976.

Bachelard, Gaston. *The Poetics of Reverie: Childhood, Language, and the Cosmos.* Daniel Russell, trans. Beacon Press, 1969.

Barzun, Jacques. *A Stroll With William James.* Harper & Row, 1983.

Bergson, Henri. *The Two Sources of Morality and Religion.* R. Ashley Audra and Cloudesley Brereton, trans. University of Notre Dame Press, 1935.

Bowker, John, ed. *The Oxford Dictionary of World Religions.* Oxford University Press, 1977.

Buchholz, Ester Schaler. *The Call of Solitude: Alonetime in a World of Attachment.* Simon & Schuster, 1997.

Byrd, Admiral Richard E. *Alone.* G. P. Putnam's Sons, 1938.

Campbell, Joseph. *The Masks of God: Oriental Mythology.* Penguin Books, 1976.

——. *The Masks of God: Primitive Mythology.* Penguin Books, 1976.

——. *The Hero With a Thousand Faces.* Princeton University Press, 1973.

Deikman, Arthur J. "Deautomatization and the Mystic Experience." In *The Nature of Human Consciousness*; Robert E. Ornstein, ed.;W.H. Freeman and Company, 1973.

Durkheim, Emile. *Suicide: A Study in Sociology.* John A. Spaulding and George Simpson, trans. Free Press, 1951.

Freud, Sigmund. *Civilization and Its Discontents.* James Strachey, trans. W.W. Norton, 1961.

Friedman, Thomas. *The Lexus and the Olive Tree: Understanding Globalization.* Farrar Straus Giroux, 1999.

Happold, F.C. *Mysticism: A Study and an Anthology*. Penguin Books, 1964.

James, William. *The Varieties of Religious Experience: A Study in Human Nature*. Modern Library, 1994.

Jung, C.G. *Modern Man in Search of a Soul*. Harcourt Brace Jovanovich, 1933.

Koch, Philip. *Solitude: A Philosophical Encounter*. Open Court, 1994.

Lasch, Christopher. *The Culture of Narcissism: American Life in the Age of Diminishing Expectations*. W.W. Norton & Company, 1979.

Maslow, Abraham H. *Religions, Values, and Peak-Experiences*. Penguin Compass, 1994.

Masson, J. Moussaieff. "The Psychology of the Ascetic." In *Journal of Asian Studies*, Vol. XXXV, No. 4, August 1976.

Moustakas, Clark E. *Loneliness*. Prentice-Hall, 1961.

Mumford, Lewis. *The Conduct of Life*. Harcourt Brace Jovanovich, 1951.

Neumann, Eric. *Origins and History of Consciousness*. Princeton University Press, 1954.

Ornstein, Robert E. *The Nature of Human Consciousness*. Viking Press, 1973.

Sayer, Robert. *Solitude in Society: A Sociological Study of French Literature*. Harvard University Press, 1978.

Schacht, Richard. *Alienation*. Doubleday & Company, 1970.

Sitter, John. *Literary Loneliness in Mid-Eighteenth Century England*. Cornell University Press, 1982.

Storr, Anthony. *Solitude: A Return to the Self*. Free Press, 1988.

Tillich, Paul. *The Eternal Now*. Charles Scribner Sons, 1963.

Toynbee, Arnold J. *A Study of History*. Abridgement by D.C. Somervell. Oxford University Press, 1946.

Underhill, Evelyn. *Mysticism*. E. P. Dutton, 1961.

Weber, Max. *The Protestant Ethic and the Spirit of Capitalism*. Anthony Giddens, trans. Charles Scribner's Sons, 1958.

Wildman, Wesley J. "In Praise of Loneliness." In Leroy S. Rounder, ed.; *Loneliness*; University of Notre Dame Press, 1998.

Winnicott, D.W. "The Capacity to Be Alone." In D.W. Winnicott, *The Maturational Processes and the Facilitating Environment*, International Universities Press, 1965.

Notes

OVERTURE

1. Nietzsche, *Genealogy and Ecce Homo*, "Why I Am So Wise," #8, 233.
2. Hayman, *Nietzsche: A Critical Life*, 21.
3. Nietzsche, *Zarathustra*, "Noontide," 307.
4. Nietzsche, *Genealogy and Ecce Homo*, 343.
5. Nietzsche, *Human, All Too Human*, #626, 259.
6. Nietzsche, *Daybreak*, #177, 179.
7. Nietzsche, *Beyond Good and Evil*, #289, 196f.
8. Ibid., #44, 55.
9. Emerson, *Essays and Lectures*, 388.
10. Byrd, *Alone*, 138f.
11. Bishop, *Petrarch and His World*, 239.
12. Petrarch, *The Life,* 298.
13. Bishop, 136.
14. Forster, *Petrarch:Poet and Humanist*, 3.
15. "Pro Archia" in *Cicero*; N. H. Watts, trans.; Harvard University Press, 1923; vol. XI, #16, 25.
16. Pound, *Spirit of Romance*, 36.
17. Ibid., 96.
18. Ibid., 126.
19. Ibid.
20. Petrarch, *The Life,* 168.
21. Petrarch, *Selections from the Canzoniere and Other Works,* "Ascent of Mount Ventoux," 17.
22. The Psalm is 45th in the Vulgate, 46th in the Protestant Bible.
23. Bishop, 234.
24. Petrarch, *The Life*, 100 and 102.
25. Ibid., 105.
26. For full text of the tale, see ibid., 109–121.
27. Ibid., 148.
28. Ibid., 150.
29. Bishop, 137.

30. Ibid., 142.
31. Bishop, 134.
32. Petrarch, *The Life,* 291.
33. Ibid., 131.
34. Ibid., 290.
35. Ibid., 153.
36. Ibid., 152.
37. Ibid., 153.
38. Ibid., 315.
39. Ibid., 130.
40. Ibid., 310.
41. Forster, *Petrarch: Poet and Humanist,* 6.
42. Number 35, first two stanzas. DB translation. For Italian originals and alternative translations of this and other selections below, see *Petrarch: The Canzoniere*; Mark Musa, trans.
43. Number 129, first stanza. DB translation.
44. Ibid., third stanza. DB translation.
45. Number 270, last stanza. DB translation.
46. Number 290; first, third, and fourth stanzas. DB translation.
47. Petrarch, *Selections from the Canzoniere and Other Works*, "Letter to Posterity," 2.
48. Ibid., "Ascent of Mount Ventoux," 15.
49. Number 366, sixth stanza. DB translation.
50. Bishop, 242.
51. Trinkaus, *The Poet as Philosopher,* 65.
52. Ibid., 65ff.
53. Ibid., 48.
54. Ibid., 68.
55. Ibid., 64.
56. Bishop, 145.
57. Trinkaus, 62.
58. Ibid., 63.
59. Ibid., 70.
60. Petrarch, *The Life,* 137.
61. Ibid., 306.

PREHISTORIC SOLITUDE

1. Rasmussen, *Intellectual Culture,* vol. 7, #1, 110f.
2. Ibid., 126.
3. Spencer and Gillen, *Northern Tribes of Central Australia*, 488.

4. Harner, *The Way of the Shaman.* See especially chap. 2, "The Shamanic Journey."
5. Petrarch, *The Life*, 266.
6. *Diogenes Laertius*, "Epimenides," vol. I, 117.
7. Gorman, *Pythagoras*, 74.
8. Guthrie, *History of Greek Philosophy,* vol. I. See section titled "The Earlier Presocratics and the Pythagoreans" for fuller discussion on these points.
9. Gorman, 26ff.
10. Eliade, *Zalmoxis*, 29.
11. Ibid.
12. Halifax, *Shamanic Voices,* 118.
13. Ibid., 118.
14. Ibid., 69.
15. Ibid., 119.
16. Ibid., 120.
17. Eliade, *Rites and Symbols,* 31f.
18. Ibid., 35f.
19. Schoolcraft, *Indian Legends,* 58ff.
20. Ibid., 106ff.
21. Evans-Wentz, *Tibetan Yoga,* 311f. Abridged.
22. Bergson, 238.
23. Clottes and Lewis-Williams, chap. 5.

ANCIENT INDIA

1. Rig Veda; O'Flaherty, trans.; 137f. See also Bhagat, 107ff.
2. Ibid.
3. Johnson, *Poetry and Speculation of the Rg Veda,* 18.
4. Upanishads; Hume, trans.; *Maitri Up.*; 145ff.
5. Ibid., 114.
6. Ibid., 113.
7. Rig Veda, 34.
8. Mahabharata; Van Buitenen, trans.; "The Book of the Forest"; vol. 2, bk. 3, 302.
9. Ibid., 303.
10. Ibid., "The Book of the Beginning," vol. 1, bk. 1, 333.
11. Ibid.
12. Ibid., vol. 1, 161. Edited by DB, changing the word "asceticism" in one instance to "tapas."
13. Malalaskera, *Encyclopedia of Buddhism*, vol. 2, #1, 159.
14. Buddha; *The Lion's Roar*; Maurice, trans.; "Advantages of a Recluse's Life"; 206ff.
15. Bhagat, 82.

16. Campbell, *Masks of God: Oriental Mythology*, 285.
17. Quoted in Bhagat, 87.
18. Upanishads; *Maitri Up.*; 431. Edited by DB.
19. Jacobi, *Jaina Sutras*, 264.
20. Buddha, *The Lion's Roar*, 221.
21. Buddha; *Dialogues of the Buddha*; Rhys Davids, trans.; "Fruits of the Life of a Recluse"; 93.
22. Petrarch, *The Life*, 259f.
23. According to the second-century Greek historian Arrian, Alexander ordered his troops to salute when the Hindu sage Calanus expired on a funeral pyre fearless of death, as bugles sounded and elephants roared. See Arrian, *The Campaigns*, 351f.
24. Ibid., 263.
25. Mahabharata; Van Buitenen, trans.; "The Book of the Beginning"; vol. 1, #4, 56ff.
26. Radhakrishnan and Moore, "The Laws of Manu," 181ff.
27. O'Flaherty, *Hindu Myths*, "The Pine Forest Sages Castrate Siva," 141ff.
28. Ibid.
29. Conze, ed.; *Buddhist Scriptures*; "The Practice of Introversion"; 100f. Excerpt.
30. Ibid., "The Advantages of Solitary Meditation," 107.
31. Ibid.
32. Ashvagosha; *Saudarananda*; Johnston, trans.; 57f.
33. Dimmit and van Buitenen, *Classical Hindu Mythology*, "The Hermitage of Atri," 323ff.
34. Ibid.
35. Thapar, *History of India*, 71.
36. Bhartrihari; *The Hermit and the Love Thief*; Miller, trans.; #104, 68.
37. Ibid., #147, 82.
38. Ibid., #177, 93.

GREECE AND ROME

1. "Philoctetes," in *The Complete Plays of Sophocles*; Moses Hadas, trans.; Bantam Books, 1967; 189.
2. Aristotle; in *The Complete Works*; Barnes, ed.; 1987.
3. "Echo and Narcissus," in Ovid, *The Metamorphoses;* Horace Gregory, trans.; New American Library, 1985, 95.
4. Aristotle; *Ethics*; Thomson, trans.; bk. 10, #7, 328.
5. Ibid., bk. 10, #8, 334.
6. Ibid., bk. 10, #7, 329.
7. Petrarch, *The Life*, 269.
8. Ibid., 269.

9. Ibid., 266.
10. In Bolton, *Aristeas,* 120ff.
11. Dodds, *Greeks and the Irrational,* 135.
12. In Bolton, *Aristeas,* 121ff.
12. See Guthrie, W.K.C., *History of Greek Philosophy*, vol. II, 1–77, for a discussion of Parmenides, his link to shamanism, and his revolutionary application of the religious experience of mystical *ekstasis* (ecstacy) to philosophy.
14. Plato, *Symposium* in *Great Dialogues of Plato*, 161.
15. Ibid., 174f.
16. Ibid, 210ff.
17. All quotes in this section are from Heraclitus; *The Art and Thought of Heraclitus*; Khan, trans.
18. Diogenes Laertius, "Democritus"; vol. II, 445ff.
19. Ibid., #38.
20. Freeman, *Ancilla*, 92.
21. Freeman, *Ancilla*, 109.
22. Diogenes Laertius, "Diogenes," vol. II, 43.
23. Ibid., #78.
24. Epicurus; *Philosophy of Epicurus;* Strodach, trans.; "Leading Doctrines"; #14, 198.
25. Lucretius, *The Way Things Are,* 86.
26. In Sedgwick, *Horace: A Biography*, 50.
27. Horace, *Satires and Epistles*; Jacob Fuchs, trans.; *Epistles* I–10, 61.
28. Horace; *The Essential Horace*; Raffel, trans.; *Epodes* 2, 110.
29. Ibid., *Epistles* I–4, 206.
30. Ibid., *Odes* IV–11, 101f. Adapted by DB.
31. Horace; *Satires and Epistles*; Jacob Fuchs, trans.; *Epistles* I-14, 65.
32. Petrarch, *The Life*, 272f.
33. Seneca, *Letters from a Stoic*; Letter VII, 41.
34. Ibid., Letter IX, 51.
35. Petrarch, *The Life*, 282.
36. Aurelius; *Meditations*; Maxwell Staniforth, trans.; 63.
37. Lucian, "The Passing of Peregrinus," 47f.
38. Ibid, 45.
39. Philo; *Philo of Alexandria*; David Winston, trans.; 45.
40. Ibid., from *De Abrahamo*, 262f.
41. Ibid., from *Quis Rerum Divinarum Heres Sit*, 211.
42. Dillon, *The Middle Platonists*, 372.
43. Rist, *Plotinus: The Road to Reality*, 19.
44. Plotinus; *The Essence*; MacKenna and Turnbull, trans.; "Beauty"; 49.
45. Ibid., "The Good or the One," 222.

ANCIENT CHINA

1. For more on this, see Bill Porter's *Road to Heaven,* chapters 1 and 2. Porter cites the recent finding of a shaman's fish-spirit mask in or near the Chungnan Mountains of central China dating back to the fifth century B.C. The mask appears to be an early form of paired dragons used to aid the shamans' heavenly journeys and is evidence of a shamanic culture from which the likes of Master Kuang would have emerged. With the onset of a more stylized and bureaucratic approach to divination, says Porter, the original shamans headed for the mountains, as it were, where Emperor Huang Ti would have gone to reconnect with their more potent wisdom (20ff).
2. Chuang Tzu; *The Complete Works*; Watson, trans.; 118ff.
3. Ibid., 33.
4. See Bill Porter, *Road to Heaven,* 1ff. Porter cites stories in the third-century *Kaoshichuan* (*Records of High-Minded Men*) of emperors following Huang Ti who sought mountain hermits to rule their kingdoms as early as the third millennium B.C. These tended to be shamanic rather than secular hermits, but in ancient China there seems to have been little difference between the two. Some refused to rule; others accepted.
5. Waley, *The Way and Its Power,* 34.
6. Analects, VIII, 13. Among others, quote based on Waley translation in Confucius, *The Analects*, 135.
7. From *Lieh-Nü Chuan*, chap. 2, #13. See A. R. Davis, *The Narrow Lane,* 4.
8. In Cyril Birch, ed.; *Anthology of Chinese Literature*; from #33, 59.
9. Hawkes, *Songs of the South,* 258. Reproduced by permission of Penguin Books, Ltd.
10. Ibid., 250ff.
11. Ibid., 209.
12. Ibid., 71.
13. Ibid., 199.
14. Waley, *The Way and Its Power,* 37.
15. Kuan Tzu; Rickett, trans.; IX.1–2, 163.
16. Ibid., XV.1–2, 168. Adapted by DB.
17. Shuhmacher and Woerner, *Encyclopedia of Eastern Philosophy*, 199 ("Lao-tzu").
18. Waley, *The Way and Its Power,* 176.
19. Chuang Tzu, "T'ien Tzu-Fang," 224.
20. Ibid., "The Great and Venerable Teacher," 82f.
21. Ibid., "Mastering Life," 205f.
22. Ibid., "In the World of Men," 57f.

THE DESERT FATHERS

1. Petrarch, *The Life*, 198, 199, then 254.
2. Eusebius, *The Ecceliastical History*, vol. II, #IX, 35.
3. Robinson, *Nag Hammadi Library*, "Teachings of Silvanus," 347.
4. Ibid., "The Gospel of Thomas," #49, 49.
5. Ibid., #75, 126.
6. Ibid., #51, 123.
7. Ibid., #70, 126.
8. Waddell, *The Desert Fathers,* "The Life of Saint Paul the First Hermit," 30ff.
9. Athanasius, *The Life of Anthony,* 42.
10. Waddell, 42f.
11. Athanasius, 87f.
12. Ibid., 42f.
13. Merton, *Wisdom of the Desert,* 63f.
14. Ibid., 64f.
15. Ibid., 72.
16. Ibid., 41.
17. Ibid., 55.
18. Ibid., 75.
19. Ibid., 47.
20. Ibid., 51.
21. Palmer, et al., *The Philokalia*; 33.
22. Ibid., 35.
23. Evagrius of Pontus, *The Praktikos*, 33f.
24. Merton, *Wisdom of the Desert,* 62.
25. Ibid., 67f.
26. John Climacus, 269.

SUFI SOLOISTS

1. Glubb, *The Life and Times of Muhammad*, "The Call," chap. IV, 84.
2. See Andre, *Garden of the Myrtles,* 14.
3. Ibid., 10f. Reformatted by DB.
4. Ibid., 11.
5. Ibid., 58.
6. Ibid., 18.
7. Ibid., 57.
8. Ibid., 59.
9. Attar, *Muslim Saints and Mystics*; Arberry, trans.; "Ibrahim ibn Adham"; 62ff.

10. Andre, 78.
11. Schimmel, *Mystical Dimensions of Islam*, 48.
12. Attar, "Dawud al-Ta'i," 141.
13. Ibid.: "Rabi'a," 42.
14. Rabi'a; *Doorkeeper*; Upton, trans.; 24.
15. Ibid.: 24.
16. John Bowker, ed.; *The Oxford Dictionary of World Religions*; 789 ("Rabi'a").
17. Rabi'a, *Doorkeeper*, 21.
18. Ibid., 22.
19. Schimmel, 46.
20. 'Iraqi; *Divine Flashes,* Chittick and Wilson, trans.; 126.
21. Ibid., 114.
22. Rumi, *The Essential Rumi*, 6. Reprinted with permission of the translator, Coleman Barks.
23. Ibid.
24. Nurbakhsh, *In the Tavern of Ruin*, 95.
25. In Kritzeck, 239. R.A. Nicholson, trans.
26. Rumi, *The Essential Rumi*, 22.
27. Al-Ghazali; *Al-Ghazali's Path to Sufism*; McCarthy, trans.; 52ff.
28. Schimmel, 36.
29. In Kritzeck, 241. R.A. Nicholson, trans.
30. In Kritzeck, 268. R.M. Rehder, trans.
31. See Hafiz, *Teachings*, "Introduction," 15f.
32. Andre, 98.
33. See Hafiz, 15.

MEDIEVAL EUROPE

1. Bede; "Life of Cuthbert"; Webb, trans.; chap. 17, 94.
2. Ibid., chap. 20, 98.
3. Jackson, *A Celtic Miscellany*, 68f.
4. Ibid., 279f.
5. "Le Moniage Gillaume"; in Brian Woledge, Geoffrey Brereton, and Anthony Hartley, eds.; *The Penguin Book of French Verse*; Penguin Books, 1980; 25ff.
6. Clay, *Hermits and Anchorites of England,* 88.
7. Ibid., 89f.
8. Ibid., 193.
9. Ibid., 85.
10. Dionysius the Areopagite; *Mystical Theology*; Rolt, trans.; 191.
11. Anonymous; *Cloud of Unknowing*; Wolters, trans.; 110.

12. In Capps and Wright, eds.; *Silent Fire*; 106. William Johnston, trans.
13. Ibid., 107f.
14. Eckhart; Blakney, trans.; "Talks of Instruction"; 9.
15. Mechthild of Magdeburg; *The Flowing Light*; Tobin, trans.; bk. I, #44, 62 and bk. I, #35, 55f.
16. Capps and Wright, *Silent Fire*, 135.
17. Ibid., 135.
18. Ibid., 138.
19. Ibid., 138.
20. Ibid., 140.
21. Rolle; *The Fire of Love*; Wolters, trans.; 45.
22. Ibid.: 72.
23. Julian of Norwich; *Revelations*; Wolters, trans.; 68.
24. Ibid.
25. DB trans. Last three quatrains.
26. DB trans. Stanzas #1 and #6.
27. John of the Cross; *The Collected Works*; Kavanaugh and Otilio, trans.; commentary, 30f.

SCHOLARS AND CH'AN MASTERS

1. In Birch, *Anthology of Chinese Literature*, "Poems of My Heart," 198. C.J. Chen and Michael Bullock, trans.
2. See T'ao Ch'ien; *The Poetry;* Hightower, trans.; 50.
3. Ibid.: 270.
4. DB trans. Chinese text in T'ao Ch'ien; *Gleanings*; Fang, trans.; 89.
5. DB trans. Chinese text in Wang Wei; *The Poetry of Wang Wei;* Yu, trans.; 230f.
6. DB trans.
7. Matthiessen, *Nine-Headed Dragon River*, 7f.
8. There are many translations of this important passage from "The Transmission of the Lamp." I have abridged the wording based on translations by D.T. Suzuki, in *Manual of Zen Buddhism,* 76f; and in another Suzuki translation at it appears in Thomas Hoover's *The Zen Experience*, 22f.
9. Han Shan; Red Pine, trans.; see poems 21, 99, and 287.
10. Ibid, #279.
11. Ibid., #4.
12. DB trans. See original Chinese in Red Pine's *The Collected Songs of Cold Mountain*, with translation of poem 57.
13. Stonehouse; *The Zen Works of Stonehouse*; Red Pine, trans.; #36, 19.
14. See Dogen; *Moon in a Dewdrop*; Tanahashi, et al., trans.; 214. Rewritten by DB.
15. See Basho; *Narrow Road*; Yuasa, trans.; 32. Rewritten by DB.

MODERN RECLUSES

1. Montaigne, *The Complete Essays,* Frame, trans.; "Of Three Kinds of Association"; 629.
2. Ibid., "Of Husbanding Your Will," 767.
3. Descartes; *Discourse on Method*; F.E. Sutcliffe, trans.; 52.
4. Ibid., 95.
5. Ibid., 48.
6. *Pensées,* #136. DB translation.
7. Rousseau; *Reveries*; Butterworth, trans.; "Fifth Walk"; 69.
8. Wordsworth, *Prelude,* Book Four.
9. Thoreau, *Journals,* December 28, 1856.
10. Ibid., June 22, 1851.
11. Whitman, *Specimen Days,* "A Sun-Bath—Nakedness," 513.
12. Flaubert; *The Temptation*; Mrosovsky, trans.; 232.
13. *Oeuvres,* I–14.
14. Valéry; *Monsieur Teste,* "Preface," 5.
15. *Notebooks,* II, 601.
16. Valéry, *The Evening With Monsieur Teste,* 17.
17. Shattuck, *Marcel Proust,* 17f.
18. Rilke; *Selected Poems*; Bly, trans.; #7, 19.
19. Rilke; *Letters to a Young Poet*; Mitchell, trans.; letter to Mr. Kappus, December 23, 1903; 54.
20. Merton, *Thoughts in Solitude,* 108.

ON CLOISTERPHOBIA

1. Kierkegaard, *Diary,* 23.
2. Petrarch, *The Life,* 88 and 92.
3. See Workman, *The Evolution of the Monastic Ideal,* 338.
4. Ibid., 351.
5. Weber, *The Protestant Ethic,* "The Religious Foundations of Worldly Asceticism," chap. 4, 95ff.
6. Ibid., 172.
7. Merton, *Confessions of a Guilty Bystander,* 222.
8. Aristotle, *The Politics,* 1253a1.
9. Quoted in Toynbee, *Study in History,* vol. II, 76.
10. David Hume, *An Enquiry Concerning the Principles of Morals,* sec. IX, pt. I, par. 3.
11. Quoted in Waddell, *The Desert Fathers,* 7.
12. Nietzsche, *Daybreak,* 52.
13. Quoted in Toynbee, *Study of History,* vol. II, 78.

14. Mahabharata; Ganguli, trans.; "Santi Parva"; sec.18, vol. VIII, 33.
15. Han Fei Tzu; Watson, trans.; 110.
16. John Evelyn, *Public Employment and an Active Life Prefer'd to Solitude, 1667.* Quoted in Koch, *Solitude,* 210.
17. Hawkes, *Songs of the South*, 245.
18. *Moby Dick*, "The Mast-Head," chap. 35.
19. Merton, *Disputed Questions*, 185.
20. Merton, *No Man is an Island,* 246.
21. Jerome; *Select Letters*; Wright, trans.; Letter 22, #7, 67.
22. Jerome, "To Rusticus," Letter 75, #16.
23. *Heart of Darkness,* chap. 3.
24. Ibid.
25. Masson, "Psychology of the Ascetic," 623.
26. Ibid., 623.
27. Ibid., 625.
28. Freud, *Civilization and Its Discontents,* chap. II. All quotes on p. 28.
29. Burton, *Anatomy of Melancholy,* end of last chapter.
30. *Decline and Fall of the Roman Empire,* chap. 50, pt. 3.
31. *Memoirs of My Life,* vol. I, 117.
32. Donne, *Poetry and Prose*, "Devotions Upon Emergent Occasions," 308. I have kept the original spelling.
33. Toynbee, vol. I, 230.
34. Campbell, *Hero With a Thousand Faces*, "The Monomyth," 30.
35. Ibid., "Departure," 64.
36. Toynbee, vol. I, 217.
37. Ibid., 224.
38. Powys, *Philosophy of Solitude,* "The Something That Infects the World," 163.
39. Storr, *Solitude,* "The Hunger of the Imagination," 72.
40. Chuang Tzu, "The Way of Heaven," 143.
41. Mumford, *Conduct of Life,* "The Need for Two Lives," 265.
42. Ibid., "The Great Good Place," 263.
43. Anthony Storr (*Solitude,* 22) tells the story of an analyst he knew personally who saw a patient three times per week over the period of one year. At every session, the patient lay down on the couch and plunged straight into free association. At the end of the year, the patient pronounced himself cured. But the analyst declared that he had offered no interpretation whatever during that period. In her book *The Call of Solitude*, Ester Schaler Buchholz makes a similar claim, supported by evidence in practice, for the psychotherapeutic value of what she calls "alonetime."
44. Merton, *No Man is an Island,* 246.
45. Ibid., 247.

46. Rilke; *Letters to a Young Poet*; Mitchell, trans.; 98f.
47. Powys, *Philosophy of Solitude*, "The Self and Its Loves," 184.
48. Petrarch, *The Life*, 130.
49. Montaigne, *Complete Essays*, "On Solitude," 174.
50. Jeffers, "Original Preface to 'The Double Axe,'" 173.
51. Friedman, *The Lexus and the Olive Tree,* 83f.
52. Seneca; *Letters from a Stoic*; Robin Campbell, trans.; Letter XVIII, 67f.
53. Petrarch, *The Life,* 143.
54. Mahler, *Stillness*, 75.

PSYCHOLOGY

1. *Walden*, "Economy," chap. 1
2. Nietzsche, *Genealogy,* "What is the Meaning of Ascetic Ideals?" sec. 1, 97.
3. Nietzsche, *Zarathustra*, "Reading and Writing," chap. 7.
4. Quoted in Barzun, *A Stroll With William James*, 248.
5. James, *Varieties*, 466.
6. Ibid., 467.
7. Nietzsche, *Genealogy and Ecce Homo*, 300.
8. Merton, *Thoughts in Solitude,* #X, 48.
9. Patanjali, *Aphorisms of Yoga*, 72.
10. Govinda, *The Way of the White Clouds*, "Trance Walking and *Lung-Gom* Training," 81.
11. Conze, *Buddhist Scriptures*, "Meditation," chap. 2, 99f.
12. Rousseau, *Reveries*, "Fifth Walk," 64.
13. See Raymond D. Gozzi, "Some Aspects of Thoreau's Personality." In Harding, ed.; *Henry David Thoreau: A Profile*; 150ff.
14. Underhill, *Mysticism*, 169.
15. Andre, *In the Garden of Myrtles*, 80.
16. Zimmerman, *Pleasures of Solitude,* "The Advantages of Solitude to a Scholar," chap. III, 42. The book was first titled *Advantages and Disadvantages of Solitude*; it is said that Henry Thoreau took along a pocket version of the volume to Walden Pond.
17. Budge, trans.; *'Anan Isho*; "Of Flight from Men"; bk. 1, chap. 13.
18. Guthrie, K. S.; *Pythagorean Sourcebook*. See especially the introduction and *The Life of Pythagoras* by Iamblichus.
19. Chuang Tzu, 58.
20. Deikman, in Ornstein, *Human Consciousness*, 216ff.
21. Arieti, *Creativity,* 13.
22. Ibid., 373.
23. Ibid., 62.
24. Quoted in Arieti, 268.

25. Storr, *Solitude,* 25.
26. Ibid.
27. Ibid., 201.
28. Rousseau, *Reveries,* "Seventh Walk," 89ff.
29. *Confessions,* bk. I. See Christopher Kelly, et al., eds.; *The Collected Writings of Rousseau,* vol. 5; University Press of New England, 1995.
30. Nietzsche, *Genealogy,* "What is the Meaning of Ascetic Ideals," sec. 8, 111.
31. Plato; *The Complete Texts*; Rouse, trans.: *Symposium,* 152.
32. Neumann, *Origins and History of Consciousness,* "The Original Unity," pt. II–A, 261ff.
33. Montaigne, "Of Solitude," 176.
34. Cited in Storr, *Solitude,* 88f.
35. Ibid., 90f.
36. Ibid., 19.
37. Lowrie, *Short Life of Kierkegaard,* 55.
38. Petrarch, *The Life,* 131.
39. David-Neel, *Magic and Mystery in Tibet,* "Mystic Theories and Spiritual Training," 256f.
40. James Boswell, *Life of Johnson,* 27 October 1779.
41. Powys, *Philosophy of Solitude,* "The Self and the Bitterness of Life," 218.
42. In Edsman, ed.; *Studies in Shamanism*; 167.
43. Ibid., 177.
44. Ibid., 179.
45. Bergson, *The Two Sources,* "Dynamic Religion," 230.
46. From poem by Robert Bly, "The Magnolia Grove: For Michael Bullock," in *Jumping Out of Bed.* This seems to be Bly's imaginative rendering of what P'ei Ti might have said. If we attribute it to Bly, who is also a Friend of Solitude, the sentiment is the same.
47. Conze, *Buddhist Scriptures,* "The Progressive Steps of Meditation," 108.
48. Mumford, *Conduct of Life,* "The Need for Two Lives," 265.
49. Thoreau, *Journals,* April 4, 1839.
50. DB trans. See Chinese original in Pauline Yu, *The Poetry of Wang Wei,* 230.
51. Ignatov, *Whisper to the Earth,* "For Yaedi," 19. Selection quoted as prose.
52. Rousseau, *Reveries,* "Fifth Walk," 64.
53. Chuang Tzu, "Discussion on Making All Things Equal," 46.
54. Epicurus; *Letters, Principal Doctrines*; Geer, trans.; "True Pleasure"; #D, 57.
55. Seneca, "On Tranquillity of Mind," *#10,* 251ff.
56. Han Shan; *The Collected Songs*; Red Pine, trans.; poem #87. Reprinted with permission from Copper Canyon Press, P.O. Box 271, Port Townsend, Washington 98368.
57. Seneca, *Letters to Lucilius,* #VII, 42f.
58. Flaubert, *Temptation of Saint Anthony,* 94.
59. In Cyril Birch, ed.; *Anthology of Chinese Literature*; "Poems of My Heart"; #4, 199.
60. Bhartrihari, *Hermit and the Love Thief,* 153.

61. From the *Gmani Samayutta.* See Malalaskera, ed; *Encyclopedia of Buddhism*; vol. 2, #1, 159.
62. Quoted in Deikman, 220.
63. Ibid.
64. Rilke; *Letters to a Young Poet*; letter to Mr. Kappus, December 23, 1903; 54ff.
65. Bachelard, *The Poetics of Reverie*, 108, 116, and 24.
66. Radhakrishnan and Moore, *Artha Sastra*, "The Institution of Spies," chap. 11, 200.
67. Nietzsche, *Joyful Wisdom*, #27, 69.
68. Masson, "The Psychology of the Ascetic," 624.
69. Ibid., 625.
70. Diogenes Laertius, "Diogenes," vol. II, 35.
71. Petrarch, *Selections from the Canzoniere and Other Works,* 10.
72. Horace; Fuchs, trans.; Epistles I–16, 68.
73. Storr, *Solitude,* 193.
74. Ibid.
75. Maslow, *Religions, Values, and Peak-Experiences,* 21 and 59ff.
76. Emerson, *Essays and Lectures,* "Fate," 956.
77. Plato; *Symposium*; in *Great Dialogues*; Rouse, trans.; 153.
78. Plotinus, *The Essence*; MacKenna, trans.; "Beauty," #7, 47.
79. Dionysius the Areopagite; *The Mystical Theology*; Rolt, trans.; "What is the Divine Gloom," 191.
80. Jacobi, trans.; *Jaina Sutras*; 261.
81. Ibid., 263.
82. Upanishads, *Brihad. Up.*, #4.4.6, 141.
83. Chuang Tzu, "Mastering Life," 197.
84. James, *Varieties,* "Saintliness," 317.
85. David-Neel, *Magic and Mystery in Tibet*, 219.
86. Ibid., 217.
87. Ibid., 218.
88. In Georgianna, *The Solitary Self,* 72.
89. John Climacus, "Step 5: On Penitence," 129.
90. Ibid., "Step 30: On Faith, Hope, and Love," 289f.
91. Bhagavadgita, "Devotion," chap. 4, verses 6 and 7.
92. Rumi, *The Ruins of the Heart*, 30.
93. Ibid.
94. Nietzsche, *Genealogy and Ecce Homo*, "Why I Am So Clever," #10, 258.
95. Merton, *Contemplative Prayer*, 90.
96. Carretto, *In Search of Beyond*, 85f. (Listed in Sources under "Christians.")
97. See Dogen; *Moon in a Dewdrop*; Kazuaki Tanahashi, ed.; "Rules for Zazen," 29f. and 314.

98. Chuang Tzu, "Knowledge Wandered North," 234f.
99. Buddha; *The Lion's Roar*; David Maurice, trans.; "The Void…of What?" 118ff.
100. Valéry, *Monsieur Teste*, 36.
101. Nietzsche, *Daybreak*, #43, 43.
102. Wittgenstein, *Tractatus*, #6.54, 189.
103. Wittgenstein, *Culture and Value*, 63.
104. Wittgenstein, *Philosophical Investigations*, #IIxi, 228.
105. Johnson, *Poetry and Speculation of the Rig Veda,* 18f.
106. Dickinson, poem #280.
107. Epicurus; *The Philosophy*; Strodach, trans.; 185.
108. Powys, *Philosophy of Solitude*, 206.
109. Ibid., 106f.
110. Ibid., 216.
111. Upanishads, *Maitri Up.*, #6–17, 435.
112. Ibid., #6–22, 437f.
113. Ibid., #6–30, 442.
114. Ibid., #619, 436.
115. Merton, *The Desert Wisdom,* 30.

SOLITUDE IN SOCIETY

1. Sayer, *Solitude in Society,* 1.
2. Ibid., 3.
3. Ibid., 5f.
4. Lasch, *Culture of Narcissism*, 21.
5. Ibid., 82.
6. Ibid., 101.
7. Ibid., 103.
8. Durkheim, *Suicide,* 378. Durkheim stressed, it should be noted, that to provide an enduring sense of community the private corporations of his day would have to be reorganized on a wholly different basis, such that they "become a definite and recognized organ of our public life" (379). To his credit, Durkheim warns further that the "too definite programs [for social change] generally embraced by our political philosophers" are "imaginative flights, too far from the complexity of facts to be of much practical value." The important thing, he adds, "is not to draw up in advance a plan anticipating everything, but rather to set resolutely to work" (390f).
9. Lasch, *Culture of Narcissism*, 396f.
10. J.C. Friedrich Von Schiller, "Letters Upon the Aesthetic Education of Man," 1794, Letter 25. Quoted in Schacht, *Alienation,* 24.
11. Schacht, *Alienation*, introductory essay by Walter Kaufmann, "The Inevitability of Alienation," lviii.

12. Quoted in Schacht, *Alienation*, 215. Tillich, *Systematic Theology*, vol. II, 44-5.
13. Tillich, *The Eternal Now*, 24.
14. Ibid., 25.
15. Rolle, *Fire of Love,* chap. 13, 82.
16. Dickinson, poem #1116.
17. Ignatov, *The One in the Many*, 163.
18. Buson, in *Zen Art for Meditation*, 79.
19. See Website: www.probe.org, specifically Kirby Anderson's 1993 article "Loneliness" at http://www.probe.org/menus/kac7.html. Publisher: Probe Ministries, 1900 Firman Drive, Suite 100 Richardson, TX 75081.
20. See Website: www.counsel.ufl.edu
21. See Website: www.deletestress.com
22. Defoe, "Serious Reflections," 6.
23. Ibid., 12f.
24. Petrarch, *The Life*, 135.
25. Bhagavadgita; Van Buitenen, trans.; chap. 2, verse 2–3, 73
26. Bhagavadgita; Miller, trans.; chap. 3, verse 5, 41.
27. Ibid., chap. 3, verse 25, 44.
28. Ibid., chap. 9, verse 9, 84.
29. Ibid., chap. 2, verse 37, 34.
30. Ibid., chap. 10, verse 7, 90.
31. Mahabharata; Ganguli, trans.; "Shanti Parva"; sect. 8, vol. VII, 11f.
32. Ashtavakragita, "The Master," selection from stanza 3, 50. From *THE HEART OF AWARENESS, a Translation of the Ashtavakra Gita* by Thomas Byrom, © 1990 by Thomas Byrom. Reprinted by arrangement with Shambala Publications, Inc., Boston, www.shambala.com.
33. Ibid., from stanza 11, 52.
34. Ibid., selections from stanza 41, 58; followed by stanza 100, 71.
35. I picked up a quote to this effect years ago in my researches on solitude in society; but I was unable to locate the source at the time of publication. I don't think I could have made it up.
36. Quoted in Bill Porter's *Road to Heaven,* 220. Porter says that the saying came to mind in the course of meeting a hundred or so hermits in the Chungnan Mountains of China, when he came across a group of monks living in the Temple of the Sleeping Dragon in the city of Sian. They asked what he was doing, and Porter replied that he was visiting hermits. "You've come to the right place," they said. "We are all hermits here."
37. Andres, 67.
38. Ibid., 68.
39. Eckhart; Blakney, trans.; "Talks of Instruction"; 5ff.
40. Kierkegaard, *Fear and Trembling*, "Problemata: Preamble from the Heart," 67f.

0-595-30990-9

CPSIA information can be obtained at www.ICGtesting.com
Printed in the USA
LVOW061014241011

251823LV00001B/23/A